中国内部控制研究中心

(辽宁省人文社会科学A类重点研究

CICRC

第2辑

会计与控制评论

刘永泽 主编

REVIEW OF ACCOUNTING AND CONTROL

Utz Schäffer

Controlling Development and State of the Art in German-speaking Countries

林 斌 周美华

内控缺陷带来的经济后果——基于公司诉讼的视角

刘永泽 张 亮

我国政府部门内部控制框架体系的构建研究

张先治 季 侃

内部报告对管理会计发展的影响研究

张 琦 王森林 张 娟

我国政府会计研究的回顾与评价

东北财经大学出版社
Dongbei University of Finance & Economics Press
大 连

图书在版编目（CIP）数据

会计与控制评论（第2辑）/ 刘永泽主编．—大连：东北财经大学出版社，2011.12
ISBN 978-7-5654-0637-9

Ⅰ．会… Ⅱ．刘… Ⅲ．①会计制度-研究 ②内部审计-研究 Ⅳ．①F233 ②F239.45

中国版本图书馆CIP数据核字（2011）第261588号

东北财经大学出版社出版
（大连市黑石礁尖山街217号 邮政编码 116025）
教学支持：（0411）84710309
营 销 部：（0411）84710711
总 编 室：（0411）84710523
网　　址：http://www.dufep.cn
读者信箱：dufep@dufe.edu.cn

大连北方博信印刷包装有限公司印刷 东北财经大学出版社发行

幅面尺寸：180mm×255mm 字数：230千字 印张：12 1/2 插页：1
2011年12月第1版 2011年12月第1次印刷

责任编辑：李 彬 王芃南 责任校对：赵 楠 王 娟
封面设计：张智波 版式设计：钟福建

ISBN 978-7-5654-0637-9
定价：34.00元

编委会

目　录

目　录

CONTENTS

CONTENTS

Controlling Development and State of the Art in German-speaking Countries

Utz Schäffer

(Institute of Management Accounting and Control of WHU—Otto Beisheim School of Management German 56179)

Abstract This paper aims to improve the basic understanding of controlling in German-speaking countries by discussing the following four topics: the emergence of controlling in practice and as an academic discipline, the different conceptions of controlling (the practice-based conception from the International Controllers Association and conceptions in the German literature) and the tasks and roles of controllers. Empirical studies from the WHU Controller Panel illustrate the tasks and roles of German controllers.

Keywords Controlling Controller Emergence Conception Tasks Roles Germany

Emergence of Controlling in Practice

The first controllers worked in the public sector in England and in the USA. As early as the 15th century, the job title "controller" was used for the role of keeping records about incoming and outgoing funds and goods at the royal court in England. Similarly, a "comptroller" was responsible for monitoring the balance between the national budget and expenditure in the USA since 1778. These origins in the areas of accounting and supervision correspond to two responsibilities of controllers whose crucial importance has not changed to the present day, as we will show later. Controller positions only became widespread much later, however, namely from the 1920s onwards. The increased importance of controlling and the institutional upgrading of the role of controllers was a consequence of the changing economic circumstances in the USA in the 1920s:

The number of large corporations grew, but they were confronted with increasing problems in terms of internal communication and coordination.

As production plants became more productive because of technological innovation, the share of fixed costs increased and thereby limited entrepreneurial flexibility.

Innovative management tools rarely used in practice and not widely known became available at the same time as the need for them increased because of the prevailing economic turbulence.

In this context, the typical tasks of controllers also changed: whereas their responsibilities as chief accountants, auditors or treasurers previously consisted of tracking transactions that had already taken place, they now also had to introduce planning procedures based on accounting language, coordinate and analyse budget-related data. By switching its focus to the user-customized collection and processing of information by controllers, accounting evolved from being a pure recording and monitoring tool to being an instrument for dealing with the future. The increasing uncertainty inherent in the company's environment required explicit planning: simply extrapolating historical data was no longer helpful in these dynamic times. The planning process and the plans resulting from it were seen to be the appropriate tool for ensuring that companies remained manageable. Newly created controller positions thereby became responsible for developing a concept for results-oriented planning, creating the required processes and providing support to management in the operation of the planning process.

In Germany, the expression "controller" remained unknown for a long time. Even early contributions to the debate in the 1950s and the resulting trips by German academics to the USA did nothing to change this (Auffermann, 1952). The dominant attitudes in Germany were rejection and a lack of understanding (Goossens, 1959). Even at the end of the 1960s, controllers were usually only found in German subsidiaries of US companies. Then, suddenly, things seemed to change. According to an often-cited study by McKinsey of 30 German companies with sales greater than 1 billion German Marks, 90 percent had controller positions by 1974, even if these were not always thus named (Henzler, 1974). The general validity of this finding—which at first glance seems excessively high—was confirmed in the following years by other empirical surveys.

The development was clarified in the 1990s by an analysis of job advertisements in the Frankfurter Allgemeine Zeitung, a major German newspaper, for the period 1949 to 1994 (Weber & Schäffer, 1998). In order to depict the way the expression might have changed over time job advertisements for positions similar to that of controller were also included in the analysis. In accordance with the functions and roles typically covered by controllers, these included all advertisements mentioning the areas of business administration, accounting and planning. Concerning the quantitative development of the job advertisements, the survey provided three key findings:

The first advertisement for a controller was published in 1954.

As was assumed in the relevant literature, the controller positions were initially mainly offered by local subsidiaries of US parent companies.

The number of controller positions developed exponentially; but only in the 1980s did it exceed the number of positions similar to that of controller.

From a task-related perspective, job advertisements for controllers were characterized by the simultaneous listing of budgeting and budgetary monitoring, planned vs. actual comparisons, variance analyses and cost monitoring. This combination of aspects differentiated them in a statistically significant way from positions similar to those of controller (Weber & Bültel, 1992). The analysis by Weber and Schäffer (1998) further shows a clear change of individual tasks over time (e. g. towards integrating controllers more strongly into strategic management issues), although there was no change in the fundamental bundle of tasks.

Tasks of Controllers

The specific combination of tasks is crucial to understanding the function of controlling/controllers in the company and the practical meaning of controlling. The simultaneous responsibility for information, planning and monitoring related tasks is characteristic of the controller's job role, independent of the size of the company or the industry sector. However, whereas there is consistency regarding the diversity of tasks, the specific characteristics of the tasks and the amount of time dedicated to them vary significantly. In this section, we will have a detailed look at the tasks of controllers using several empirical findings.

One of the first studies on the tasks of controllers in Germany was conducted by von Landsberg and Mayer (1988). Among other things, controllers were asked the degree of importance they placed on specific tasks and how much effort they invested in them. The result confirmed the findings of the analysis of job advertisements: controllers are inextricably linked to the ongoing operational planning of companies (budgeting, investment and planning). They design and manage the planning process and they are involved in defining goals. They report on whether the objectives of the firm have been achieved, they are responsible for the ongoing monitoring of planned values and they feedback the results to management. In addition, they provide management support in the form of comprehensive information services and they are responsible for building and maintaining the required systems. They act as coaches, consultants and counterparts to managers on all issues related to business administration. In a typically German fashion, other financial functions are carried out by other departments. For example, controllers do not see themselves as being responsible for balance sheets, taxes, finances and insurance—at least, this was the case in 1988. Nevertheless, the overall impression was that the job role had a broad spectrum of tasks with a solid core, but rather unclear boundaries.

Stoffel (1995) compared the tasks of controllers in Germany, the US and France found considerable differences. The bundling of planning, monitoring and information supply tasks in controller positions differed significantly from country to country. The large accounting share in the USA results in a focus dominated by financial figures. In France, controllers usually also report to the finance department, but are only at the third management level (at most) and, therefore, have relatively little influence. Where planning, monitoring and information supply tasks tend to be seen as being of equal importance, as is the case in Germany, a significant part of controllers' tasks consists of influencing and accompanying the planning processes themselves. Correspondingly, controllers are ranked at a higher level in the company's organizational structure. As a result, controllership becomes a phenomenon that is determined greatly by context and culture.

The range of tasks for which controllers are responsible was also highlighted in a recent empirical study conducted by the WHU Controller Panel in 2008. Study participants were asked how much time they spend on various tasks. Figure 1 shows the task areas provided and the corresponding percentage of working time allocated. Below is a summary of the main results:

Supplying management with information continues to be a core element of controllers' activities. The largest percentage of a controller's resources is needed for ongoing reporting, followed by budgeting and control. Even though controlling is no longer a pure supplier of information and other tasks are considered to be of greater importance, reporting and the corresponding regular information updates to management continue to be the task areas that take up the greatest amount of a controller's time. Moreover, there continues to be a considerable gap between the management of information and the next highest entry, budget planning and monitoring. Although the workload caused by this task fluctuates, controllers dedicate the equivalent of almost a day per week to it.

Consulting and project-related tasks are increasing in importance. Management consulting and collaborating on specific projects jointly fill up another working day each week. These tasks now occupy a growing share of a controller's time, mainly at the expense of cost accounting. Performing these two tasks provides controllers with the opportunity to establish close contact with management and to influence decisions actively. It is thus not surprising to find out that controllers who also see themselves as crucial counterparts to management perform these tasks at a higher level of intensity. In spite of this development, cost accounting with a slight lag—continues to occupy the fifth position in the ranking of task areas.

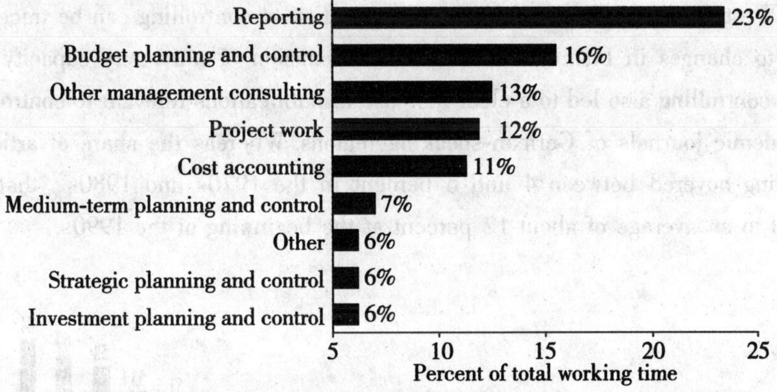

Figure 1 Segmentation of A Controller's Working Time According to The Range of Activities

Development of Controlling as an Academic Discipline

In parallel with its impressive development in practice, controlling has become a recognized discipline in German academia as well—in spite of some reservations (Küpper & Wagenhofer, 2002). According to a study by Binder and Schäffer (2005), there were no fewer than 72 chairs explicitly carrying the label "controlling" at the 92 business administration faculties of German language universities and business schools in 2004. Furthermore, some aspects of controlling as a subject are often covered by other chairs that do not explicitly use the expression controlling as part of their names. A closer analysis of the chairs' labels shows that only 15 percent of the 72 chairs are "pure" controlling chairs. The remaining 85 percent of chairs are linked to other subjects. This diversity of combinations clearly shows that controlling can be linked to very different aspects—and thereby represents a classical cross-sectional function. Combinations with accounting (36 percent) and auditing (13 percent) head the list. According to Hirsch (2003), "the combination of controlling and accounting in a chair's name is an indication of the great closeness of these two disciplines". (p. 225) Nevertheless, 36 percent of chairs are characterized by other combinations (see Figure 2).

The institutional development of German language controlling at universities and business schools began in 1973, when Péter Horváth was offered the newly created chair of controlling at the Darmstadt Technical University. After that, progress was slow until the end of the 1980s. In 1989, just 17 of today's 72 controlling chairs existed. Then, things started speeding up. In just a few years, 14 controlling chairs were established in the former East Germany, while the number grew by 41 in the former West Germany. This rapid institutionalisation of controlling can be traced back mainly to changes in business practice. The expansion of university capacity in the field of controlling also led to a clear increase in publications relevant to controlling in the academic journals of German-speaking regions. Whereas the share of articles on controlling hovered between 4 and 6 percent in the 1970s and 1980s, that figure doubled to an average of about 12 percent at the beginning of the 1990s.

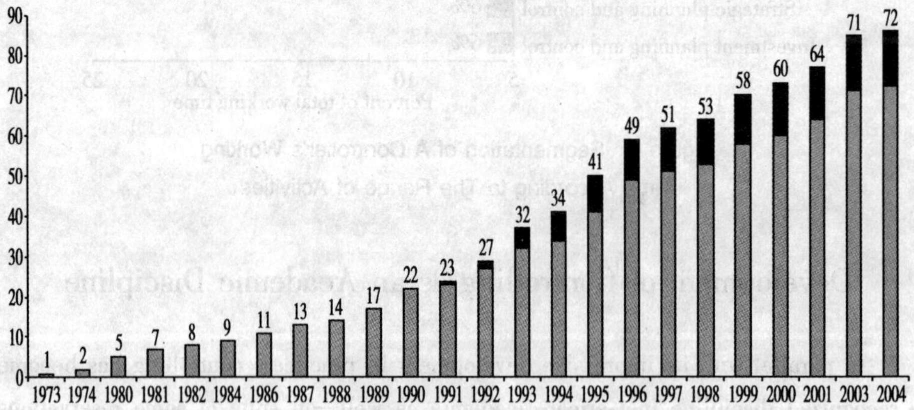

Figure 2　The Development of Controlling Chairs

Source　Binder & Schäffer, 2005a, p. 102.

Controlling Conceptions

There are many different controlling conceptions in the relevant German-language literature and there is no such thing as a unified understanding of controlling, much less a "generally accepted controlling principle" (Küpper, Weber, & Zünd, 1990, p. 282). The structure shown in the following, therefore, cannot claim to be representative.

Controlling as an Information Supply Function

Early controlling conceptions usually focused on information supply as the essence of controlling. Such an understanding is shown in the following two statements, for instance: controlling as "management support through information" (Hoffmann, 1972, p. 85) or controlling as "obtaining, preparing and coordinating information to be used by management in directing business to achieve certain goals" (Heigl, 1989, p. 3).

The point of reference is usually accounting, although in contrasting forms. Some authors have equated controlling with an American type of accounting, there by including areas such as statistics, budgeting, taxes and internal auditing within the ambit of controlling. Other authors have viewed the idea of controlling as not so much a functional expansion of accounting but rather as a material change to it. Their point of reference is a technocratic understanding of accounting.

This becomes particularly clear in Bannow's (1983) statement, who sees "the responsibility of a head of accounting as lying essentially in capturing and recording the information (figures) underlying the business processes of a company in accordance with accepted accounting principles to enable the accounts to be drawn up at a later stage so that management can be granted discharge at the end of defined periods (financial year)" (p. 20). Apart from mixing an institutional and a functional perspective, such statements negate the control function that has been inherent in accounting since its origins (Schneider, 1992b) as well as the evolution of cost accounting into a management tool. From a theoretical perspective, it makes little sense to relabel the established concept of decision-oriented accounting controlling.

This criticism applies in a similar way to approaches that try to derive the essence of accounting as controlling from an intensive analysis of information use, i. e. the recipients of the financial data. The image of "customer-unfriendly" accounting that underlies such a definition is relevant in practice. In theory, however, the question of how the "proper" financial information should be shown to different information recipients in the company has already been assigned to an area of research, namely the different types of behavioural research that deal with this issue (Schweitzer & Küpper, 2003).

The attempt to define controlling as a "central unit of company information systems" (Müller, 1974, p. 683) is also problematic. According to this and similar conceptions, controlling is associated with a set of tasks ranging from determining information requirements in cooperation with those who need them, to information acquisition, to preparing information in a manner that addresses the problems and recipients, to explaining the information. Sometimes controlling is limited to an "essentially information-related dimension" in the hopes that the "appearance of omnipotence" (Link, 1982) can thereby be effectively counteracted. However, there are good reasons for doubting that this is a sensible way of addressing the question of demarcation. The approach essentially offers nothing more than relabeling a field of research (information systems and management) that has long been studied. This is not really convincing, particularly if one considers that the responsibilities of controllers go far beyond pure information tasks in practice.

Controlling As Results-oriented Control

The second type of early controlling conceptions emphasise controlling as a subarea of corporate management that is tasked with results-oriented control or with consistently aligning the company with its goals. Mann (1973, p. 13), for instance, explicitly described controlling as "profit control".

In this generalised form, however, the approach is not helpful. It is not only controlling, but also the entire management of a for-profit company that directs all its energies towards making a profit. It also remains unclear whether the exclusive reference to the profit goal purposefully excludes other company goals or stands for an abbreviated representation. Such a limitation oriented towards the profit goal makes little sense. It implies that non-profit organizations such as state hospitals, would by definition not be able to use controlling. It is hard to see a sufficient reason for this. However, if one extends "profit-oriented" to "results-oriented", the added value of the explanation is, in practical terms, equal to zero.

A possible meaningful interpretation of this controlling conception does not address profit orientation itself, but rather the way in which it is realised. This becomes clear from Hahn's (1987) definition: "The way in which controlling works as a management philosophy includes … results-oriented planning, and supervision by means of target agreements … and analyses of goal achievement … using the figures provided by accounting and finance" (p. 3). This conception is based on a view of management that describes it in terms of a control cycle, as shown below.

The starting point lies in defining the objectives that the company and its units want to achieve. These are generated in a planning process and provided to the respective managers at various levels in the company in the form of plans. The managers try to achieve their objectives through their daily management activities. The extent to which they succeed in their efforts is recorded, for instance, through cost accounting as a means of measuring outputs. The values thus identified then form the basis for comparing planned with actual values. If any deviations are found, the information can be fed in two directions: the newly gained knowledge can be used in a feedback loop to modify execution in such a way that the goals are achieved after all or in the case of feed-forward loop, the deviation data is used to question the validity or achievability of the plans.

Viewing controlling as such a control cycle converts it into a synonym for "managing by plans", which at the same time creates strong links to the roots of controllership. Controller positions were introduced when entrepreneurs had to change their management behaviour for reasons of size and dynamics, namely when plans started replacing (or at least accompanying) personal instruction. Management that focuses heavily on individuals, as is typically the case in medium-sized companies, or bureaucratic, rule-based management structures, as found in the public sector, are marked other "management philosophies". Controlling would thereby have to be defined as a specific form or philosophy of management. A large part of the management literature already deals with "plan-based" management, however.

A further potentially sustainable delimitation is provided by Krüger's (1979) definition: "Controlling is a system of coordinated measures, principles, goals, methods and techniques used for system-internal, results-related control and monitoring" (p. 158). Siegwart (1986) similarly equated controlling with "profit-oriented control and monitoring" (p. 109). Such definitions prove to be useful when a further management function is identified in addition to control/steering and monitoring/supervision, namely goal-setting or decision making. Such a differentiation is by no means uncommon in the literature; it is, in fact, widely known. However, the innovative contribution of such a controlling definition would only consist in the shared perspective on existing management elements, especially monitoring (of results) and parts of planning (e. g. the relationships between planning levels).

Controlling As A Coordination Function

The controlling conceptions in this, the third group, see the central task of controlling as lying in the coordination between different subsystems of management. This perspective, in which controlling is linked exclusively to a coordination function, was to a large degree formed by Horváth (1978) and Küpper (1987). Horváth argued for a systems-based approach by differentiating a company's management system into a planning and monitoring system on the one hand and an information (supply) system on the other hand. This differentiation generates a need for coordination, which is covered by controlling. It thus becomes the third management subsystem. Horváth saw the task of coordination as not being limited to relationships between systems (e. g. matching planning and monitoring information), but that it also included coordination within the planning and monitoring system as well as within the information supply system as part of the responsibility of the controlling function (e. g. coordinating strategic with operational planning). Schmidt

(1986) extended Horváth's approach by focusing not on coordination itself, but rather on the objects of coordination: "The coordination function of controlling relates to the management system and to the phases of the management process. Its activities aim primarily at the company-wide internal coordination and integrative linking of the information, goal, planning and monitoring and organization systems" (p. 73). This structural approach was adopted—with slight modifications—by Küpper (1987). The benefit of such greater differentiation is that it uncovers additional coordination problems waiting to be solved. By taking on such a coordination task, controlling aims to achieve exactly the same with regard to management as management does with regard to execution. Controlling deals with efficiency (achieving an objective with the least inputs) and effectiveness (using inputs to achieve objectives that provide the highest utility). Coordination deficits within the management system lower both. For instance, if a new remuneration system is introduced without first ensuring that the required information is available in the necessary quality, demotivation, performance drops and management opportunism result. The coordination task reaches its limits when it becomes too expensive to carry out or when the knowledge needed to execute it adequately is lacking.

If controlling is defined in this way, it enters into any form of the management of a (productive) institution. The existence of the function (coordination) is at its core influenced neither by the concrete objective nor by specific leadership styles or models. Consequently, controlling has to exist in "classical', bureaucratically organised public administrations as much as in medium-sized companies managed personally by the head of the company. Under such a broad perspective, the range of tasks related to coordination in the management system is very wide.

However, coordinating management in "normal" large companies—with the concomitant importance of systematic, results-oriented planning and monitoring—is subject to requirements completely distinct from those in a bureaucracy or a typical medium-sized company. The concept of controlling then only matches the limited way it is understood in practice. In classical bureaucracies, one finds neither controlling as a concept nor people whose job title is controller.

Weber (1992) thus proposed that the coordination task of controlling should be limited to management systems where the planning system is of exceptional importance, in other words where operations are mainly coordinated through plans. In this case, the coordination tasks of controlling are concentrated on the planning system. The monitoring system, human resources management system and organizational and information systems are primarily coordinated towards the planning system and the need to coordinate direct interdependencies between the other management subsystems becomes less pronounced.

The coordination-based perspective on controlling is—independent of the definition used in each case—not undisputed in the current debate. The criticism starts with the systems-based perspective, which is considered to provide descriptive rather than explanatory value. A further criticism addresses the fact that there are usually no clear statements about where the exact boundaries of the subsystems lie and how these are formed (or should be formed) (Weber & Schäffer, 2000). In this way, both Küpper (2005) and Horváth (2006) defined the set of subsystems over time in different ways. Furthermore, in the practical reality of companies, there are already problems with separating management from operational systems (e. g. in modern group concepts in production). The lacking theoretical attention dedicated to defining system boundaries denies an answer to the question of the completeness as well as the meaningfulness of the differentiation. Furthermore, the coordination-based controlling approach is also not immune to overlaps with traditional subdisciplines of business administration. Instead, if taken to its logical conclusion, it leads to a counterintuitive separation from management, allocating to controlling the entire task of management design (meta-management) (Weber, 1997; Zenz, 1999). Finally, the coordination-based approach—especially in its interpretation by Küpper—is far removed from the focus of controllers' activities (Weber et al., 2006) and thereby from the empirical roots of controlling (Schneider, 1992; Schäffer, 1996; Kappler & Scheytt, 1999; Wall, 2000; Becker, 2003).

Controlling As Assuring the Rationality of Management

Based on a critical discourse around the coordination approach (Weber & Schäffer, 2000), a new approach has been developed according to which controlling deals with assuring the rationality of management (Weber & Schäffer, 1999; Schäffer & Weber, 2004). A specific management perspective forms the basis of this view. Management is performed by economic actors (especially managers) who strive to achieve individual goals and who are endowed with cognitive abilities. These are subject to individual limitations. Deficits of rationality may result from a manager's limited abilities (skill) and motivation (will). Starting from these inherent deficits, assuring rationality means acting to increase the likelihood that the execution of management actions corresponds to the anticipated means-end relationship regardless. To this end, the function deals with how to recognise rationality deficits and how to reduce or eliminate them. This understanding of controlling also corresponds to a large degree with the "classical" definition of management control by Anthony (1965): "Management control is the process by which managers assure that resources are obtained and used effectively and efficiently in the accomplishment of the organization's objectives" (p. 28).

Rationality is a key concept, and not just in business administration. Much older disciplines also discuss it (for instance, philosophy and the theory of science). Not surprisingly for anyone who has read this far, rationality is another expression that is defined in different ways in the literature. However, this lack of uniformity can easily be circumvented by referring back to means-end (or instrumental) rationality, which holds a dominant position in economics. In this case, rationality is measured by the yardstick of efficiently using means to achieve given ends. These ends are usually means for achieving higher-order ends, so that means-end rationality aims at the efficiency and effectiveness of actions (Schäffer & Weber, 2004).

The ICV's Practice-based Conception of Controlling

Although a vast number of conceptions have been developed in academia, only one originated in practice, namely the International Controller Association (Internationale Controller Verein, ICV), which is by far the largest association of controllers in German-speaking countries. It was founded and strongly influenced by Albrecht Deyhle, the best-known trainer of German-speaking controllers. His understanding of controlling played a key role in the development of controlling in German companies, not least because of the large number of controllers he coached. The International Group of Controlling (IGC), which is closely linked to the ICV, formulated a position paper (Leitbild Controller) that begins with a short introductory statement: "Controllers design and accompany the management process of defining goals, planning and controlling and thus have a joint responsibility with management to reach their objectives". This means that:

Controllers ensure the transparency of business results, finance, processes and strategy and thus contribute to higher economic effectiveness.

Controllers coordinate secondary goals and the related plans in a holistic way and organise a reporting system that is future-oriented and covers the enterprise as a whole.

Controllers moderate and design the controlling process of defining goals, planning and management control so that every decision maker can act in accordance with his or her agreed objectives.

Controllers provide necessary company management data and information.

Controllers develop and maintain controlling systems.

Roles of Controllers

Understanding controlling conceptions and controllers' tasks offers an initial notion of the roles controllers play. Actually, practical implementations and academic discussions have both agreed that controllers can be bean counters, inspectors, internal consultants, navigators and many other roles. However, which are the main roles of the controller generally? Which roles do managers expect controllers to play? And how have the roles of controllers changed over time? To search for the answers, the WHU Controller Panel conducted a longitudinal study.

Roles As Perceived by Managers

The 2010 survey asked controllers to assess how controllers' roles were perceived by managers (see Figure 3). The participants were of the view that management already predominantly perceives controlling in the sense of the more modern understanding of controlling. Accordingly, the perceived roles of internal consultant (in 67 percent of companies) and of the economic conscience (59 percent) predominated. By contrast, the negatively perceived role images of sniffer dog (22 percent), bean counter (12 percent) and brake (6 percent) were seen only in a minority of companies. The extensive prevalence of the inspector role image was notable. But when controlling is perceived to be purely a monitoring and inspection agency, it is hard to achieve collaboration between controlling and anagement based on trust and cooperation. Controlling continues to be seen as focusing on historical data rather than the future, as evidenced by the low prevalence of the change agent (8 percent), innovator (4 percent) and architect (2 percent) roles.

Current Role Images Vs. Desirable Role Images

A comparison between the studies conducted in 2006 and 2010 on the statuses and perspectives of controlling, which included a survey of role images, shows the extent to which the desired changes may already have occurred during the past few years. Contrasting current role images with those considered desirable in the future highlights how the perceptions of controllers in their companies should change (see Figure 4).

The intended significant reduction of the inspector role is particularly noteworthy (129 fewer mentions). This traditional—and common—perception of controlling is increasingly being seen as an obstacle to collaboration between controlling and

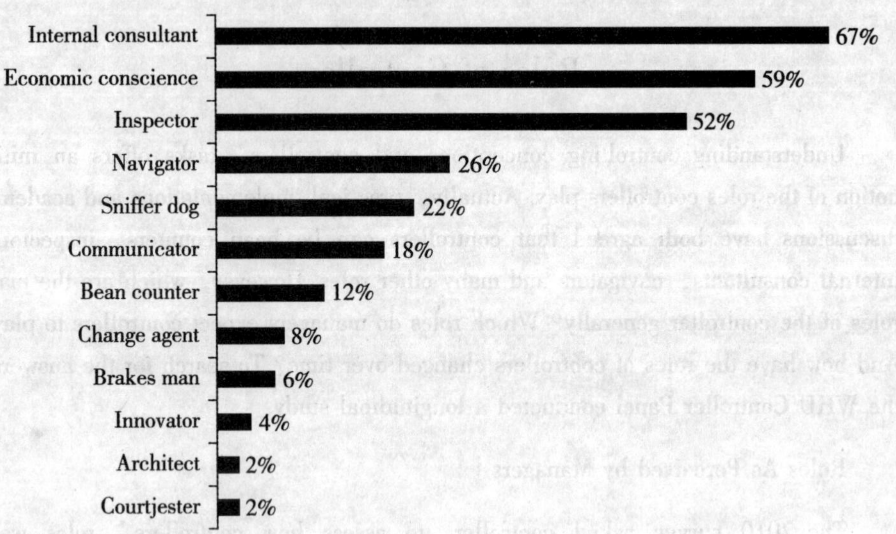

Figure 3 Controllers' Roles from Managers' Perspectives

Source WHU Controller Panel 2010, p. 13.

management based on trust and cooperation. Conversely, the perceived role image of the internal consultant, which is already predominant, is expected to grow further. The greatest increase was found for the "pilot" function. The future-oriented roles of change agent and innovator are also expected to increase in importance.

A clear concordance between the desired state described in the previous study and the current reality was only found with regard to the role of the internal consultant. This role image has become more prevalent in 2010 compared with 2006. Conversely, an opposite trend can be identified for the roles of the inspector and sniffer dog. Although controllers expressed a desire for these roles to become less important, they have in fact become more widespread (considerably so in the case of the inspector role image).

Skills Demanded for Role Fulfilment

The various tasks assumed by controllers require a well-rounded and balanced skill set. Both controllers' personalities (soft skills) and their capabilities (hard skills) shape controlling in companies. They are the key success factors and, at the same time, a possible cause of the lacking acceptance of performance by controlling. What skills are demanded to mould a fully equipped controller?

This question can be answered by the longitudinal study conducted by the WHU Controller Panel. The study result showed that the characteristics of a "typical controller", such as age, education and work experience, are relatively constant over time and have also not changed as a result of including additional participants in

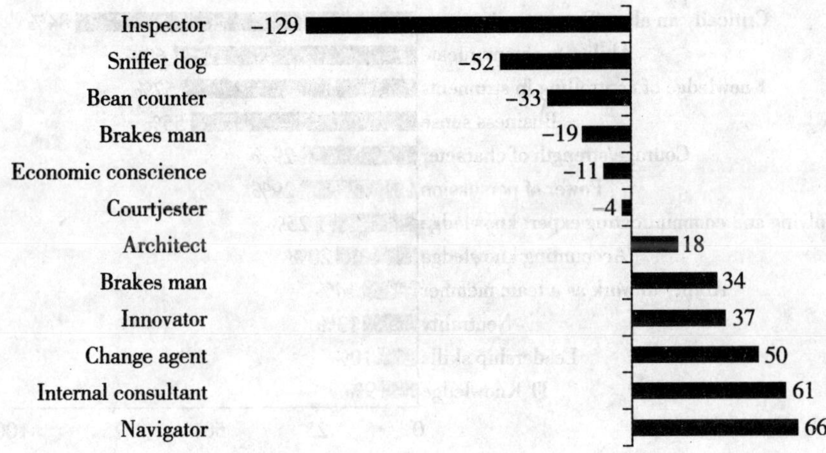

Figure 4 Comparison Between the Desired Roles and Actual Roles of Controllers

Source WHU Controller Panel 2010, p. 15.

the study. The only exception is represented by the controlling training courses given by the Controller Academy, of which members of the ICV make significantly greater use. The education level of controllers can be summarised as "highly qualified". The participants in the survey acquired their specific, controlling-related skills from a broad range of sources, of which the most important is on-the-job learning. An even more interesting question than that of educational profile is that of which skills controllers should be acquiring in order to be successful at what they do.

In 2008, controllers in the WHU Controller Panel were offered four groups of skills to which they were asked to allocate their answers. The results confirmed the findings from previous studies and from the literature (see Figure 5), which are summarised below:

Controllers need to have a balanced spectrum of skills. In order to explore the optimum mix of skills for controllers in greater depth, the survey provided a list of individual skills from which participants could choose the four most important skills for a controller. The results shown in Figure 5 confirm that technical skills are just as important as business acumen, management skills and personal qualities.

A considerable amount of controllers act as critical counterparts to management. The ability to ask critical questions and identify weak spots was mentioned by 84 percent of participants. Lagging behind considerably were communication skills (60 percent), domination of controlling tools (57 percent) and business acumen (55 percent). This assessment matches the modern understanding of controllers as critical counterparts who are no longer just "number crunchers".

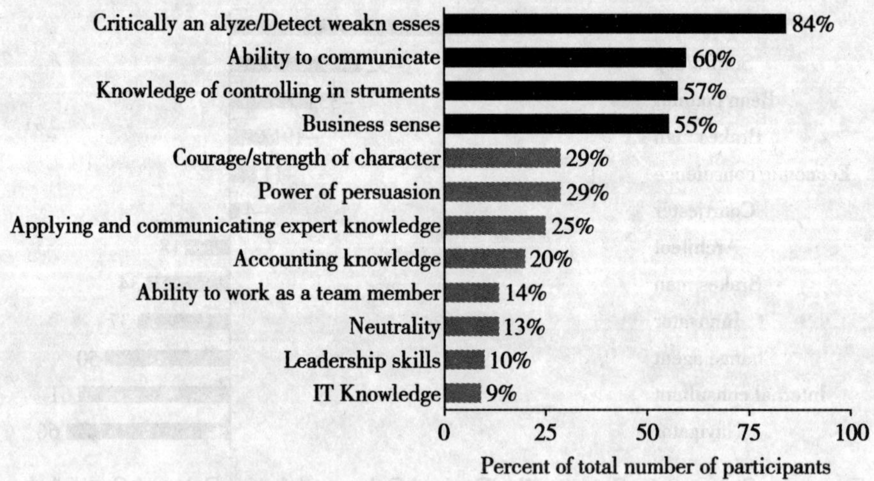

Figure 5 Most Important Capabilities of Controllers

Source WHU Controller Pance 2008, p. 10.

Summary

Controlling in German-speaking countries has gained recognition and legitimacy in both practice and academia, although initially it was found in practice, which caught researchers' attention and advanced research discussion. Today, German controllers assume a wide range of tasks from regular operational tasks such as reporting, budgeting and planning to special tasks such as internal consultancy and project-related tasks. Controlling research understands controlling predominantly either as a coordination function or as a function that is aimed at assuring the rationality of management with the controller acting as economic conscience and internal consultant. Finally, we must not forget what we learned from Stoffel's (1995) comparison study between Germany, France and US, which concluded that controllership is determined greatly by context and culture.

References

[1] Anthony, R. N., Planning and Control Systems, Boston, 1965.

[2] Auffermann, J. D., Vorwort, in: Rationalisierungs-Kuratorium der Deutschen Wirtschaft (RKW) (Ed.): Rechnungswesen im Dienst der Werkleitung, RKWAuslandsdienst, Vol. 3 (1952), p. 6.

[3] Bannow, W., Controlling ist wichtiger denn je, Harvard Manager, Vol. 5 (1983), pp. 20-25.

[4] Becker, A., Controlling als reflexive Steuerung von Organisationen, Stuttgart, 2003.

[5] Binder, C. /Schäffer, U., Deutschsprachige Controllinglehrstühle an der Schwelle zum Generationswechsel, in: Zeitschrift für Controlling und Management, Vol. 49(2005), pp. 100-104.

[6] Goossens, F., Der Controller, Chef des Unternehmens ohne Gesamtverantwortung, Mensch und Arbeit, Vol. 11(1959), pp. 75-76.

[7] Hahn, D., Controlling: Stand und Entwicklungstendenzen unter besonderer Berücksichtigung des CIM-Konzeptes, in: Scheer, A. -W. (Eds.): Rechnungswesen und EDV (8. Saarbrücker Arbeitstagung), Heidelberg, 1987, pp. 3-39.

[8] Heigl, A., Controlling: Interne Revision (2nd edition), Stuttgart et al., 1989.

[9] Henzler, H., Der Januskopf mußweg, in: Wirtschaftswoche, Vol. 28(1974), pp. 60-63.

[10] Hirsch, B., Zur Lehre im Fach Controlling, in: Weber, J. /Hirsch, B. (Eds.): Zur Zukunft der Controllingforschung: Empirie, Schnittstellen und Umsetzung in der Lehre, Wiesbaden, 2003, pp. 249-266.

[11] Hoffmann, F., Merkmale der Führungsorganisation amerikanischer Unternehmen: Auszüge aus den Ergebnissen einer Forschungsreise 1970, in: Zeitschrift für Organisation, Vol. 41 (1972), pp. 3-8, 85-89 and 145-148.

[12] Horváth, P., Controlling: Entwicklung und Stand einer Konzeption zur Lösung der Adaptions-und Koordinationsprobleme der Führung, in: Zeitschrift für Betriebswirtschaft, Vol. 48 (1978), pp. 194-208.

[13] Horváth, P., Controlling (10th edition), Munich, 2006.

[14] Institute of Management Accounting and Control (IMC): WHU Controller Panel Study Report, www. whu-controllerpanel. de(Studien), 2008.

[15] Institute of Management Accounting and Control (IMC): WHU Controller Panel Study Report-Roles of Controllers, www. whu-controllerpanel. de(Studien), 2010.

[16] Kappler, E. /Scheytt, T., Auf dem Weg nach Jenachdem: Controlling postmodern organisieren, in: Schreyögg, G. (Eds.): Organisation & Postmoderne, Wiesbaden, 1999, pp. 211-234.

[17] Krüger, W., Controlling: Gegenstandsbereich, Wirkungsweise und Funktionen im Rahmen der Unternehmenspolitik, in: Betriebswirtschaftliche Forschung und Praxis, Vol. 31 (1979), pp. 158-169.

[18] Küpper, H. -U., Konzeption des Controlling aus betriebswirtschaftlicher Sicht, in: Scheer, A. -W. (Eds.): Rechnungswesen und EDV, 8. Saarbrücker Arbeitstagung, Heidelberg, 1987, pp. 82-116.

[19] Küpper, H. -U., Controlling: Konzeption, Aufgaben, Instrumente (4th edition), Stuttgart, 2005.

[20] Küpper, H. -U. /Wagenhofer, A., Vorwort der Herausgeber, in: Handwörterbuch Unternehmensrechnung und Controlling (4th edition), Stuttgart, , 2002, pp. X-XI.

[21] Küpper, H. -U. /Weber, J. /Zünd, A., Zum Verständnis und Selbstverständnis des Controlling, in: Zeitschrift für Betriebswirtschaft, Vol. 60(1990), pp. 281-293.

[22] Link, J., Die methodologischen, informationswirtschaftlichen und führungspolitischen Aspekte des Controlling, in: Zeitschrift für Betriebswirtschaft, Vol. 52(1982), pp. 261-279.

[23] Mann, R., Praxis des Controlling, Munich, 1973.

[24] Müller, W., Die Koordination von Informationsbedarf und Informationsbeschaffung als

zentrale Aufgabe des Controlling, in: Zeitschrift für betriebswirtschaftliche Forschung, Vol. 26 (1974), pp. 683-693.

[25] Schäffer, U., Controlling für selbstabstimmende Gruppen?, Wiesbaden, 1996.

[26] Schäffer, U./Weber, J., Thesen zum Controlling, in: Scherm, E./Pietsch, G. (Eds.): Controlling: Theorien und Konzeptionen, Munich, 2004, pp. 459-466.

[27] Schmidt, A., Das Controlling als Instrument zur Koordination der Unternehmensführung, Frankfurt et al., 1986.

[28] Schneider, D., Theorien zur Entwicklung des Rechnungswesens, in: Zeitschrift für betriebswirtschaftliche Forschung, Vol. 44 (1992), pp. 3-31.

[29] Schneider, D., Controlling im Zwiespalt zwischen Koordination und interner Misserfolgsverschleierung, in: Horváth, P. (Eds.): Effektives und schlankes Controlling, Stuttgart, 1992, pp. 11-35.

[30] Schweitzer, M./Küpper, H.-U., Systeme der Kosten- und Erlösrechnung (8th edition), Munich, 2003.

[31] Siegwart, H., Controlling-Konzepte und Controller-Funktionen in der Schweiz, in: Mayer, E./Landsberg, G. v./Thiede, W. (Eds.): Controlling-Konzepte im internationalen Vergleich, Freiburg i. Br., 1986, pp. 105-131.

[32] Stoffel, K., Controllership im internationalen Vergleich, Wiesbaden. Vellmann, K.-H. (1990): Organisation des Controlling in einem Konzern, in: Mayer, E./Weber, J. (Eds.): Handbuch Controlling, Stuttgart, 1995, pp. 535-563.

[33] Wall, F., Koordinationsfunktion des Controlling und Organisation, in: Kostenrechnungspraxis, Vol. 44 (2000), pp. 295-304.

[34] Weber, J., Die Koordinationssicht des Controlling, in: Spremann, K./Zur, E. (Eds.): Controlling: Grundlagen-Informationssysteme-Anwendungen, Wiesbaden, 1992, pp. 169-183.

[35] Weber, J., Zur Abgrenzung von Führung und Controlling, WHU working paper No. 45 (1997), Vallendar.

[36] Weber, J./Bültel, D., Controlling: Ein eigenständiges Aufgabenfeld in den Unternehmen der Bundesrepublik Deutschland-Ergebnisse einer Auswertung von Stellenanzeigen aus den Jahren 1949-1989, in: Die Betriebswirtschaft, Vol. 52 (1992), pp. 535-546.

[37] Weber, J./Schäffer, U., Controlling-Entwicklung im Spiegel von Stellenanzeigen 1990-1994, in: Kostenrechnungspraxis, Vol. 42 (1998), pp. 227-233.

[38] Weber, J./Schäffer, U., Sicherstellung der Rationalität von Führung als Aufgabe des Controlling?, in: Die Betriebswirtschaft, Vol. 59 (1999), pp. 731-747.

[39] Weber, J./Schäffer, U., Controlling als Koordinationsfunktion?, in: Kostenrechnungspraxis, Vol. 44 (2000), pp. 109-118.

[40] Zenz, A., Strategisches Qualitätscontrolling: Konzeption als Metaführungslehre, Wiesbaden, 1999.

德语区国家管理控制的发展与现状

乌茨·舍费尔

（WHU 管理学院管理会计与管理控制研究院　德国　56179）

摘　要　本篇文章旨在帮助读者了解管理控制在德语区国家的发展和现状。文章涉及以下四个方面：第一，管理控制的实务起源与学术制度；第二，管理控制的概念（国际管理控制师协会所提出的基于企业实务的概念以及德语文献中所提出的学术概念）；第三，管理控制师的职责；第四，管理控制师在企业中所扮演的角色。

关键词　管理控制　管理控制师　起源　概念　职责　角色　德国

Effects of ISO 9001 Requirements on the Performance of Korean Companies: From the Viewpoint of BSC Perspectives

Do, Sangho Park, Moo-Hyun

(Keimyung University, Korea)

Abstract The objective of this study is to analyze the effects of quality management systems constructed by ISO 9001 requirements from viewpoint of BSC perspectives. Evaluation of quality management system based on BSC perspectives considers both short-term financial and nonfinancial performance, which eventually will foster future long-term financial results.

Data collected from small to medium-sized Korean companies with ISO certificates were analyzed to examine the relationships among BSC perspectives. Structural equation model was used to test research hypotheses.

The results of data analysis reveal that, from the learning and growth perspective, quality management systems does not have positive direct influence on the business performance. Instead, quality management systems have positive indirect influence on the business performance through the quality performance, a part of internal business perspective, and the customer satisfaction, a part of customer perspective. In addition, the relationships between quality management systems and its four sub-constructs were examined. Implications of this study and future research are also suggested.

Keywords Balanced Scorecard Quality Management Systems ISO 9001

Introduction

The ISO 9000 family of standards provide standardized procedures and guidelines for constructing sound Quality Management Systems (hereafter, QMS) and have been amended three times over the years (in 1994, 2000 and2008) since the first introduction in 1987. The standards play a significant role in helping firms establish sound QMS. ISO 9000 compliance certification means that the products or services satisfy the minimum requirement for QMS (Kim, 2004). As a result, the concept and its sub-constructs of quality management became central to business management (Won, 2010; Kim, 2004 and 2007).

Of the various ISO 9000 standards, ISO 9001 certification includes requirements for international certification. Since it provides standard procedures and suggestions for sound QMS systems regardless of sizes, types and/or specialties of firms, it is of great interest to firms which try to improve the quality of products and services (Won, 2010).

The firms in the competitive market are pressed for the establishment of QMS partly because of the worldwide trends of standardization rather than their own will in order to meet the requirements (Kim and Yoon, 2004). Particularly, ISO 9001 certification becomes increasingly mandatory for small and medium companies in Korea as they try to avoid unnecessary conflicts with their customers, i. e., usually big firms in Korea. Those relying heavily on exports also need certification to satisfy foreign customers (Kang, 2002).

Such environment surrounding them led to a sharp increase in the total number of Korean firms to acquire ISO 9001 certification in a short period of time. Despite the fact that firms invested much resources including time and personnel in building QMS, the effectiveness of ISO 9001 is still in question because the performance results were mixed (Kim and Yoon, 2004; Kang, 2002).

Kang (2002) argued establishment of sound QMS conforming to ISO 9001 standards provides only the foundation for systematic and continuous improvement in the quality of products and services, but not the improvement itself. Therefore, maintenance and regular upgrades of QMS is necessary to achieve substantial results and ISO 9001 certification should be regarded as a means for quality management rather than a goal.

The effectiveness of ISO 9001 requirements drew attentions from practitioners and academics in the fields of quality management, operations management and management accounting. For example, corporate culture for the implementation of ISO 9001 certification (Kim and Yoon, 2004), the relationships between the ISO 9001 certification and the competitiveness of quality (Hur and Koh, 2007), customer satisfaction and performance of firms (Kim, 2004 and 2007), employee satisfaction (Lee et al., 2007), and the relationship between the principles of quality management and ISO 9001 (Won, 2010) have been documented. Such studies tried to test the positive effects of the ISO 9001 certification and effectiveness of the systems in improving quality.

Based on the prior research, this study purports to evaluate the effectiveness of QMS established with the introduction of ISO 9001 certification from the Balanced Score Card (BSC) perspectives. It is particularly of interest, the growth rate of firms with ISO 9001 certification has been declined from 2003 while they need to make a strategic transition from quantitative growth to practical values (Won, 2010). BSC framework has the advantage in evaluating the effectiveness of QMS not only from the internal and external viewpoints but also from the perspectives of the firms' present and future.

Secondly, according to Kwon et al. (2006), firms that implemented QMS standards achieved better quality. However, it was also found that those firms lacking in activities of maintaining effective QMS such as continuous improvement, resolution of customer complaints and appropriate response to customers' escalating expectations.

Kaplan and Norton (2001) contended that learning and growth perspective affects internal process perspective, which in turn leads to the improved performance in financial perspective. This study is expected to provide understanding as to what extent the performance of QMS affects the various perspectives of BSC and to help identify areas of competency which the company should focus on.

Thirdly, ISO 9001 certification are directed at the cycle of Plan-Do-Check-Act as they are consistent with requirements such as management responsibility, resource management, product realization, and measurement, analysis and improvement. Therefore, the four elements included in the ISO 9001 requirements improve the performance through their operation as the whole cycle rather than each element affects the performance. The research models in most of previous studies on QMS, however, focused on individual effects of these four activities on customer satisfaction or quality performance. This study distinguishes itself from previous studies by modeling effects of these four activities on the performance simultaneously.

Previous Studies and Development of Hypotheses

Quality Management Systems (QMS)

QMS is a collection of activities designed to satisfy the needs of customers and is aimed at achieving and maintaining quality standards of ISO 9001 (Hur and Koh, 2007). Specifically, the ISO 9001 centers its requirements on four areas of management responsibility, resource management, product realization, and measurement, analysis and improvement.

ISO 9001 lists eight principles for quality management that the top management should implement in order to successfully operate QMS and achieve the desired results (Won, 2010). The principles are: customer-orientation, leadership, employee participation, fairness, management system, continuous improvement, decision making based on facts, relationship with the suppliers. Establishment of good QMS guided by these principles would help ensure the quality of business performance in terms of effectiveness, efficiency, flexibility and adaptability. (Park et al., 2007)

Based on this supposition, research has been conducted on how QMS leads to quality performance, customer satisfaction, employee satisfaction and financial performance. There are also other studies focusing on developing a model combining TQM, Six Sigma and Malcolm Baldridge National Quality Award.

The results of these studies would have certain contribution both in practical and theoretical senses. Few studies, however, focused on the present and future performance of firms from the BSC perspectives. This study would investigate the effects of QMS by utilizing BSC conceptual framework.

Balance Score Card (BSC)

BSC was first introduced by Kaplan and Norton (1992) and has been applied to various areas including manufacturing, service and public sectors. BSC is designed as an innovative model of performance evaluation that encompasses financial and non-financial activities. It consists of learning and growth, internal business process, customer and financial perspectives (Kaplan and Norton, 1992).

The perspectives of BSC are linked by causal relationships, and are used to better predict the performance of firms in the future. This overcomes the shortcoming by traditional model of performance evaluation based on the financial indicators only, i. e., past-orientation (Kaplan and Norton, 1996). The BSC perspectives emphasize that performance evaluation by nonfinancial indicators focuses on long-term performance more than by financial indicators, which, in turn, improves the future performance.

In summary, the performance evaluation based on non-financial indicators provides the manager better understanding of the interactive relationships between areas of management. This enables the management to allocate resources strategically based on the understanding of priorities among various management activities (Kaplan and Norton, 2001 and 1996).

Performance Evaluation of Quality Performance System based on BSC

In an increasingly competitive environment, firms that try to secure competitive advantages utilize BSC in order to diagnose its comprehensive status and evaluate the key success factors from various perspectives. The performance evaluation by BSC framework is considered to play a positive role in improving the performance (Malina and Selto, 2001).

From this context, this study examines the effectiveness of establishing the QMS from the BSC perspective. As explained earlier, the ISO 9000 family of standards enumerate quality management principles which include an idea of customer orientation. The idea of customer orientation has positive impacts on improving the customer satisfaction from the BSC perspective. In addition, ideas of continuous improvement, employee participation, decision making based on facts, and relationships with suppliers are consistent with the values of quality management. Therefore, the QMS would have positive impact on the quality improvement. Hence, it appears that the results of QMS with ISO 9001 certification is linked to the BSC perspectives.

The four perspectives suggested by Kaplan and Norton (1992; 1996) have causal relationships and have sequential impacts in the order of learning and growth perspective, internal business process perspective, customer perspective and financial perspective (Kaplan and Norton, 2001).

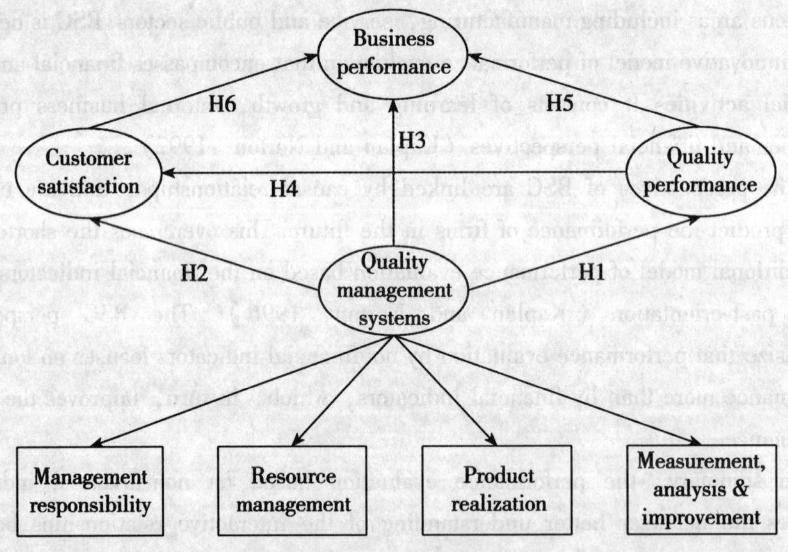

Figure 1 Research Model

Based on the work of Kaplan and Norton (2001), this study proposes the research model illustrated in Figure 1 by hypothesizing the relationships among the establishment of QMS that satisfy the requirements of ISO 9001 (learning and growth perspective), (internal business perspective), customer satisfaction (customer perspective), business performance (financial perspective).

Hypothesis 1. Quality management systems have significantly positive effects on quality performance.

Hypothesis 2. Quality management systems have significantly positive effects on customer satisfaction.

Hypothesis 3. Quality management systems have significantly positive effects on financial performance.

Hypothesis 4. Quality performance has significantly positive effects on customer satisfaction.

Hypothesis 5. Quality performance has significantly positive effects on business performance.

Hypothesis 6. Customer satisfaction has significantly positive effects on business performance.

Research Methodology

To test the causal relationships among the QMS, quality performance, customer satisfaction, and financial performance from the four BSC perspectives, data were collected from companies that implemented and met the requirements of ISO 9001 standards. Questionnaire was distributed to the managers. Questionnaire includes measurement items for each of variables from BSC perspectives and sub-constructs of quality management systems as shown in Table 1.

Some of them were interviewed face to face in a quiet room. Others were contacted by the phone to get the responses. Still others were requested to complete and mail back the questionnaire over the phone. The structured equation model was applied to analyze data.

Operationalization of Variables

This study adopted structured measurement scales which were proved to have validities in the previous studies. First of all, QMS is operationalized by the elements included in the ISO 9001 certification requirements, i. e. , quality management, resource management, product realization, and measurement, analysis and improvement.

Operationalization of research variables, i. e. , quality performance, customer satisfaction and financial performance are taken from the previous studies. (Sohn, 2009; Lee and Lee, 2007; Kim, 2004, 2007; and Kim and Yoon, 2004) The detailed descriptions of measurements are shown in Table 1. The variables are measured by 7 point rank scale.

Table 1 **Operationalization of Research Variables**

Variables	Operationalization	Items of Measurements*
Management responsibility	Management leadership	Management's will (mr 1) Customer-orientation (mr 2) Policies on quality (mr 3) Quality planning (mr 4) Responsibility, authority and communication (mr 5) Management review (mr 6)
Resource management	Support for implementation and maintenance of continuous improvement	Acquisition of resources (rm 1) Human resource management (rm 2) Infrastructure (rm 3) Work environment (rm 4)
Product realization	Process planning and implementation	Product realization planning (pr 1) Customer-related process (pr 2) Research and development (pr 3) Purchasing (pr 4) Production and services (pr 5) Monitoring and management of measurement tools (pr 6)
Measurement, analysis and improvement	Implementation of continuous development	Process development (mai 1) Monitoring and measuring (mai 2) Management of defective products (mai 3) Data analysis (mai 4) Quality improvement (mai 5)
Quality performance	Improvement of technology and productivity to ensure competitiveness	Decrease in defective units (qp 1) Decrease in reworks (qp 2) Decrease in production lead time (qp 3) Improvement of technology (qp 4) Improvement of quality (qp 5)
Customer satisfaction	Meeting the needs of customers to satisfy customers	Response to customer needs (cs 1) Processing customer complaints (cs 2) Monitoring customer information (cs 3) Surveying customer satisfaction (cs 4) Compliance with product liability regulations (cs 5)
Business performance	Business performance through continuous improvement activities	Increase of efficiency (bp 1) Decrease in inventory costs (bp 2) Improving management quality (bp 3) Increase of productivity (bp 4) Reduction in costs (bp 5)

Note: * Items of measurement are classified in each category of variables for brevity and cross reference.

Descriptive statistics

Of the 457 questionnaire collected, 118 were discarded due to insincerity and 339 were useful for empirical analysis. The descriptive statistics of data collected is shown in Table 2.

Table 2 Demographic Characteristics of Sample

	Classification	Frequency	Percentage (%)
Rank	Manager in charge	116	34. 2
	Head of department	135	39. 8
	Director	88	26. 0
Industry	Metal	51	15. 0
	Machinery	112	33. 0
	Electrical / Optical	10	2. 9
	Textile	11	3. 2
	Rubber / Plastic	13	3. 8
	Chemical	1	0. 3
	Other	141	41. 6
Number of employees	<5	42	12. 4
	5≤ ~ <10	91	26. 8
	10≤ ~ <100	193	56. 9
	100≤ ~ <300	7	2. 1
	300≤ ~ <500	5	1. 5
	500≤	1	0. 3
Duration of ISO certification	≤1 year	57	16. 8
	1 year< ~ ≤4 years	168	49. 6
	5 years≤	114	34. 6

As shown in Table 2, ranks of respondents are well spread among managers in charge, heads of departments, and directors. The most responses were collected from the firms in machinery. Most of these companies got ISO certifications for more than a year and are small and medium-size companies with employees of 10 to 100.

Reliability and Validity of Constructs Measured

The reliability and validity of variables included in the model were examined and the results are shown in Table 3 and Table 4.

Cronbach's α coefficient was used to test the reliability of measurement items. Those with coefficients greater than Cronbach's α were eliminated as they were considered to undermine the internal consistency. The items eliminated in the process are: quality planning (mr 4), responsibility, authority and communication (mr 5), management review (mr 6) of the 'management responsibility' variable; acquisition of resource (rm 1) in the 'resource management' variable; purchasing (pr 4), and monitoring and management of measurement tools (pr 6) in the 'product realization' variable; monitoring and measurement in the 'measurement, analysis and improvement' variable; quality improvement (qp 5) in the 'quality performance' variable; and monitoring of customer information (cs 3) and compliance with product liability law (cs 5) in the 'customer satisfaction' variable; and, finally, increase of productivity (bp 4) in the business performance variable. After eliminating these items, Cronbach's α's were measured at the level of 0.7 or above, and the measurements were considered to be reliable.

Table 3 **Scale Reliability and Validity**

Variables	Measurement Items	Factor Loading	t-value	R-square	α*	C.R**	AVE***
Management responsibility	mr 1	0.874	24.035	0.764	0.909	0.913	0.778
	mr 2	0.940	–	0.884			
	mr 3	0.829	21.601	0.687			
Resource management	rm 2	0.752	16.548	0.566	0.865	0.870	0.692
	rm 3	0.850	20.069	0.723			
	rm 4	0.888	–	0.789			
Product realization	pr 1	0.810	19.853	0.656	0.911	0.912	0.722
	pr 2	0.896	–	0.803			
	pr 3	0.842	21.378	0.709			
	pr 5	0.848	21.722	0.719			
Measurement, analysis and improvement	mai 1	0.836	19.700	0.699	0.905	0.906	0.706
	mai 3	0.805	18.452	0.648			
	mai 4	0.856	–	0.733			
	mai 5	0.863	20.824	0.745			
Quality performance	qp 1	0.852	22.252	0.726	0.929	0.929	0.767
	qp 2	0.895	24.794	0.801			
	qp 3	0.899	–	0.808			
	qp 4	0.856	22.474	0.733			
Customer satisfaction	cs 1	0.839	13.380	0.704	0.804	0.824	0.613
	cs 2	0.834	13.311	0.696			
	cs 4	0.662	–	0.438			
Business performance	bp 1	0.839	19.989	0.704	0.904	0.905	0.705
	bp 2	0.851	20.495	0.724			
	bp 3	0.873	–	0.762			
	bp 5	0.794	18.220	0.630			

Note: * Cronbach's α.

* * Assessing the Composite Reliability of Measurement Models.

* * * Coefficient of average variance extracted.

Table 4 **Correlation Coefficients and Discriminant Validity**

Variables	(1)	(2)	(3)	(4)	(5)	(6)	(7)
(1) Management responsibility	**0. 882**						
(2) Resource management	0. 641	**0. 832**					
(3) Product realization	0. 593	0. 808	**0. 850**				
(4) Measurement, analysis and improvement	0. 549	0. 715	0. 843	**0. 840**			
(5) Quality performance	0. 566	0. 674	0. 648	0. 759	**0. 876**		
(6) Customer satisfaction	0. 526	0. 674	0. 762	0. 935	0. 792	**0. 783**	
(7) Business performance	0. 487	0. 638	0. 724	0. 784	0. 737	0. 838	**0. 840**

Note: Bold numbers on the diagonal are the square root of AVE.

To test the validity, confirmatory factor analysis was conducted. The result satisfies the requirements of factor loading coefficients being greater than 0. 60 and is statistically significant (3rd and 4th rows) and coefficient of average variance extracted is greater than 0. 50 as illustrated in Table 3.

The discriminant validity test comparing the correlation coefficients with the square roots of AVE shows that the correlation coefficient between the variable of measurement, analysis and improvement and the variable of customer satisfaction is 0. 935. The correlation coefficient between the variable of business performance and the variable of customer satisfaction is 0. 838. Both coefficients are greater than the root of AVE.

In the studies of Kim (2004; 2007), Kim and Yoon (2004), the variable of measurement, analysis and improvement was found to be the most influencing factor on the customer satisfaction. The high correlation between the two variables in the current study appears to support the results of those studies. The variable of customer satisfaction usually brings about a positive long term relationship with customers, which, in turn, leads to improvement in business performance. In this regards, the high correlations between some variables of interest are judged to be reasonable and not to threaten the validity.

The fit indices of CFA used in this study were $\chi 2$ (d. f.) = 478. 283 (254), $\chi 2$/d. f. = 1. 883, RMR = 0. 050, GFI = 0. 894, AGFI = 0. 865, NFI = 0. 937, CFI = 0. 969, RFI = 0. 925, RMSEA = 0. 051, which satisfy the fit index standards required in social sciences in general.

Test of Hypotheses

The structural equation model and AMOS 18. 0 were used in this study to test research hypotheses. To test if the research model was fit, the fit indices were calculated: χ2 (d. f.) = 584. 191 (265), χ2/d. f. = 2. 204, RMR = 0. 067, GFI = 0. 873, AGFI = 0. 844, NFI = 0. 923, CFI = 0. 956, IFI = 0. 956, RFI = 0. 912, RMSEA = 0. 060. It is considered that the research model meets the fit index standards.

The tests of hypotheses found that QMS with ISO 9001 certification have significantly positive influence on quality performance (path-coefficient = 0. 789, t = 14. 720) and customer satisfaction (path-coefficient = 0. 771, t = 8. 821) at 0. 01 level. The QMS with ISO 9001 certification do not have significantly positive influence on business performance.

Quality performance has significantly positive influence on customer satisfaction (path-coefficient = 0. 183, t = 0. 689, $p<0.01$) and business performance (path-coefficient = 0. 158, t = 2. 202, $p<0.05$). Finally, customer satisfaction was found to have statistically significantly positive influence on business performance (path-coefficient 0. 521, t = 3. 191) at the 0. 01 level. These results are summarized in Figure 2.

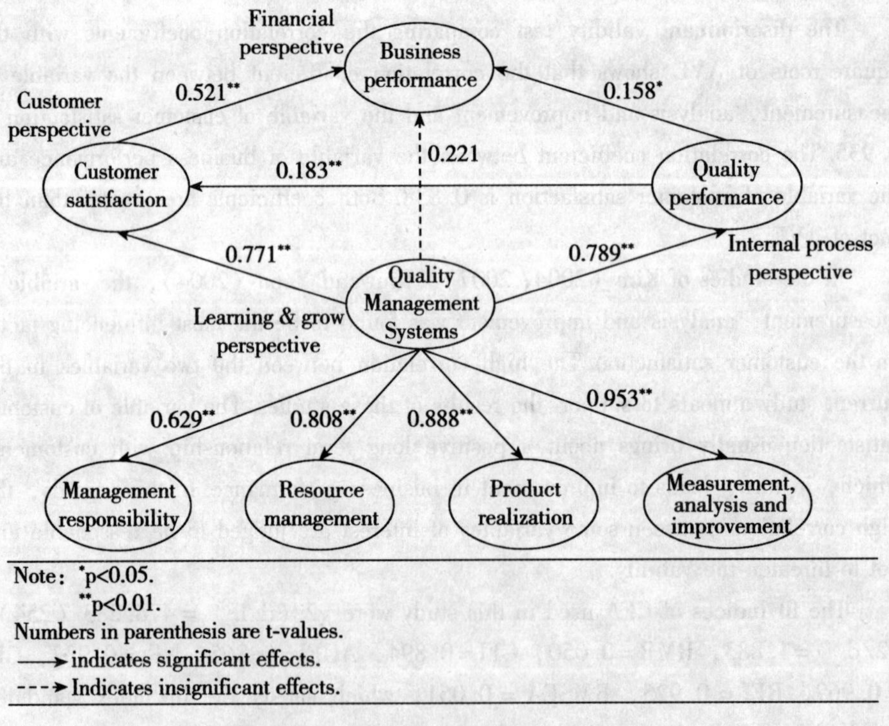

Note: *p<0.05.
**p<0.01.
Numbers in parenthesis are t-values.
——→ indicates significant effects.
- - -→ Indicates insignificant effects.

Figure 2 Results of Structural Analysis

Discussions and Conclusion

This study empirically tests the impact of the QMS of firms that satisfied the ISO 9001 certification requirements. As the number of firms with new ISO 9001 certificates declines in recent years, there are contentions that there needs development in practical value of the system rather than quantitative growth of ISO 9001 certificates (Won, 2010). A number of studies have made both theoretical and empirical contributions by testing the impact of QMS through ISO 9001 certificates.

This study is distinguished from others by applying the BSC perspectives. This study takes into consideration both short term financial performance evaluation and non-financial performance evaluation for future performance.

The earlier argument in this line of research for causal relationships between the four perspectives in BSC framework was later developed into cyclical influences starting from learning and growth perspective, internal business process perspective, customer perspective and to financial perspective (Kaplan and Norton, 2001).

This cyclical view of perspectives was also reflected in the results of this study. The QMS, i.e., learning and growth perspective, do not have direct impact on the business performance, i.e., financial perspective; instead, the systems have indirect impacts on business performance through quality performance and customer satisfaction.

While the business process perspective, operationalized as quality performance, was found to direct impact on business performance, i.e., financial perspective, it also showed indirect impacts on business performance through customer satisfaction.

The primary implication of this study is that QMS improve the efficiency and effectiveness of internal management activities and the external customer satisfaction. Such a complicated and cyclical process, rather than a simple process, ultimately leads to improved business performance. While the short-term benefits of QMS are minimal, the long-term benefits are more evident.

Future studies in this area could focus on the mediating effects of the time period since the adoption of QMS. In addition, the comparison between firms which keep up with ISO 9001 requirements and those which discontinued maintaining ISO requirements is needed.

References

[1] Kang, S., "The Effect of the Type of ISO 9000 Certification on Organizational Performance", Korean Management Review, Vol. 31, No. 1(2002), pp. 211-238.

[2] Kwon, B. G., Y. Y. Won and H. G. Kim, "Effect Analysis of Certification of ISO 9000 Quality Management System", Journal of Korean Society for Quality Management, Vol. 34, No. 2 (2006), pp. 1-11.

[3] Kim, Y. and J. Yoon, "The Effect of the Organizational Leadership and Corporate Culture Type, ISO 9001:2000 System, the Quality Culture Formation on the Corporate Performance", Journal of Korean Society for Quality Management, Vol. 32, No. 2(2004), pp. 37-58.

[4] Kim, J. H., " A Study on the Effects of ISO 9001/2000 Certification Factors on Performance of Service Quality and Customer Satisfaction" Journal of Korean Society for Quality Management, Vol. 32, No. 4(2004), pp. 64-77.

[5] Kim, J. H. " A Study on the Effects of ISO 9001/2000 Quality Factors to Customer Satisfaction and Customer Behavior", Journal of the Korean Production and Operations Management Society, Vol. 8, No. 4(2007), pp. 147-171.

[6] Park, D. J., H. G. Kim and Y. Y. Won., " Quality Management systems and global standard; Research Trend and Future of ISO 9000 Quality Management System: Literature Review", Journal of Korean Society for Quality Management, Vol. 35, No. 3(2007), pp. 1-20.

[7] Sohn, S. J., "The Effects of Corporate Culture, TQM, and Six Sigma Quality Management on Non-financial Performance and Financial Performance", Korean Management Review, Vol. 38, No. 6(2009), pp. 1691-1719.

[8] Won, H. G., " An Analysis of Relationship between ISO 9000 Quality Management Principles and ISO 9001 Requirements", Journal of Korean Society for Quality Management, Vol. 38, No. 2(2010), pp. 276-283.

[9] Lee, J. C. and S. J. Lee, " Causal Relationship between Learning Promotion Factor and TQM Implementation Factor in the Quality Management of SME", Korean Small Business Review, Vol. 29, No. 4(2007), pp. 19-41.

[10] Lee, H. S., Y. J. Choi and Y. R. Kim, "A Study on the Influence of ISO 9001 Quality Management System (QMS) on Employee`s Satisfaction", Journal of Korean Society for Quality Management, Vol. 35, No. 4(2007), pp. 16-25.

[11] Hur, S. and H. Koh, "A Study on the Evaluation Model for Quality Competitiveness of Management System", Productivity Review, Vol. 21, No. 4(2007), pp. 1-29.

[12] ISO 9001: 2000 (E). Quality management system-Requirements. ISO, Geneve, Switzerland: 2000.

[13] Kaplan, R., and D. P. Norton., "Balanced Scorecard-Measure that drive performance", Harvard Business Review, Jan. -Feb. (1992), pp. 71-79.

[14] Kaplan, R. S., and D. P. Norton, " Using the balanced scorecard as a strategic management system", Harvard Business Review, Jan. -Feb. (1996), pp. 75-85. 1996.

[15] Kaplan, R. S., and D. P. Norton, "Transforming the balanced scorecard form performance measurement to strategic management: Part I", Accounting Horizons, Vol 15, No. 1 (2001), pp. 87-104.

[16] Malina, M. A. and F. H. Selto, "Communicating and Controlling Strategy: An Empirical Study of the Effectiveness of the Balanced Scorecard", Journal of Management Accounting Research, Vol. 13 (2001), pp. 47-90.

基于平衡计分卡的 ISO 9001 要求对韩国公司的影响研究

都相浩　穆珲

韩国启明大学

摘　要　本研究的目的在于基于平衡计分卡视角，分析根据 ISO 9001 要求构建的质量管理体系的影响。基于平衡计分卡视角对质量管理体系进行评价，能够同时考虑对未来长期的财务结果产生影响的短期财务与非财务业绩。本文在从具有 ISO 证书的韩国中小企业收集数据以分析平衡计分卡各个维度之间的关系的基础上，应用结构方程模型来验证假设。分析结果表明，从学习和成长维度看，质量管理体系对企业绩效不存在积极的直接影响，而是通过质量绩效（内部流程维度的一部分）、顾客满意度（顾客视角的一部分）对企业绩效产生积极的直接的影响。本文还对质量管理体系与其四个分支的关系，以及本研究的政策建议与未来有待进一步研究的内容进行了论述。

关键词　平衡计分卡　质量管理体系　ISO 9001

内控缺陷带来的经济后果
——基于公司诉讼的视角①

林斌　周美华

（中山大学管理学院　中国广州　510275）

摘　要　利用2000年到2007年公司诉讼（corporate lawsuit）的数据，本文研究了内部控制、公司诉讼与企业价值之间的关系。结果显示：（1）企业内部控制存在重大缺陷、公司绩效越差、财务杠杆越高和规模越小的公司，其被诉的概率越大；（2）相比其他公司，内部控制存在重大缺陷的公司，其企业价值更低；（3）和其他公司相比，由于高额的诉讼成本，陷入诉讼纠纷的企业，其企业价值更低。

关键词　内部控制　重大缺陷　公司诉讼　企业价值

一、引言

学术界和实务界都把安然（Enron）和世通（WorldCom）等公司的失败归咎于它们的内部控制存在重大缺陷，同样的，发生在新加坡的中航油事件也是企业内部控制失败的结果（金彧昉等，2005）。具体到我国，吴水澎等（2000）运用COSO报告的标准和评价方法，从内部控制的五要素出发分析了郑州亚细亚集团的倒闭，他们认为，其内部控制的极端薄弱是促成倒闭的主要原因之一。这种由于内部控制存在重大缺陷而导致严重后果，例如中航油（新加坡）公司申请了破产保护，而公司诉讼作为解决纠纷的终极手段，在公司失败之前就会大量的出现。另一方面，《企业内部控制基本规范》（以下简称《基本规范》）第一章第三条定义了内部控制和内部控制的目标，其目标是“合理保证企业经营管理合法合规、资产安全、财务报告及相关信息真实完整，提高经营效率和效果，促进企业实现发展战略”。和COSO报告一样，都强调了经营的合法合规以及财务报告的可靠性，从现有的文献看，大部分都是关注内部控制缺陷对财务报告质量的影响（例如，Ashbaugh-Skaife et al.

---

①　本文系国家自然科学基金项目（70972076）和教育部人文社会科学基金项目（09YJA790199）研究成果。感谢中山大学管理学院博士生李万福、王林坚、刘瑾、舒伟、曹健、林东杰、肖海莲等参与讨论；感谢中山大学会计学术论坛上葛锐博士和蔡祥副教授的批评和建议，文责自负。

(2008) 和 Doyle et al (2007) 研究的是内控缺陷及其补救对应计质量的影响，ogneva et al. (2007) 和 Ashbaugh-Skaife et al. (2009) 研究了内控缺陷对权益资本成本的影响)，而鲜有文献研究内部控制缺陷和企业经营的合规合法性的关系，本文拟研究内部控制、公司诉讼和企业价值之间的关系。具体来说，我们主要研究以下三个问题：第一，当公司的内部控制存在重大缺陷时，是否会给企业价值带来负面的影响？第二，研究内部控制重大缺陷是否是公司诉讼的原因？第三，在控制内部控制重大缺陷后，考察公司诉讼是否还对企业价值存在负面的影响？

内部控制缺陷将会导致有意的和无意的误述，进而会影响公司报告的会计信息质量，从而影响投资者做出投资决策，所以，我们首先从会计信息质量方面研究内控重大缺陷对企业价值的影响；针对第二个问题，我们从风险的角度讨论内控重大缺陷和公司诉讼的关系，Ogneva et al. (2007) 和 Ashbaugh-Skaife et al. (2009) 都认为，当公司的内部控制存在重大缺陷时，企业的风险会增加，而风险超过某个阈值后，公司遭遇诉讼的概率将会大大的增加；最后，公司诉讼会带来高额的成本，这些成本既有支付给律师等的成本也有由于陷入诉讼而带来的声誉损失和惩罚，所以最后一个问题我们从诉讼的成本方面分析公司诉讼给企业价值造成的影响。

上市公司的诉讼纠纷既是一个法学问题，也是一个经济学问题。法学界对上市公司的研究一般采用案例研究的范式，强调其典型性和特殊性，而忽视其普遍性。受此影响，Cutler 和 Summers (1988) 研究了 Texaco 和 Pennzoil 对 Getty Oil 的控制权之争对企业价值的影响，在这篇广为引用的关于公司诉讼的文章中，被人诟病的就是只研究了一个案例，同时，Engclmann 和 Corncll (1988) 采用相似的方法，研究了五个案例。他们的研究结果发现，被告股价显著下跌，原告的股价有轻微上涨，在每个配对案例中，原告公司价值的增加远远地小于被告损失，也就是说存在严重的价值流失 (leakage)。对此，上述两篇文章都进行了细致的分析，他们认为，诉讼导致的财务困境成本是价值流失的最重要原因。和上述两篇文献一致，Bhagat et al. (1994) 采用大样本分析了公司之间的诉讼，他们认为低效率的谈判是公司诉讼的原因，财务困境成本 (the cost of financial distress) 导致了公司价值的流失。Bizjak et al. (1995) 研究的是私人反垄断诉讼，所谓的私人反垄断是指原告也是公司而不是政府部门，据我们所知，这是唯一的一篇原告具有显著正收益的文献，其原因可能和诉讼的类型相关，当被告败诉后，其垄断的市场份额可能会被原告瓜分，这促使原告的股价上升。在国内，王彦超等 (2008) 研究了公司诉讼对盈余管理的影响，祝继高 (2011) 利用银行起诉上市公司违反债务契约的诉讼数据，研究了债权人对会计稳健性的需求。

基于以下两点理由，我们的研究只关注重大缺陷带来的影响：第一，从内控缺陷的影响程度看，重大缺陷是最严重的缺陷，其对公司的影响最大，也最有代表性；第二，因为我国还没有要求强制披露内部控制信息，所以我们只能找其他变量作为内部控制重大缺陷的替代，依据《企业内部控制审计指引》，我们可以确定当某些迹象出现后，可能存在内部控制重大缺陷，以此作为替代变量，而其他的重要缺陷和一般缺陷更难找到替代变量，在 Doyle et al.（2007）中也只研究重大缺陷。

本文对现有文献的贡献如下：第一，现有文献还甚少有研究内部控制对企业价值的影响，本文从会计信息质量方面对此进行了检验；第二，前人对公司诉讼的研究都集中在其产生经济后果方面，而甚少有人研究其产生的原因，本文从内部控制角度对此进行了补充；第三，对于公司诉讼对企业价值的影响，国外的研究主要是从短期的市场反应方面进行研究，而甚少从长期的角度或者采用会计数据进行分析，本文从这两方面进行了补充。

二、理论分析和研究假设

1. 内部控制重大缺陷和公司诉讼

现代企业理论认为，企业是一系列（不完全）合约的有机结合，这组契约治理企业发生的各种交易，使企业内部发生的交易费用低于由市场组织这些交易时所发生的交易费用。但是，在现实世界中，由于未来事件的不确定性、人的有限理性和机会主义行为，以及存在交易成本，实际交易中签订的合约往往是不完全的，直观上很容易理解这点，因为合约不可能列出所有未来发生的可能事件，只能把许多决策和交易交给未来去做。刘明辉等（2002）认为，企业内部控制能弥补上述企业合约的不完全性，以保证企业的正常运作和发展。林钟高等（2007）也认为，内部控制是企业内部各个控制主体之间为实现其财富最大化而做出的合约安排，其本质属性是一种持续均衡利益关系的契约装置。而当内部控制存在导致企业严重偏离控制目标的内控缺陷时，合约的不完备性将更加严重，对未来事件的估计更不确定。

私人惩罚机制从两个方面促使了合约双方履约：一是直接与交易者终止交易关系有关的未来损失；二是与交易者在市场上的声誉贬值有关的损失（克莱因，1990）。而在不完全契约的自我履行上，法律的仲裁和强制执行起到了一种对私人惩罚机制的补充作用。诉讼机制和私人惩罚机制一起拓宽了不完全契约的自我履约边界，从而使得交易双方的利益博弈在“帕累托”意义上得到改进（潘琰、辛清泉，2003）。

另外，在《企业内部控制基本规范》中的风险评估要素中，强调了企业应及时识别、系统分析经营活动中与实现内部控制目标相关的风险，合理确定风险应对策略，确定相应的风险承受度。Ogneva et al.（2007）认为至少存在三个原因导致了财务报告的误述，进而增加了公司的风险：（1）内控缺陷可能增加了会计错误的概率：（2）系统的内部控制问题可能增加组织中各个层面对盈余的操控，例如，和合约相关的内控问题能使得经理人员更容易操控收益的确认；（3）重大内控缺陷也能增加财务舞弊的概率。而 Ashbaugh-Skaife et al.（2009）的研究发现，内部控制存在重大缺陷的公司，有更高的异质风险，风险越高的公司，公司的股价将可能会下跌的越多，这会招致外部股东的集体诉讼。这种情况在我国还比较少见，但是同样的，当公司的风险越高时，其经营的稳定性将会产生较大的波动，进而影响到现金的流入，这样也会招致公司的供应商和债权人的起诉。

从内控缺陷的决定因素看，财务状况是其中非常重要的因素，绩效差的公司可能对内部控制的投资不够，该投资表现在两个方面：一是财务上的支持；二是管理层的时间（Doyle et al.，2007）。Krishman（2005）的研究也发现报告的内控问题和亏损相关。而糟糕的财务状况也是公司被诉的最主要原因（陈晓、王建军，2011）。

由于我国法制不健全，以及执行力度等问题，我国上市公司一般是由于经济纠纷，而且主要是由于公司或控股股东为第三方提供担保，和向金融机构借款逾期未还，发生诉讼、仲裁事项（姚胜琦等，2006）。此外应付账款到期未付也是公司被起诉的重要原因。和其他条款相比，《企业内部控制应用指引》（下称指引）第6号资金活动、第7号采购业务、第9号销售业务和第16号合同管理更可能和公司被诉相关，例如资金活动中规定，在筹资（投资）时企业应当对筹资（投资）方案进行科学论证，重大筹资（投资）方案应当形成可行性研究报告，全面反映风险评估情况；企业应当对筹资（投资）方案进行严格审批，重点关注筹资（投资）用途的可行性和相应的偿债能力（获利能力）。在担保业务中，要注意担保申请人的风险和资信情况，企业应该建立担保授权和审批的制度，以及担保合同的执行和监控。所以当这些内部控制制度存在缺陷或者有制度而执行力度不强，超出公司的风险承受度时，公司可能会陷入被诉的风险。因此，我们提出以下假设：

H1：内部控制重大缺陷和公司诉讼概率正相关。

2. 内部控制重大缺陷和公司价值

财务报告内部控制是一个过程，为财务报告的可靠性和按照公认会计原则编制对外财务报告提供合理保证。具体的，财务报告内部控制包括了以下的政策和程序（PCAOB，2004）：

（1）保持以合理的细节准确、公允地反映公司资产的交易和处置记录；

（2）为对交易进行必要的记录以容许按照公认会计原则编制财务报表，以及公司的收入和支出都经过了公司管理层和董事会的授权批准提供合理保证；

（3）为防止或及时发现未经批准取得、使用或处置那些可能会对财务报表产生重要影响的公司资产提供合理保证。

产生低质量的会计信息可能基于以下两个原因：一是管理人员故意的误述

或者疏忽，这些非随机误述有典型的高估当前的盈余，或者“洗大澡”式的低估当前盈余。例如通过重要的会计估计政策选择（比如担保负债，销货退回的储备，应收账款坏账备抵金等）来操控应计项目。员工的舞弊可能是由于内部控制责任的不恰当分工，在宽松的控制环境下，不恰当的分工可能会导致资产的挪用和会计记录的更改，并且由于没有足够的人员进行监控而不能被发现。此外，虚假陈述也可能是管理层强调盈余目标导致的结果。二是由于员工缺少恰当的政策、培训或者勤勉而导致的随机的，非故意的误述，例如存货的计算和定价误差，这会导致误报库存商品和相关销售成本的分配，由于缺乏特定的收益变化记录政策导致收益确认的差错，应该资本化的却费用化，或者反过来，存货跌价准备的不确定估计等，这些随机的误述可能导致应计或盈余向上或向下的波动（Ashbaugh-Skaife，et al.，2009）。

总之，好的内部控制将降低故意的和非故意的差错，从而产生可靠的财务报告，其目的是防止和发现导致财务报告虚假陈述的错误和舞弊。反过来，弱的内部控制会导致会计数据的噪音甚至偏差。正如Lambert，Leuz和Verrecchia（2007）的理论模型证明的那样，会计信息通过直接效应和间接效应影响公司的价值，其中直接效应为高质量的会计信息不会影响公司的现金流，但是会影响市场参与者对公司现金流的方差和协方差①的评价。间接效应为高质量的信息和更好的内部控制会影响公司的决策，例如运营决策和经理人员挪用的资源等。财务报告披露的会计信息对投资者意义重大：一方面，投资者可以借助这些信息了解投资对象的运营情况和绩效水平，以决定是否值得投资；另一方面，投资者在解读企业运行情况的基础上更好地监督和评价管理者，降低潜在的代理成本和由于信息不对称带来的风险（Bushman 和 Smith，2001；Healy 和 Palepu，2001）。所以当公司的内部控制存在重大缺陷时，我们认为这些缺陷可能会导致财务报告的质量下降，进而影响市场参与者对公司价值的评估，基于此我们提出如下假设：

H2：内部控制重大缺陷和公司价值负相关。

3. 公司诉讼和企业价值

公司诉讼作为解决利益冲突的终极机制，其成本是非常高的（王彦超等，2008）。据调查，在美国，直接的诉讼成本远远地高过债务或者和解本身的偿付。Massin 和 Brothers（1994）的研究发现，公司成为被告时，在每个案件中的花费超过60万美元，在有些案例中，甚至迫使被告公司进入破产程序（Bhagat 和 Romano，2001）。

在此，我们把诉讼产生的成本分为显性的和隐性的两部分，显性的成本包括律师的费用、法院收取的诉讼费用、被告诉讼失败的赔偿、争议的标的，如果是向银行借贷的话，可能还有罚息等。隐性的成本包括对将来公司行为的限

① 和整个市场上其他公司相比。

制，比如下一次借贷会对金额和利息进行限制，或者对进入某行业进行限制；供应商也许会缩短应收账款的天数；公司诉讼对声誉的损害表现在两个方面（Engelmann 和 cornell，1988）：其一，当成为上市公司的被告败诉后，可能被法院判为非法，这会导致商业合作伙伴怀疑公司将来也会对其采用同样的非法或机会主义行为，降低其对公司的信心；其二，如果法院判决被告进行赔偿，这可能会导致公司陷入现金短缺的困境，这样合作伙伴会担心公司的付款速度或者降低产品的质量等。此外还会转移管理层专注于经营管理的精力。股东预期公司未来的现金流发生损失，公司未来投资价值下降，可能会抛售股票，公司在资本市场上的总体价值将会下降。正如 haslem（2005）所述，诉讼的成本最终将由公司的股东承担。因此，我们提出下面的假设：

H3：公司诉讼和企业价值负相关。

三、研究设计和变量

1. 内部控制重大缺陷的计量

根据财政部印发的《企业内部控制配套指引》中的《企业内部控制评价指引》（第四章），内部控制缺陷按其影响程度分为重大缺陷、重要缺陷和一般缺陷。其中，重大缺陷是指一个或多个控制缺陷的组合，可能导致企业严重偏离控制目标。

依据《企业内部控制审计指引》，表明内部控制可能存在重大缺陷的迹象主要包括：

（1）注册会计师发现董事、监事和高级管理人员舞弊；

（2）企业更正已经公布的财务报表；

（3）注册会计师发现当期财务报表存在重大错报，而内部控制在运行过程中未能发现该错报；

（4）企业审计委员会和内部审计机构对内部控制的监督无效。

本文以公司或高管违规，从而被监管层处罚作为内部控制存在重大缺陷的替代变量之一，这和审计指引中的第一条重大缺陷迹象相同。第二个替代变量为年报的重述，在 Doyle et al.（2007）对内控缺陷的决定因素的研究中，最后以财务报告的重述作为重大缺陷的替代变量，以进行敏感性检验。第三个替代变量为审计意见，我们认为审计意见表明了审计师对财务报告的评价，综合了更多的信息，如果注册会计师出具非标准的审计报告，则说明财务可靠性较差或根本不可靠，这也和第三条迹象相关。最后一个替代变量为是否设立了审计委员会，审计委员会的会计专业属性让其承担了对内部控制监察的职能。在 Carcello et al.（2002）的研究中，91%的随机样本的审计委员会章程都列示了对内部控制进行评价是他们的职能之一。我国的《企业内部控制基本规范》第十三条也规定了“企业应当在董事会下设立审计委员会。审计委员会负责审查企业内部控制，监督内部控制的有效实施和内部控制自我评价情况，协调内部控制审计及其他相关事宜等”。本文的内控缺陷变量选择也和李万福等（2011）相似。

2. 样本和变量

（1）公司诉讼

本文首先选取了2000—2007年的所有A股上市公司的诉讼案件作为研究对象，按以下要求剔除样本：①金融行业的上市公司；②部分数据缺失的样本。公司诉讼样本来自于WIND数据库，研究中用到的其他财务数据来自CSMAR数据库。2000—2007年的公司诉讼样本为3 629家，减去金融企业71家，原告890家，最终的样本为2 668家，因为一家公司可能在一年内遭遇多起诉讼纠纷，如表1所示在一年内涉诉6次以上的公司多达1 126家，也就是说公司诉讼主要集中在某一些公司，所以最后进入我们回归分析的公司诉讼样本为892家（其中还删除了其他数据缺失的观测值）。从表1B栏的诉讼类型中也可以看出，我国的公司诉讼主要是经济纠纷，这反映了我国公司诉讼的可能原因之一是公司陷入了财务困境，而在西方文献中经常见到的是因为虚假陈述而被外部股东提起诉讼的样本很少，这可能和我国的法律制度相关，目前我国对上市公司信息披露违规的处罚手段还是以行政处罚为主的罚款，而民事赔偿和刑事处罚的规定还缺乏实施细则和有效机制，例如在我国证券市场建立之初就已经存在的《民法通则》就未对证券违法做出规定①。

（2）公司违规

CSMAR把公司违规和高管违规分开处理，但是对数据分析发现，监管机构在处罚公司的时候，一般也会涉及高管人员的处罚，我们发现只对16家公司的高管进行单独处理。同时在公司违规的处罚中，会同时披露公司违规年度，但是在19家公司对高管违规的数据中却没有披露什么时候违规，我们采用监管机构披露公告的日期作为高管违规的年度。此外，从公司违规到被监管机构处罚往往会存在时间上的滞后，比如公司在2008年违规，但是可能在2010年才会被查处，滞后的区间大约为两年。在本文中，我们的研究区间从

---

① 虽然。2002年1月15日，最高人民法院下发了《关于受理证券市场因虚假陈述引发的民事侵权纠纷案件的有关问题的通知》（下面简称《通知》），但是由于该通知为此类案件的审理设立了行政决定前置程序，即人民法院受理的虚假陈述民事赔偿案件，其虚假陈述行为须经中国证监会及其派出机构调查并做出生效处罚决定，当事人依据查处结果作为提起民事诉讼事实的依据，人民法院方予以依法受理。同时规定了诉讼时效为两年，并且不能以集体诉讼的形式受理。2003年1月9日，最高人民法院又公布了《最高人民法院关于审理证券市场因虚假陈述引发的民事赔偿案件的若干规定》（以下简称《规定》），该规定降低了投资者起诉的门槛，以及可以提起共同诉讼，但是《规定》限定了“被告举证证明原告在虚假陈述揭露日或者更正日之前已经卖出证券的，人民法院应当认定虚假陈述与损耗结果之间不存在因果关系”。这意味着，在揭露日或者更正日前将股票抛售的原告即使积极诉讼也不可能胜诉，而事实上，有不少投资者出于止损的目的，都可能在揭露日前将股票抛出，此外，对于“揭露日”的确定，各个方面还存在不同理解，而揭露日的不同，将直接造成原告人数和损失金额的不确定（上海证券交易所研究中心，2008），我们认为上述的两个文件是我们较少见到虚假陈述民事诉讼的重要原因之一。

2000 年开始，到 2007 年结束，之所以以 2000 年作为我们研究的起点是因为 1999 年 10 月 31 日颁布的《中华人民共和国会计法》①从 2000 年 7 月 1 日开始实施，这是我国经济活动中基本的法规之一，是会计工作的基本大法，具有重要的影响和意义。以 2007 年结束主要存在两个理由：第一是违规数据的滞后，其中 2008 年和 2009 年分别为 69 家和 49 家，这明显比前两年少；第二，到 2007 年的时候，绝大部分的上市公司都已经设立了审计委员会，而审计委员会是我们研究中的一个重要的替代变量，这些变量只有存在变化时才有意义，到 2007 年只有 157 家公司没有设立审计委员会。从表 2 中可以看出，从 2004 年开始，随后的违规次数逐年递减，这可能是我国法规逐步健全，执行力度加大的结果，但是更可能是因为违规和被监管者发现之间的时滞造成的结果。

表 1　公司诉讼的概要分布

A 栏

诉讼次数	1	2	3	4	5	6	6 次以上
公司年	554	364	210	212	130	72	1 126
比率	20.76%	13.64%	7.78%	7.95%	4.87%	2.70%	42.2%

B 栏

类型	借款②	担保	贷款	欠款	虚假陈述	其他	合计
公司年	871	906	230	118	21	495	2 668
比率	32.6%	34%	8.6%	4.4%	0.0078%	18.6%	100%

C 栏

年度	2000	2001	2002	2003	2004	2005	2006	2007
公司年	83	326	264	132	460	645	462	296
比率	3.11%	12.22%	9.9%	4.95%	17.24%	24.18%	17.32%	11.09%

（3）年报重述

我们从巨潮资讯网检索年度报告中，手工查看每一个“年度报告更正公告”或“年度报告补充公告”或“年度报告更正及补充公告”或年报的修正版等，看其是否涉及重大的会计差错更正，把元写成万元的该类录入错误当做非重大缺陷，还有某一年度共同性的错误也作为非重大缺陷，例如在 2007 年度就经常遇到补充管理层的基本资料和薪酬的重述。在巨潮资讯网中，只存在 9 家公司 2000 年的年报，所以财务重述的数据从 2001 年开始。

① 参见中国证监会网站：http：//www.csrc.gov.cn/pub/newsite/xxfw/fgwj/gjfl/200802/t20080227_77627.htm.

② 该借款是指向银行借款，也就是说其原告专指银行。

表2 **内控缺陷年度分布**

年度	2000	2001	2002	2003	2004	2005	2006	2007
违规次数	112	196	153	153	168	129	99	96
年报重述		142	153	110	119	62	59	79
非标意见	174	153	156	100	146	163	140	118
审计委员会	11	57	267	167	125	52	90	593

以上的公司违规、非标审计意见和审计委员会设立的数据都来自国泰安数据库。需要说明的是，只要公司在某一年至少有一次出现在违规数据或者公司诉讼数据中，我们就认定其违规或者涉诉，所以我们在实证结果中看到违规的次数从1 106次降到了729次，而成为被告的次数从2 668次降到了892次。这样处理的好处是避免夸大我们的实证结果，这和Doyle et al.（2007）的处理一样。

除了上述变量外，我们还参考了王彦超等（2008）和陈信元等（2007）的研究结果，在我们的研究模型中加入其他控制变量，具体的定义见表3。

表3 **变量定义**

变量类型	变量符号	变量名称	变量定义
因变量	Tobin'sQ	企业价值	股权市值+净债务市值/期末总资产，非流通股权市值用净资产代替
	EPS	每股收益	净利润/总股数
	Lawsuit	公司诉讼	公司在某年度至少一次被诉时取值为1，否则为0
自变量（ICD）	Illegality	公司违规	公司或高管被监管部门处罚时取值为1，否则为0
	Restatement	年报重述	年报发生重述时取值为1，否则为0
	Audit	审计意见	非标意见时取值为1，否则为0
	Auditcommittee	审计委员会	未设立审计委员会取值为1，否则为0
	Icd1	内控缺陷	当公司存在违规、年报重述和非标审计意见任意一项时取值为1，否则为0
	Icd2	内控缺陷	公司违规、年报重述、非标审计意见和是否设立了审计委员会的加总，其取值为0、1、2、3、4
控制变量	ROA	资产报酬率	（利润总额+财务费用）/平均资产总额
	Cashflow	现金流量	现金及现金等价物净增加额/总股数
	Lev	财务杠杆	负债总额/资产总额
	Log（size）	公司规模	资产总额的自然对数
	Ind	行业	中国证监会公布的行业分类
	Year	年度	年度虚拟变量

注：表3中的控制变量主要参考王彦超（2008）和陈信元（2007）。

(4) 实证结果

①描述性统计和相关系数

我们从公司诉讼、公司违规、审计意见、是否设立了审计委员会和年报是否发生了重述五个方面，对公司规模、每股收益、财务杠杆、现金流量以及资产报酬率进行了比较，从表4的各栏中可以看出来，各个变量不管按什么情况分类，其均值和中位数绝大部分都存在显著差异，并且和预测方向一致，同时在25%和75%分位数上的比较也和预测方向一致。D栏中（是否设立了审计委员会）财务杠杆和现金流的均值T检验都不显著，这可能和下面的原因相关：如果公司在某年设立了审计委员会，那么之前的年度我们就把公司归于未设审计委员会，而设立当年和之后的年度就归于设立了审计委员会，也就是说，D栏的比较不只是公司之间的比较，也包括了同一家公司在设立了审计委员会前后的比较，这可能会干扰到我们的比较结果，而如果我们把设立审计委员会之后的年度排除在我们的样本之外，上述的两个变量都和预测的方向一样变得显著了。

表5是单变量之间的相关系数及其显著性，我们关注的公司诉讼、公司违规、审计意见、是否设立了审计委员会和年报重述五个变量中，没有和Tobin'sQ负相关的，公司诉讼、审计意见和Tobin'sQ显著正相关，这可能和我国的国情相关，在我国，要获得上市的资格比较难，而需要上市的公司较多，从而产生了我国独有的“壳资源”现象，人们预测到绩效差的公司可能会被未上市的公司收购，所以即使涉诉的公司和非标意见的公司其市场价值也不会下跌到其资产价值之下，我们的检测也看到非标意见的公司其Tobin'sQ显著大于标准意见的公司（其均值分别为4.57和1.55）。EPS和上述五个变量显著的负相关，这和我们的预期一致。而除了是否设立审计委员会（Auditcommittee）这个变量外，公司违规、审计意见和年报重述这三个变量都和公司诉讼显著正相关。四个内控缺陷的替代变量之间都显著相关，但是相关系数不大，其他控制变量的符号和显著性大体和我们预测的相一致。

②回归分析

A. 内部控制重大缺陷和公司诉讼

本部分采用以下模型来分析内控缺陷和公司诉讼之间的关系：

$$Lawsuit_{it} = \beta_0 + \beta_1 ICD_{it} + \beta_2 Roa_{it} + \beta_3 Lev_{it} + \beta_4 Cashflow_{it} + \beta_5 Logsize_{it} + \sum_{j=1}^{11} \beta_j Ind + \sum_{k=1}^{7} \beta_k Year + \varepsilon_{it} \quad 1$$

表6是上述模型的混合数据回归结果，方程（1）、（2）、（3）、（4）分别对应着内部控制重大缺陷的四个替代变量：公司违规、年报重述、审计意见和审计委员会。方程（5）中的Icd1表示，只要公司违规、年报重述、审计意见中三项有一项出现时取值为1，否则为0，方程（6）中的Icd2表示上述四项加总的取值（其取值为0，1，2，3，4），结果显示，除审计委员会变量外，其

表4 **主要变量的描述性统计**

A栏

变量	涉讼公司(892)					预测方向	未涉诉公司(9 048)				
	均值	中位数	标准方差①	25%	75%		均值②	中位数③	标准方差	25%	75%
Size	1.58e+09	8.36e+08	3.66e+09	4.34e+08	1.55e+09	<	3.69e+09 ***	1.47e+09 ***	1.94e+10	8.45e+08	2.94e+09
EPS	-.1593	.05	.9192	-.175	.15	<	.1845 ***	.18 ***	.4786	.0559	.34
Lev	2.332	.6432	29.94	.4929	.8551	>	.5152 **	.4761 ***	.7110	.3377	.6062
Cashflow	.0361	.0011	.5249	-.1043	.1304	<	.1785 ***	.03753 ***	.82693	-.1493	.3177
ROA	.0519	.0357	.1190	-.0395	.0661	<	.0622	.0568 ***	2.394	.0299	.0888

B栏

变量	违规公司(729)					预测方向	未违规公司(9 211)				
	均值	中位数	标准方差	25%	75%		均值	中位数	标准方差	25%	75%
Size	1.71e+09	1.08e+09	2.44e+09	6.16e+08	1.92e+09	<	3.65e+09 ***	1.44e+09 ***	1.92e+10	8.11e+08	2.89e+09
EPS	-.2541	.04	1.173	-.31	.17	<	.1860 ***	.171 ***	.4408	.051	.3356
Lev	.7689	.5877	1.360	.4162	.7189	>	.6709	.4818 ***	9.343	.3438	.6148
Cashflow	-.0113	-.0077	.8008	-.2474	.1989	<	.1798 ***	.0349 ***	.8041	-.1364	.3098
ROA	-.0385	.0292	.2675	-.0558	.0613	<	.0602 ***	.0567 ***	.7578	.0299	.0887

① 标准方差为均值检验时的标准方差。
② 均值的星号为T检验的显著性，*** $p<0.01$，** $p<0.05$，* $p<0.1$，单尾检验。
③ 中位数的星号 Wilcoxon 秩和检验的显著性，*** $p<0.01$，** $p<0.05$，* $p<0.1$。

续表

C 栏

变量	重述公司(679)					预测方向	未重述公司(9 058)				
	均值	中位数	标准方差	25%	75%		均值	中位数	标准方差	25%	75%
Size	2.27e+09	1.23e+09	6.24e+09	6.63e+08	2.42e+09	<	3.63e+09 ***	1.42e+09 ***	1.93e+10	8.08e+08	2.82e+09
EPS	-.0005	.09	.7906	.011	.22	<	.1662 ***	.17 ***	.5178	.05	.3338
Lev	.6619	.5348	.8542	.3884	.6811	>	.6725	.4835 ***	9.415	.3451	.6171
Cashflow	.0468	.0078	.7152	-.1427	.2013	<	.1760 ***	.0344 ***	.8159	-.1447	.3076
ROA	.0033	.0415	.2295	.0157	.0681	<	.0566 ***	.0562 ***	.7576	.0288	.0884

D 栏

变量	非标公司(1 119)					预测方向	标准意见公司(8 821)				
	均值	中位数	标准方差	25%	75%		均值	中位数	标准方差	25%	75%
Size	1.40e+09	8.49e+08	1.76e+09	4.00e+08	1.66e+09	<	3.77e+09 ***	1.48e+09 ***	1.97e+10	8.56e+08	2.98e+09
EPS	-.4396	-.0816	1.114	-.62	-.0539	<	.2290 ***	.19 ***	.3517	.07	.35
Lev	2.320	.6942	26.78	.5109	.9702	>	.4700 **	.4710 ***	.2379	.3359	.5969
Cashflow	-.0707	-.0086	.5609	-.1489	.0527	<	.1959 ***	.0497 ***	.8266	-.1419	.3387
ROA	-.0325	-.0076	2.190	-.1519	.0405	<	.0636 *	.0594 ***	.0749	.0337	.0905

E 栏

变量	未设审计委员会公司(5 566)					预测方向	设立审计委员会公司(4 171)				
	均值	中位数	标准方差	25%	75%		均值	中位数	标准方差	25%	75%
Size	2.29e+09	1.28e+09	3.68e+09	7.46e+08	2.43e+09	<	5.19e+09 ***	1.63e+09 ***	2.82e+10	8.88e+08	3.37e+09
EPS	.1161	.15	.5001	.04	.294	<	.2059 ***	.185 ***	.5914	.0563	.39
Lev	.5838	.4717	2.161	.3309	.6089	>	.7892	.5055 ***	13.65	.3598	.6353
Cashflow	.1687	.0278	.7896	-.144	.303	<	.1646	.0347	.8364	-.1455	.3006
ROA	.0374	.0521	.1782	.0247	.0816	<	.0736 **	.0593 ***	1.101	.0316	.0953

表5 主要变量的皮尔逊相关系数

	Tobin'sQ	lawsuit	Illegality	Audit	Auditcommittee	Restatement	EPS	ROA	Cashflow	Lev	Log(size)
Tobin'sQ	1										
lawsuit	0.0494***	1									
Illegality	-0.0024	0.0065***	1								
Audit	0.0530***	0.2552***	0.2498***	1							
Auditcommittee	-0.0136	0.0001	0.0247**	0.0731***	1						
Restatement	-0.0041	0.0990***	0.0942***	0.1190***	0.0382***	1					
EPS	-0.0196*	-0.1863***	-2110***	-0.3905***	-0.0818***	-0.0782***	1				
ROA	0.1939***	0.0040	-0.0352***	-0.0412***	-0.0244**	-0.0185*	0.1558***	1			
Cashflow	-0.0018	-0.0515***	-0.0632***	-0.1049***	0.0025	-0.040***	0.2507***	0.0265***	1		
Lev	0.9769***	0.0580***	0.0016	0.0632***	-0.0112	-0.0003	-0.0475***	0.0818***	-0.0061	1	
Log(size)	-0.1373***	-0.1931***	-0.0896***	-0.2224***	-0.1338***	-0.0528***	0.2626***	-0.0297***	0.0518***	— 0.1179***	1

他回归模型中的内控缺陷变量都显著和公司诉讼相关，这说明当公司的内部控制存在重大缺陷时，可能会导致公司陷入诉讼纠纷。而审计委员会不显著的原因可能有两个：第一，公司在设立了审计委员会之后的年度，审计委员会都会一直存在，而不像其他三个替代变量，在其后的年代是变化的。而我们在进行回归时，把审计委员会存在的年度都加进来了，也就是说，该回归不但比较了是否设立审计委员会的差异，而且把同一家公司在设立了审计委员会之后的影响也加入了我们的模型，这降低了方程（4）的解释力。第二，审计委员会变量不显著也可能因为是否设立审计委员会确实和公司遭遇诉讼的概率不相关。

方程（1）、(2)、(4)、(5) 和（6）的所有控制变量和我们的预测方向都显著一致，资产报酬率（ROA）显著为负，说明公司的绩效越差公司被诉的概率越高；财务杠杆（Lev）显著为正，说明公司的负债比率越高，被诉讼的概率越高；每股现金流（cashflow）和公司被诉的概率显著负相关，说明用于自身发展或者用于偿债的现金越少，其被诉的概率越高；而规模越小的公司更可能被诉，这说明了小规模公司抵抗风险的能力差，上述控制变量的检验结果和王彦超等（2008）基本一致。方程（3）中的控制变量只有公司规模是显著的，其他三个变量都不显著（审计意见显著为正 z 值达到 13.36），其可能的原因是审计意见概括了其他变量对公司诉讼的信息，同时我们也看到 Pseudo R2 在四个回归方程中的值是最大的，所以我们初步推测，在我们选择的四个内部控制重大缺陷替代变量中，对公司诉讼最具解释力的可能是审计意见。

B. 内部控制重大缺陷和公司诉讼对企业价值的影响

本部分采用下述 OLS 回归模型来分析内部控制重大缺陷和公司诉讼对企业价值的影响：

$$\mathrm{Value}(\mathrm{Tobin'sQ},\ \mathrm{Eps})_{it} = \alpha_1 + \alpha_2\mathrm{ICD}_{it} + \alpha_3\mathrm{Lawsuit}_{it} + \alpha_4\mathrm{Roa} + \alpha_5\mathrm{Lev}_{it} + \alpha_6\mathrm{Cashflow}_{it} + \alpha_7\mathrm{Logsize}_{it} + \sum_{k=1}^{11}\alpha_k\mathrm{Ind} + \sum_{j=1}^{7}\alpha_j\mathrm{Year} + \varepsilon_{it} \qquad 2$$

表 7 和表 8 分别是以 Tobin'sQ 和 EPS 作为企业价值替代的 OLS 回归结果，为避免内生性，我们只能把内控缺陷和公司诉讼两个变量同时放入回归模型中。表 7 的回归结果显示，内控缺陷的替代变量中，年报重述边际显著为负（T 值为 1.93），其他的至少在 5% 的水平上显著和预期一致。六个方程中的公司诉讼变量都至少在 1% 的水平上显著，这说明内部控制缺陷和公司诉讼都会降低公司的价值。同时，控制变量中的财务杠杆（Lev）显著为正，而公司规模（Log（size））显著为负，这和 Tobin'sQ 的计算方法相关，也和陈信元等（2007）的研究结果一样，而公司绩效（ROA）也都显著为正，这说明绩效越好的公司其公司价值越大。表 7 中的 R-squared 至少都达到 97.3%，说明自变量对因变量的解释力度很强，而当我们把财务杠杆排除出我们的回归方程后，R-squared 降到了 2.3%。当我们用财务杠杆对 Tobin'sQ 进行单变量回归时，其 R-squared 也达到了 95.37%，而在其他的文献中，我们也发现他们的

R-squared都达到了40%水平以上（陈信元等，2007）。

表6 内部控制重大缺陷对公司诉讼的logistic回归结果（因变量为Lawsuit）

VARIABLES	(1) Lawsuit	(2) Lawsuit	(3) Lawsuit	(4) Lawsuit	(5) Lawsuit	(6) Lawsuit
Illegality	0.368***					
	(0.124)					
Restatement		0.761***				
		(0.114)				
Audit			1.387***			
			(0.104)			
Auditcommittee				-0.00469		
				(0.0854)		
Icd1					1.084***	
					(0.0890)	
Icd2						0.482***
						(0.0534)
ROA	-0.373***	-0.345***	-0.0573	-0.393***	-0.179*	-0.231**
	(0.129)	(0.123)	(0.185)	(0.133)	(0.0924)	(0.105)
Lev	0.322***	0.297***	0.0947	0.336***	0.162*	0.210**
	(0.115)	(0.110)	(0.0716)	(0.119)	(0.0828)	(0.0947)
Cashflow	-0.112**	-0.141***	-0.0498	-0.125***	-0.0668	-0.0808*
	(0.0464)	(0.0458)	(0.0453)	(0.0471)	(0.0464)	(0.0463)
Log（size）	-0.608***	-0.605***	-0.525***	-0.614***	-0.535***	-0.556***
	(0.0464)	(0.0468)	(0.0461)	(0.0466)	(0.0456)	(0.0456)
Constant	10.05***	9.969***	8.283***	10.19***	8.385***	8.877***
	(1.002)	(1.010)	(0.985)	(1.010)	(0.979)	(0.979)
Ind	yes	yes	yes	yes	yes	yes
Year	yes	yes	yes	yes	yes	yes
Wald chi2	483.53***	470.50***	727.85***	472.81***	681.57***	623.32***
Pseudo R2	0.1258	0.1225	0.1558	0.1243	0.1514	0.1409
Observations	9 675	8 640	9 675	9 675	9 675	9675

注：括号内为稳健标准误，*** p<0.01，** p<0.05，* p<0.1。

方程（2）中的观测值比其他三个都少，这是因为年报重述的数据是从2001年到2007年。

表7　内部控制重大缺陷和公司诉讼对企业价值 OLS 回归结果（因变量为 Tobin'sQ）

VARIABLES	(1) Tobin'sQ	(2) Tobin'sQ	(3) Tobin'sQ	(4) Tobin'sQ	(5) Tobin'sQ	(6) Tobin'sQ
Illegality	−0.328 ***					
	(0.104)					
Restatement		−0.168 *				
		(0.0871)				
Audit			−1.073 ***			
			(0.142)			
Auditcommittee				−0.192 **		
				(0.0836)		
Icd1					−0.598 ***	
					(0.0709)	
Icd2						−0.349 ***
						(0.0451)
Lawsuit	−0.938 ***	−0.932 ***	−0.703 ***	−0.951 ***	−0.804 ***	−0.828 ***
	(0.178)	(0.184)	(0.165)	(0.176)	(0.171)	(0.172)
Roa	0.188 ***	0.189 ***	0.190 ***	0.189 ***	0.189 ***	0.189 ***
	(0.0282)	(0.0281)	(0.0278)	(0.0282)	(0.0280)	(0.0281)
Lev	2.328 ***	2.330 ***	2.332 ***	2.329 ***	2.330 ***	2.330 ***
	(0.0777)	(0.0773)	(0.0766)	(0.0776)	(0.0772)	(0.0773)
Cashflow	0.0224 *	0.0144	−0.00906	0.0292 **	0.00532	0.00815
	(0.0130)	(0.0147)	(0.0137)	(0.0133)	(0.0132)	(0.0129)
Log (size)	−0.234 ***	−0.197 **	−0.280 ***	−0.233 ***	−0.263 ***	−0.263 ***
	(0.0902)	(0.0963)	(0.0846)	(0.0892)	(0.0869)	(0.0886)
Ind	yes	yes	yes	yes	yes	yes
Year	yes	yes	yes	yes	yes	yes
Constant	6.158 ***	5.398 ***	7.170 ***	6.145 ***	6.811 ***	6.837 ***
	(1.926)	(2.055)	(1.804)	(1.905)	(1.854)	(1.892)
F	1 109.38 ***	1 182.48 ***	1 226.28 ***	1 165.61 ***	1 167.80 ***	1 181.70 ***
R-squared	0.973	0.973	0.973	0.973	0.973	0.973
Observations	9 678	8 643	9 678	9 678	9 678	9 678

注：括号内为稳健标准误，＊＊＊ $p<0.01$，＊＊ $p<0.05$，＊ $p<0.1$。

方程（2）中的观测值比其他三个都少，这是因为年报重述的数据是从 2001 年到 2007 年。

表7中我们以Tobin'sQ为因变量，Tobin'sQ代表的是资本市场对企业的估价，而表8中我们采用每股收益（EPS）作为企业价值的替代变量，每股收益是指企业的获利能力，是一个会计指标。我们在采用市场指标后再采用会计指标进行相同研究，可以使得我们的研究结果更具有说服力。表8的结果和表7的基本一致，内控缺陷和公司诉讼都和企业价值显著负相关，四个控制变量都显著为正。六个模型都在1%水平以下显著（F值最小为41.16），说明模型设定得较好。

表8 内部控制重大缺陷和公司诉讼对企业价值OLS回归结果（因变量为EPS）

	(1)	(2)	(3)	(4)	(5)	(6)
VARIABLES	EPS	EPS	EPS	EPS	EPS	EPS
Illegality	-0.347***					
	(0.0394)					
Restatement		-0.0809***				
		(0.0281)				
Audit			-0.555***			
			(0.0298)			
Auditcommittee				-0.0279**		
				(0.0129)		
Icd1					-0.318***	
					(0.0169)	
Icd2						-0.179***
						(0.0114)
Lawsuit	-0.214***	-0.220***	-0.0996***	-0.228***	-0.149***	-0.165***
	(0.0293)	(0.0319)	(0.0271)	(0.0303)	(0.0285)	(0.0289)
ROA	0.00270***	0.00279***	0.00328***	0.00277***	0.00299***	0.00301***
	(0.000575)	(0.000545)	(0.000212)	(0.000586)	(0.000392)	(0.000441)
Lev	0.00498***	0.00532***	0.00689***	0.00521***	0.00593***	0.00573***
	(0.00146)	(0.00139)	(0.000636)	(0.00149)	(0.00104)	(0.00115)
Cashflow	0.141***	0.161***	0.128***	0.148***	0.135***	0.137***
	(0.0150)	(0.0180)	(0.0149)	(0.0156)	(0.0153)	(0.0150)
Log (size)	0.109***	0.116***	0.0885***	0.115***	0.0971***	0.0974***
	(0.00627)	(0.00698)	(0.00582)	(0.00663)	(0.00612)	(0.00606)
Ind	yes	yes	yes	yes	yes	yes
Year	yes	yes	yes	yes	yes	yes
Constant	-2.002***	-2.159***	-1.553***	-2.129***	-1.727***	-1.729***
	(0.134)	(0.149)	(0.124)	(0.142)	(0.131)	(0.129)
F	41.42***	41.16***	59.41***	41.96***	50.01***	46.11***
R-squared	0.188	0.167	0.252	0.161	0.211	0.211
Observations	9678	8643	9678	9678	9678	9678

注：括号内为稳健标准误，*** $p<0.01$，** $p<0.05$，* $p<0.1$。

方程（2）中的观测值比其他三个都少，这是因为年报重述的数据是从2001年到2007年。

③稳健性检验

A. 依据表1B栏的诉讼类型分类，重复模型1和模型2的回归，结果基本上没有变化。

B. 以被证监会处罚的ST作为内部控制重大缺陷的替代，重复模型1和模型2的回归，结果没有变化。

C. 以Altman（1968）的Z-SCORE来替代模型1中的ROA，除公司违规变得不显著，而其他变量（审计意见、年报重述、Icd1和Icd2）仍然显著为正。

四、结论和不足

内部控制存在重大缺陷时会带来严重的后果，最严重的会导致企业破产，那么内部控制存在缺陷时还会带来其他的恶劣后果吗？公司诉讼可能是其中之一，本文从内部控制角度出发，研究了公司诉讼的决定因素和经济后果，研究发现，企业内部控制存在重大缺陷、公司绩效、财务杠杆和公司规模是其主要的决定因素。和其他公司相比较，当内部控制存在重大缺陷，其企业的市场价值和会计价值都显著降低，在控制内控缺陷后，由于诉讼的高额成本，公司诉讼仍然会给企业价值带来显著的负面影响。该研究的意义体现在，加强企业内部控制的建设能降低公司被诉的风险，提升企业的价值。

由于我国暂时还未强制要求披露经审计的内部控制状况，所以对于内部控制缺陷我们只能找来一些替代变量，虽然从文献上来看，这些替代变量都有其合理之处，但是其能否恰如其分地反应内部控制的重大缺陷还需要等以后有了该方面的数据进行检验。

主要参考文献

[1] 陈晓、王建军:《基于上市公司因重大债务欠债不还被提起诉讼事件的财务危机预测》,载北京2011年四校博士生论坛(4)。

[2] 陈信元、黄俊:《政府干预、多元化经营与公司业绩》,载《管理世界》。2007(1),92～97页。

[3] 金彧昉、李若山、徐明磊:《COSO报告下的内部控制新发展——从中航油事件看企业风险管理》,载《会计研究》,2005(2),32～38页。

[4] [美]克莱因:《契约与激励:契约条款在确保履约中的作用》,载科斯等:《契约经济学》,李风圣译,北京,经济科学出版社,1999。

[5] 李万福、林斌、宋璐:《内部控制在公司投资中的角色:效率促进还是抑制?》,载《管理世界》,2011(2)。

[6] 林钟高、郑军:《基于契约视角的企业内部控制研究》,载《会计研究》,2007(10),53～61页。

[7] 刘明辉、张宜霞:《内部控制的经济学思考》,载《会计研究》,2002(8),54~56页。

[8] 美国公众公司会计监督委员会(PCAOB):《第5号审计准则——与财务报表审计相结合的财务报告内部控制审计》,张宜霞主译,刘玉廷主审,大连,东北财经大学出版社,2008。

[9] 潘琰、辛清泉:《论审计合约与审计质量——基于不完全契约理论的现实思考》,载《审计研究》,2003(5),38~41页。

[10] 上海证券交易所研究中心:《中国公司治理报告(2008):透明度与信息披露》,上海,复旦大学出版社,2008。

[11] 王彦超、林斌、辛清泉:《市场环境、民事诉讼与盈余管理》,载《中国会计评论》,Vol.6,No.1(2008),21~40页。

[12] 吴水澎、陈汉文、邵贤弟:《论改进我国企业内部控制——由"亚细亚"失败引发的思考》,载《会计研究》,2000(9),43~48页。

[13] 姚胜琦、童菲、周晓辉:《上市公司诉讼仲裁信息的披露与股票非系统波动性的变化》,载《系统工程》,2006(7)。

[14] 祝继高:《会计稳健性与债权人利益保护——基于银行与上市公司关于贷款的法律诉讼的研究》,载《会计研究》,2011(5),50~57页。

[15] Altman Edward I., "Financial ratios, discriminant analysis and the prediction of corporate bankruptcy", The journal of finance, Vol. 23, No. 4(1968), pp589-609.

[16] Ashbaugh-Skaifea, Hollis, Daniel W. Collins, William R. Kinney Jr., "The Discovery and Reporting of Internal Control Deficiencies Prior to SOX-mandated Audits", Journal of Accounting and Economics 44(2007), pp. 166-192.

[17] Ashbaugh-Skaife Hollis, Daniel W. Collins, William R. Kinney Jr. and Ryan Lafond, "The Effect of SOX Internal Control Deficiencies Prior to SOX-mandated Audits", Journal of Accounting and Economics44(2008), pp. 166-192.

[18] Ashbaugh-Skaife Hollis, Daniel W. Collins, William R. Kinney Jr. and Ryan Lafond, "The Effect of SOX Internal Control Deficiencies on Firm Risk and Cost of Equity", Journal of Accounting Research. Vol. 47, No. 1(2009).

[19] Bhagat Sanjai, James A. Brickley and Jeffrey L. Coles, "The Costs of Inefficient Bargaining and Financial Distress—Evidence from Corporate Lawsuits", Journal of Financial Economics35(1994), pp. 221-247.

[20] Bhagat Sanjai and Roberta Romano, "Event studies and the Law: Part I: Technique and Corporate Litigation", Yale Law School Working Paper Series, 2001.

[21] Bizjak John M. and Jeffrey L. Coles, "The Effect of Private Antitrust Litigation on the Stock-Market Valuation of the Firm", The American Economic Review, Vol. 85, No. 3 (1995), pp. 436-461.

[22] Bushman, Robert M. and Abbie J., "Smith Financial Accounting Information and Corporate Governance", Journal of Accounting and Economics, No. 32(2001), pp. 237-333.

[23] Carcello Joseph V., Dana R. Hermanson and Terry L. Neal, "Disclosures in Audit Committee Charters and Reports", Accounting Horizons, Vol. 16, No. 4(2002).

[24] Cutler, David and Lawrence Summers, 1988, The Costs of Conflict Resolution and Financial Distress: Evidence from the Texaco-Pennzoil Litigation, Rand Journal cf Economics 19, 157 -172.

[25] Doyle, Jeffrey T., Weili Ge, Sarah McVay, "Accruals Quality and Internal Control over Financial Reporting", The Accounting Review, Vol. 82, No. 5(2007), pp. 1141-1170.

[26] Engelmann Kathleen and Bradford Cornell, "Measuring the Cost of Corporate Litigation: Five Case Studies", Journal of Legal Studies. Vol. XVII, 1988, June.

[27] Haslem Bruce, "Managerial Opportunism During Corporate Litigation", The Journal of Finance. Vol. LX. No. 4(. 2005, August), pp. 2013-2041.

[28] Healy Paul M. and Krishna G. Palepu, " Information Asymmetry, Corporate Disclosure, and the Capital Markets: A Review of the Empirical Disclosure Literature" Journal of Accounting and Economics31(2001), pp. 405-440.

[29] Krishman Jayanthi, " Audit Committee Quality and Internal Control: An Empirical Analysis", The Accounting Review. Vol. 80, No. 2(2005), pp. 649-675.

[30] Lambert Richard, Christian Leuz, and Robert E. Verrecchia, "Accounting Information, Disclosure, and Cost of Capital", Journal of Accounting Research, Vol. 45(2007), pp. 385-420.

[31] Massin S. Scott and Norman M. Brothers Jr., "Surviving the Litigious '90s: What Corporate Officers and Directors Can Do to Minimize the Risks of Lawsuits", SAM Advanced Management Journal. 59(1994), p. 27.

[32] Ogneva Maria, K. R. Subramanyam and K. Raghunandan, " Internal Control Weakness and Cost of Equity: Evidence from SOX Section 404 Disclosures", The Accounting Review, Vol. 82, No. 5(2007), pp. 1255-1297.

我国政府部门内部控制框架体系的构建研究

刘永泽　张亮

（中国内部控制研究中心/东北财经大学会计学院　辽宁大连　116025）

摘　要　目前，我国企业内部控制规范体系基本建成，而政府部门内部控制规范体系却尚属空白，不利于其职能转变、风险防范。因此，如何构建适应我国国情的政府部门内部控制规范体系成为亟待解决的重要问题。而作为政府部门内部控制规范体系研究的起点，内部控制框架体系的构建显然成为理论研究的关键问题。因此，本文在对我国政府部门的范围进行界定的基础上，构建了以政府部门内部控制的概念、目标、原则和要素为核心的内部控制框架体系。另外，本文在结合政府部门特点的基础上，建立了以国家立法为保障、内部审计为辅助、信息披露为抓手、外部审计为促进的内部控制实施机制，保证政府部门内部控制的有效实施。

关键词　政府部门　内部控制　框架体系　实施机制

改革开放30多年来，我国的经济发展取得了举世瞩目的伟大成就，经济总量一跃超过法国、英国、德国和日本等发达国家，成为仅次于美国的第二大经济体。但是，经济的高速发展没能掩盖行政体制存在的诸多问题，如政府职能不明确、行政管理效率低下、政府权力失控、贪污腐败现象严重等。因此，我国迫切需要推进行政体制改革，正如《十二五规划纲要》中指出的“大力推进经济体制改革，积极稳妥推进政治体制改革”、“深化政府机构改革、转变政府职能、加强依法行政、强化社会管理和公共服务来进一步创新政府管理体制”。政府内部控制建设实践证明，健全有效的内部控制，是政府部门切实加强内部管理、提高公共资金使用效益和为人民服务水平的重要举措（刘玉廷，2008）。一套科学完善的政府部门内部控制规范体系，可以有效地减少和规避政府风险，提高政府部门的运作效率，改善政府部门的行政管理水平，更好地履行政府部门的职责。而作为政府部门内部控制研究的起点，内部控制框架体系的构建显然成为亟待解决的关键问题。然而，目前国内外学者对于我国政府部门内部控制框架体系构建的研究甚少，因此，有必要对政府部门内部控制框架体系的构建作进一步的深入研究。

一、我国政府部门范围的界定

由于我国国情和历史背景的原因，政府部门的范围一直处于模糊不清的状态。因此，在研究我国政府部门内部控制框架体系之前，需要对我国政府部门的范围进行界定。按照当前流行的社会学理论，社会法人组织根据其性质不同可以划分为三个紧密联系又相互独立的部门：第一部门是政治部门，包括权力机关、行政机关和司法机关；第二部门是企业部门，包括公司制企业和非公司制企业；第三部门是非营利部门，包括各种社会团体、行业协会、慈善机构、社会服务机构等。另外，由于我国的特殊国情，我国设立了事业单位这一组织。按照《事业单位登记管理暂行条例》的规定：事业单位是指国家为了社会公益目的，由国家机关举办或者其他组织利用国家财政创办的从事教育、科技、文化、卫生等活动的社会服务组织。由于事业单位的职能定位不明确，导致了政事不分、事企不分。因此，若想确定政府部门的范围，需要对事业单位进行合理的划分，确保政事分开。按照《关于事业单位分类试点的意见》，根据现有事业单位的社会功能，将其划分为承担行政职能的、从事公益服务的和从事生产经营活动的三个大类。承担行政职能的事业单位，逐步转为行政机构；从事生产经营活动的事业单位，逐步转为企业；从事公益服务的事业单位，按原则保留在事业单位序列。因此，事业单位分类改革后，现有的事业单位将分别归属于第一部门、第二部门和第三部门。具体情况，如图 1 所示。

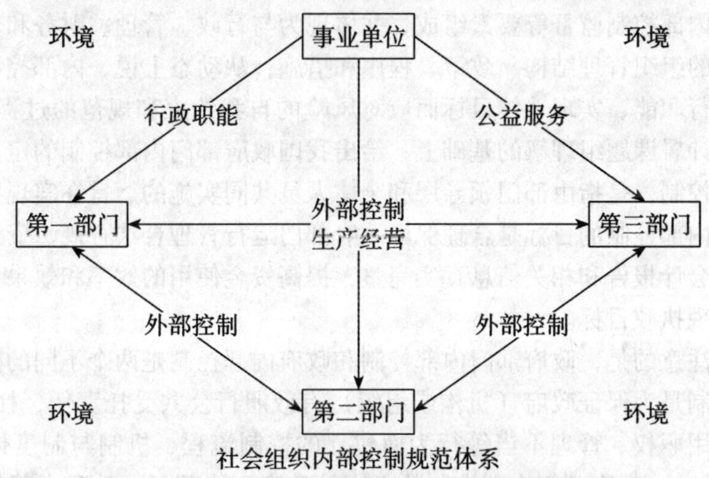

图 1　社会组织内部控制规范体系图

这样，我国就基本形成了和其他国家一致的三个部门的社会组织结构，而环境则是社会组织和内部控制存在的基础，包括政治环境、经济环境、法律环境、文化环境和技术环境等。相应的，社会组织的内部控制规范体系也应当包括第一部门、第二部门和第三部门的内部控制规范，而三个部门之间的联系就是外部控制。所谓外部控制，是相对于内部控制而言的，指的是组织外部的组织对组织施加的一种控制行为。但是，我国目前只制定了第二部门的内部控制规范，第一部门和第三部门的内部控制规范尚未制定，本文选取了第一部门中的政府部门作为我们研究的对象。政府部门和行政机关是两个相互联系又相互区别的概念。行政机关也可称为政府，强调的是政府总体，是广义的政府概念。政府部门特指各级政府下辖的职能部门，是狭义的政府概念。在确定了我国政府部门的范围之后，需要进一步明确内部控制框架体系的内容，才能构建适应我国国情的内部控制框架体系。根据政府部门的特点，本文认为，我国政府部门内部控制框架体系的内容包括：内部控制的概念、目标、原则和要素。虽然政府部门和企业的内控框架内容基本一致，但是两者的内涵却相去甚远。

二、我国政府部门内部控制的概念

概念是人们认识事物的最小单位和基本工具，人们只有通过概念才能把握事物的本质及发展规律（杨清香，2010）。因此，在我们讨论我国政府部门内部控制框架体系的构建问题之前，有必要对政府部门内部控制的概念进行清晰地界定。2006年，审计署《政府部门内部控制研究》课题组对政府部门内部控制的内涵给出了比较权威的理解："政府部门内部控制是内部控制要素与过程的统一。从静态上讲，内部控制是指政府部门为履行职能、实现总体目标而建立的保障系统，该系统由内部控制环境、风险评估、内部控制活动、信息及其沟通和内部控制监督等要素组成，并体现为与行政、管理、财务和会计系统融为一体的组织管理结构、政策、程序和措施；从动态上说，内部控制是政府部门为履行职能、实现总体目标而应对风险的自我约束和规范的过程。"我们在参考审计署课题组理解的基础上，给出我国政府部门内部控制的定义：政府部门内部控制，是指由部门领导层和全体人员共同实施的、旨在实现控制目标的过程。内部控制的目标是合理保证政府部门运行管理合法合规、资源分配公平公正、会计报告和相关信息真实完整，提高资金使用的效率和效果，促进政府部门实现执政目标。

值得注意的是，政府部门内部控制和政府内部控制是两个不同的概念。政府内部控制是为保证政府（机构或组织）有效履行公共受托责任，杜绝舞弊、浪费、滥用职权、管理不当等行为而建立的控制流程、机制与制度体系（王光远，2009）。政府部门内部控制的主体是政府职能部门，政府内部控制的主体是政府总体。因此，政府内部控制是更高层次的内部控制，其以满足公共利益为目标，以追求社会效率和公平之间的平衡为价值取向，而且能产生影响宏观经济效果和政府公众信誉的社会效应，在政府管理中发挥制约、规范公共行为的作用（审计署，2004）。政府内部控制在目标、属性和作用方面都更加宏观，从这个角度来说，政府部门内部控制从属于政府内部控制。

三、我国政府部门内部控制的目标

内部控制是因满足特定需求而产生，特定需求就是内部控制所要达到的目标，没有明确的目标，内部控制就失去了明确的指向。因此，目标是构建政府部门内部控制框架体系的起点和核心。根据我国政府部门的特点，本文认为，我国政府部门内部控制的目标是：合理保证政府部门运行管理合法合规、资源分配公平公正、会计报告及相关信息真实完整，提高资金的使用效率和效果，促进政府部门实现执政目标。在正式论述五个内部控制目标的涵义之前，有必要先对内部控制目标之间的关系加以明确。政府部门内部控制目标之间的关系主要体现在两个方面。首先，根据内部控制目标的层次不同，可以划分为治理层次目标和管理层次目标。促进政府部门实现执政目标是治理层次目标，其余四个目标是管理层次目标。治理层次目标在实施过程中需要分解成管理层次的目标，相应的，管理层次目标的实现最终会促成治理层次目标的实现。其次，管理层次的四个目标之间既相互独立又相互联系。一方面，这四个目标分别体现了政府部门面临的主要风险，代表了政府部门内部的不同需求，体现了不同管理人员的职责。另一方面，这四个目标之间又相互联系、相互影响，一个目标的实现与否会直接影响到另一个目标的实现情况。明确了政府部门内部控制目标之间的关系之后，我们将分别论述政府部门内部控制目标的内涵。

（一）合理保证政府部门的运行管理合法合规

该目标与符合相关的法律法规有关，强调政府部门要在法律法规允许的范围内运行管理，严禁违法违规行为的发生。该目标是政府部门内部控制最基本的目标，是其他四个目标存在的前提和基础。该目标取决于外部因素，在一些情况下对所有政府部门而言都很类似，而在另一些情况下只对某个政府部门有要求。政府部门的行政管理活动必须符合相关的法律法规，通常情况下要采取必要的措施保证其合法合规。适用的法律法规确定了其最低的行为准则，政府部门须将合法合规目标纳入内部控制目标之中。例如，政务公开要求政府部门根据《政府信息公开条例》来披露相关的政务信息；廉洁行政决定党员领导干部必须根据《廉洁从政若干准则》进行日常行政管理，保证政府部门的清廉。因此，政府部门需要制定政策和程序来处理相关法律法规要求的事项。政府部门的合法合规记录会对其社会形象产生巨大影响，对于提高政府部门的执政能力和社会公信力具有重要意义。

（二）合理保证政府部门的资源分配公平公正

该目标与政府部门资源分配的合理性有关。公平强调地位上“一视同仁”和衡量标准的“同一个尺度”，带有明显的工具性，用以防止社会对待中的双重标准或多重标准，即在普遍人权、独立人格、人与人之间地位等方面保证平等（吴忠民，2003）；公正强调资源分配是每个人得其所应得，所涉及的对象是社会资源，主要是社会权利和义务（陆树程，2010）。公平可分为起点公平、过程公平和结果公平三个层次，公正应分为实质公正和程序公正（顾肃，

2004)。公平公正目标的含义是:政府部门平等地对待各相关利益主体,将社会资源合理地分配给各利益主体。在这里,最突出的是部门预算的内部批复。只有将部门预算公平公正地批复给内部各单位,才能有效地实现财权与事权的匹配,发挥部门预算的引导和监督作用。公平公正目标要求政府部门同等地对待相关利益主体,将有限的公众资源投向正当合理的方向,以发挥政府部门的公共管理职能。正如温家宝总理所言“公平公正比太阳更有光辉”。

(三)合理保证政府部门的会计报告及相关信息真实完整

该目标与会计报告和相关信息的可靠性有关,强调政府部门要提供真实可靠的会计报告和相关信息。会计报告和相关信息反映了政府部门的运行管理情况和预算的执行情况,是政府部门财务信息的主要载体。同时,会计报告及相关信息作为社会公共产品,完整地反映了政府部门履行社会责任的情况,是政府部门借以解除受托责任的主要依据。另外,由于政府部门的特殊性和利益相关者的高度分散性,更加突出了政府部门会计报告和相关信息的重要性。因此,政府部门必须要合理保证会计报告和相关信息的真实完整,客观地反映部门的运行管理情况和预算的执行情况,为领导层的决策提供可靠依据,也为其解除受托责任提供依据。政府部门编制的报告既是管理的一种要求,也是一种有效的监督机制,有利于政府部门履行职责,完成工作任务。另外,预算报告是政府部门的重要报告之一,具有法定效力,这是政府部门和企业在报告上的很大不同。

(四)提高资金的使用效率和效果

该目标强调财政资金的使用效率和效果,包括保证政府部门资产的安全。该目标与成熟先进的管理理念和方法、最新的科学技术的发展(尤其是信息技术)以及科学有效的机制和体制密切相关,是实现政府部门发展战略的落脚点。在这里需要说明的是,该目标不仅仅指提高资金的使用效率和效果,也包括提高运行管理的效率和效果。之所以强调资金的使用效率和效果,是因为政府部门所有行为的效率和效果最终都体现为资金的使用效率和效果,这是由政府部门以预算管理为中心的特点决定的。预算管理反映了政府活动的范围和内容,是政府部门根据政治、经济和社会发展目标,筹集、分配与监督预算资金的管理活动,是政府部门筹集和使用集中性财政资金的重要分配杠杆,是政府部门实现其职能的重要工具。简而言之,预算是政府部门资金的使用依据,而政府部门的运行管理是围绕资金的使用展开的。因此,政府部门运行管理的效率和效果最终都体现在资金的使用效率和效果上。

(五)促进政府部门实现执政目标

执政目标是对政府部门管理活动预期取得的主要成果的期望值,是政府部门职能和宗旨的展开和具体化，是宗旨中确认的行政运行目的、社会使命的进一步阐明和界定，也是政府部门在既定的职能领域展开活动所要达到水平的具体规定。该目标与政府部门的职能和中长期规划相关，是政府部门内部控制的最高目标和终极目标，属于政府部门治理层次的目标。内部控制的战略目标是由组织的目标决定的。政府部门的目标是有效地履行政府职能，完成政府部门的既定任务。因此，其内部控制的战略目标是追求社会效益的最大化。战略目标与政府部门的使命或愿景相协调，并支持使命和愿景的实现，反映了政府部门为了更有效地履行本部门的职责、完成既定的工作任务所作的目标定位。政府部门只有在切实保证运行管理合法合规、资源分配公平公正、会计报告及相关信息真实完整、资金的使用效率和效果稳步提高的基础上，才能促进其实现发展战略。

四、我国政府部门内部控制的原则

原则是指观察问题、处理问题的基本准则。政府部门内部控制的原则，是政府部门建立与实施内部控制应当遵循的基本准则。内部控制的原则是内部控制的精髓所在，是内部控制经过长期实践而总结出来的规律性的东西（李连华，2007)，它是连接内部控制理论与实务的桥梁，为政府部门建立与实施内部控制以及评价内部控制的有效性确立了标准。本文认为，内部控制的原则包括全面性原则、重要性原则、制衡性原则、适应性原则和权责一致原则。政府部门内部控制的原则，分别从不同方面对内部控制的建立与实施给予指导，对内部控制有效性的评价提供参考标准，是政府部门内部控制得以有效实行的重要保证。

（一）全面性原则

全面性原则强调内部控制应当贯穿决策、执行和监督全过程，覆盖政府部门及其所属单位的各种业务和事项。首先，行政权力按照其属性可以划分为决策权、执行权和监督权，行政权力的这种划分符合大部制改革的核心思想，即建立决策权、执行权、监督权相互制约又相互协调的运行机制。大部门体制的实质是一种政府治理模式，利益的划分取决于决策，利益的实现取决于执行，利益的矫正取决于监督。具体说来，领导办公会议决策重大事项，各职能部门和二级单位根据自身职能行使执行权，预算委员会、审计委员会、党委纪检和监察部门分别从不同方面行使行政监督权。全面性原则强调内部控制应当贯彻决策、执行和监督全过程，即要求政府部门的决策要科学民主、执行要强调效率、监督要有力有效。其次，全面性原则强调内部控制的主体要覆盖所有的部门和单位，包括本级各职能部门和二级单位，同时也包括所有部门和单位各层级的全体员工，内部控制的对象要涵盖各项业务和事项，包括部门预算管理、固定资产管理、政府采购业务、工程基建项目、专项资金管理和非税收入管理等。因此，全面性原则是将相关控制渗透到政府部门决策、执行和监督的各个过程，避免存在内部控制盲区和空白，从而实现全面、全员和全过程控制。

（二）制衡性原则

政府部门内部控制应当在治理结构、机构设置及权责分配、业务流程等方面相互制约、相互监督，同时兼顾运行效率，实现服务目标和公益目标。相互制衡是建立和实施内部控制的核心理念，制衡性原则主要体现为不相容机构、岗位和人员的相互分离和制约。首先，政府部门应当建立相互制约、相互协调的治理结构。治理结构是对行政权力进行的纵向分解，如前所述，政府部门的治理结构主要体现为决策权、执行权和监督权的相互制约、相互协调。政府部门的决策权由领导办公会议行使，执行权由各职能部门和二级单位行使，监督权根据权力的性质分别由预算委员会、审计委员会、党委纪检和监察部门分别行使。比如说，部门预算编制和批复中涉及的重大事项由主任办公会议决策，部门预算的执行则由各相关部门、单位负责，部门预算的监督权主要由预算委员会和审计委员会行使。其次，政府部门应当根据职能特点合理设置机构。机构设置是对行政权力的横向分解，机构内部按照岗位和人员的不同，将行政权力进一步分解落实到各个岗位和人员，建立明确的岗位责任制度，实现权力和责任的有效匹配，机构设置和岗位授权应当体现不同职能机构之间的相互协调和相互制约。最后，政府部门应当兼顾效率，实现服务目标和公益目标。制衡性原则强调行政权力、机构设置、岗位设置和人员安排的制衡，减少滥用职权和串通舞弊的机会，将政府部门的风险控制在合理的范围内。但是，制衡性原则的目标不是为了制衡而制衡，其根本目标是提高政府部门的运行效率，从而实现服务目标和公益目标。

（三）适应性原则

适应性原则要求内部控制应当与部门规模、管理模式、业务范围和风险水平等相适应，并随着情况的变化加以调整。首先，内部控制的建立和实施要考虑部门规模和管理模式。按照我国宪法的规定，我国政府分为国务院、省级政府、县市级政府和乡镇级政府共四级政府。相应的，我国政府部门也划分为四级，不同级次的政府部门的规模和管理模式差异很大，内部控制的建立与实施要考虑这些差异，将不同级次的政府部门按照其规模和管理模式分别建立和实施内部控制。其次，内部控制的建立和实施要考虑业务范围和风险水平。比如说，大部制改革后的交通运输部门负责交通运输的行政管理，涉及海、陆、空等整个立体式的交通运输管理，呈现业务范围广、业务流程复杂等特点。另外，交通运输部门建设项目多、资金规模大、审批事项多，社会关注度高，存在很大的风险。因此，交通运输部门需要构建完善的内控体系，并实现内控系统的信息化，为领导层的决策提供支撑。最后，适应性原则强调内部控制应当在保持相对稳定的基础上，根据内外部环境的变化，不断地加以优化和改进。比如说，2011 年年初以来，国务院大力推行中央及地方财政预算的公开，其中“三公经费”（出国（境）费、车辆购置及运行费、公务接待费）成为需重点公开的项目。因此，政府部门要将“三公经费”列入内部控制的重点管控对象。

（四）重要性原则

内部控制应当在全面控制的基础上，关注重要业务事项和高风险领域，切实防范重大风险。重要性原则强调政府部门建立与实施内部控制应当突出重点、兼顾一般，着力防范能对政府部门产生重大影响的风险。比如说预算管理，既是政府部门重要的业务事项，也是重要风险点。预算是政府部门工作的起点和中心，是政府部门实现其职能的主要工具。从某种意义上来说，政府部门的重要性原则体现为以预算为主线的原则，政府部门的内部控制体系应围绕预算管理循环的各环节展开，贯穿于预算编制、预算批复、预算执行、预算调整、预算分析与预算决算等预算管理工作的全过程。同时，通过预算管理主线，衔接政府采购、借款报销、资金管理、合同管理、资产管理、会计核算等业务环节，从而形成有效的部门预算内部控制体系。再比如说，行政腐败是政府部门长期面临的重要问题，因此，政府部门应当将遏制腐败作为内部控制建设的一个重点。正如温家宝总理在 2011 年的政府工作报告中所强调的：“建设廉洁的政府是一项持久而又紧迫的任务，是人民的殷切期望。要加快解决反腐倡廉建设中的突出问题，扎实推进惩治和预防腐败体系建设，同时更加注重制度建设。”

（五）权责一致原则

权责一致原则是指政府部门在行政决策、执行和监督过程中掌握的权利要与承担的责任相一致。从另一个角度来说，权责一致原则是指让掌握和行使公共权力而产生消极后果的人承担否定性或对其不利的行政或法律后果、遭受制裁或惩处的原则（王放放，2000）。权责一致原则不仅强调权力和责任相匹配，也强调权力和责任的强度相对等。另外，权责一致原则也包含了财权与事权相匹配的原则。所谓财权与事权相匹配，是指政府部门履行行政职能时，根据规划和履行事项的多少合理安排财政预算，以保证行政职能的有效履行。下面，以部门预算为例来说明权责一致原则，政府部门依据其职能及工作计划，将部门预算细化批复至各业务处室及具体项目，实现财权与事权的有效匹配。通过权限与职责的分解落实，建立部门预算由各责任单位自我控制、自我约束的运行机制，从而实现政府部门的职能。权责一致原则是政府部门区别于企业的重要原则之一。按照委托代理理论，政府部门代表全体人民来管理公共事务，从而掌握着公共权力，不同部门管理的事务不同，其掌握的权力也相应不同。因此，只有做到权责一致，才能保证财权与事权的匹配，才能有效地履行政府部门的职能，创造巨大的社会效益。

五、我国政府部门内部控制的要素

内部控制的目标指明了内部控制的方向，而内部控制要素则明确了什么才能实现目标，因此，内部控制要素是政府部门建立和实施内部控制的基础。总体上来说，政府部门和企业都包括五个要素，分别是内部环境、风险评估、控制活动、信息与沟通和内部监督，但是，两者在各个要素的内涵上却差别很大，这是由于两者不同组织形态的特点决定的。

（一）内部环境

内部环境决定了内部控制的基调，是政府部门建立和实施内部控制的基础。内部环境影响着政府部门内部控制的各个方面，是内部控制其他四个要素的基础，在政府部门内部控制建立与实施中发挥着基础性的作用。根据政府部门的特点，本文认为，政府部门内部环境包括：治理结构、机构设置及权责分配、内部审计、人力资源政策和政府部门文化等。下面，我们将分别论述政府部门内部环境的各项内容。

首先，构建政府部门的组织架构。组织架构是政府部门明确内部各层级机构设置、职责权限、人员编制、工作程序和相关要求的制度安排。组织架构在内部环境中处于基础地位，包括治理结构、内部机构设置和权责分配。政府部门的治理结构主要包括决策机构、执行机构和监督机构以及这三者之间的权责分配。首先，政府部门的决策机构根据决策事项性质的不同划分为领导办公会议和预算委员会。领导办公会议负责对预算和资金使用以外的重大事项的决策，如对重要人事安排的决策，领导办公会议成员由政府部门的主要领导构成；而预算委员会则负责对预算和资金使用方面重要事项的决策，由政府部门主要领导和各职能部门的负责人构成。预算委员会和领导办公会议的最大区别是两者的成员构成不同，预算委员会在领导办公会议成员的基础上增加了财务部门和其他职能部门的负责人，一方面提高了决策的科学性，另一方面也提高了决策的透明度。其次，政府部门的监督机构应当包括审计委员会、党委纪检和监察机构。审计委员会直属预算委员会，以确保其地位上的独立性，审计委员会负责对政府部门的预算执行情况、会计报告的编制和披露情况进行监督检查。党委纪检负责对党员进行监督，严格执行党的纪律，抓好党风廉政建设，坚决同腐败现象作斗争。监察机构负责对国家行政机关和国家公务人员的监督检查，保证政令畅通，促进监察对象正确履行职责，依法办事，廉洁奉公，恪尽职守，勤政高效地为人民服务。

其次，制定政府部门的人力资源政策。人力资源是内部环境的重要组成部分，是政府部门发展的源泉和动力。在内部控制系统中，人既是实施内部控制的主体，又是内部控制的控制对象，即内部控制的客体，因此，人的观念和行为直接影响内部控制的最终效果，这是由人的主观能动性决定的。人力资源政策应当强调，将职业道德修养和专业胜任能力作为选拔和聘用员工的重要标准，切实加强员工培训和继续教育，不断提升员工的素质。另外，由于政府部门提供的是公共服务，其服务对象是广大的人民大众，因此，人力资源政策还应当强调员工的服务意识和反腐倡廉精神。

最后，营造和谐进取的政府部门文化。文化是指在政府部门内部逐渐形成的被整体团队所认同并遵守的价值观、管理意识和文化精神，以及在此基础上形成的行为规范的总和。政府部门文化在其运行管理过程中的作用日益凸显，营造和谐进取的部门文化是其内部控制建设的重要方面。政府部门应当加强文化建设，培育积极向上的价值观和社会责任感，倡导团队协作精神，树立风险意识。同时，强化依法办事，廉洁奉公，恪尽职守，勤政高效地为人民服务的意识。

（二）风险评估

政府部门的运行管理因为内部或外部的各种因素而存在风险，从而影响内控目标的实现。因此，领导层必须要时刻关注政府部门各层次的风险，并对面临的各方面风险进行评估，以有效地应对各种危机。风险评估过程是全面而复杂的，必须考虑政府部门内部和外部的全部重大风险。识别和分析风险是一个重复不断的过程，是有效内部控制制度的关键组成部分。领导层必须认真关注部门各层次的风险并采取行动来管理风险。本文认为，政府部门面临的风险可以分为两个层次的风险：宏观层次的风险和微观层次的风险。宏观层次的风险是指政府部门面临的比较宽泛的，涉及面较广的风险，微观层次的风险是指政府部门业务活动和业务流程方面的风险，涉及面较窄。下面，本文将分别论文这两个层次的风险。

首先，确定宏观层次的风险。政府部门面临的宏观层次的风险很多，主要包括滥用职权的风险、资金使用效率低下的风险、资源配置不合理的风险和道德寻租风险等。首先，政府部门面临着滥用职权的风险，特别是行政腐败的风险。政府部门是公共部门，掌握着巨大的公共权力，在当前我国法律法规尚不完善、公共权力缺乏有效制约的情况下，滥用职权甚至行政腐败的现象非常严重，每年因此而落马的高官不计其数，正如阿克顿勋爵所言“权力导致腐败，绝对的权力绝对地导致腐败”。其次，政府部门面临着资金使用效率低下的风险。政府部门作为社会公共部门，是公共产品的唯一供应方，导致了政府部门提供的公共产品没有竞争对手，因此资金的使用效率没法得到有效保证。再次，政府部门面临着资源配置不合理的风险。当前的情况下，政府部门职能转变不到位，行政手段配置资源的领域和比重较大，公共工程建设、土地使用权立项等稀缺资源的配置权，基本都掌握在相关政府部门手中。为了争夺稀缺资源，各种行贿弄权手段应运而生，最终影响资源的合理配置。最后，政府部门面临着寻租和道德风险。寻租是指人们凭借政府保护而进行的寻求财富转移的活动。从根本上来说，寻租是与劳动和公平原则相违背的，也是对公共资源的侵害和浪费。道德风险是指从事经济活动的人在最大限度地增进自身效用的同时做出不利于他人的行动。

其次，确定微观层次的风险。微观层次的风险是指业务活动和业务流程方面的风险。根据政府部门的特点，本文将其业务活动归纳为如下七项：预算管理、工程建设、政府采购、资产管理、专项资金、财政收支和非税收入。预算管理的主要风险是预算编制是否规范，各责任单位在预算管理中的职责权限是否清晰，预算执行、预算分析和预算考评是否科学规范等。工程建设的主要风险是政府工程项目管理模式是否科学合理，工程项目建设的各个环节的管理是否规范，风险是否可控等。政府采购的主要风险是采购模式是否科学、有效，政府采购的执行、支付等是否规范，职责分工是否明确及风险是否可控等。资产管理的主要风险是资产在购置、使用和处置等环节是否合规、合理，风险是否可控等。专项资金的主要风险是专项资金的计划、执行、结（决）算、工程审计等环节是否科学、规范、合理，风险是否可控等。财政收支的主要风险是财政收入和财政支出的流程是否规范，收支是否平衡等。非税收入的主要风险是非税收入是否合法合规、是否严格执行收支两条线管理、发票及许可收费制度是否规范、风险是否可控等。

（三）控制活动

在确定内部控制目标和风险之后，政府部门需要考虑实施怎样的控制活动来规避或者降低风险，从而实现控制目标。控制活动是确保政府部门的风险应对得以实施的政策和程序。政策确定应该做什么，程序确定应该怎么做，政策是程序的基础。控制活动的发生贯穿于整个政府部门，遍及各个层级和职能机构，包括一系列不同的活动，例如预算控制、信息系统控制、授权审批控制、不相容职务分离控制、财产保护控制和绩效考评控制等。控制活动与业务活动是紧密联系的，对于不同的业务活动，需要采取不同的控制活动。因此，在论述政府部门控制活动之前，需要对其业务活动进行梳理。政府部门的业务活动如图2所示，可以概括为：以预算管理为主线，划分事前规划、事中控制和事后记录三个阶段，业务活动要符合外部要求和内部管理需要。在论述完业务活动后，本文选取了颇具政府部门特点的几项控制活动重点论述，包括预算控制、授权审批控制和会计信息系统控制等。

首先，政府部门应当建立“以预算管理为主线，以资金管控为核心”预算管理体系。预算管理体系的控制活动主要是预算控制，预算控制是政府部门最重要的控制活动。预算是政府部门工作的起点和依据，是建立和实施内部控制的核心环节，政府部门所有业务最终都要通过预算管理衔接起来，从而实现预算管理的全过程控制。根据图2，预算管理体系分为三个阶段：事前规划阶段、事中控制阶段和事后记录阶段。事前规划阶段包括预算的编制和审核。预算编制是预算管理的起点，预算审核是预算管理的重要环节，有效的衔接了预算编制和预算批复。事中控制阶段包括预算批复、执行申请、借款报销和支付审核。预算批复是预算管理的核心环节，是将外部财政指标批复到内部预算指标的过程。执行申请是预算管理的关键环节，是落实工作计划和预算安排的起点。借款报销和支付审核是对预算资金使用的管理。事中控制阶段实现了预算与财务的有效衔接，是连接了事前规范阶段和事后记录阶段的桥梁。事后记录阶段包括出纳受理和会计核算。出纳受理是对资金的记录，会计核算是对事项的记录。通过事后记录，能够分析预算执行情况，及时发现问题、解决问题。

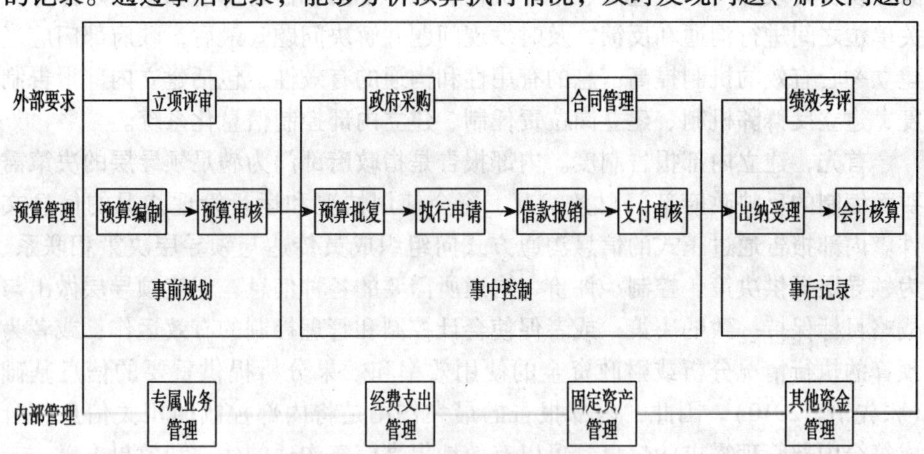

图2　政府部门内部控制系统

其次，政府部门应当建立严格的授权审批控制。授权审批控制是政府部门非常重要的控制活动，授权审批控制直接关系着财政资金的使用效率和效果，对控制目标的实现产生直接影响。授权审批控制要求政府部门根据常规授权和特别授权的规定，明确各岗位办理业务和事项的权限范围、审批程序和相应责任。建立授权审批控制时，要遵循权责一致的原则，确保行使的权力和承担的责任相一致。另外，建立“三重一大”事项决策审批机制，强化集体决策。政府部门应当在各级单位实行集体决策审批制度，对重大决策、重大事项、重要人事任免及大额资金支付业务建立科学完善的集体决策机制。

最后，建立会计信息系统控制。会计信息系统控制要求政府部门严格执行行政单位会计制度，加强会计基础工作，明确会计凭证、会计账簿和会计报告的处理程序，保证会计资料真实完整。会计信息系统控制直接关系着会计报告及相关信息的真实完整。会计信息系统控制是政府部门重要的控制活动，也是区别于企业的特殊控制活动，因为政府部门的会计信息系统要和预算管理系统相匹配对接。因此，政府部门会计信息系统不仅要满足行政单位会计制度的要求，还要在某种程度上满足预算管理的要求。

（四）信息与沟通

政府部门应当建立信息与沟通制度，明确内部控制相关信息的收集、处理和传递程序，确保信息及时沟通，促进内部控制有效运行。信息与沟通贯穿于内部环境、风险评估、控制活动和内部监督，是连接这四个要素的重要手段。信息与沟通能够提高政府部门内部控制的效率和效果，为内部控制的有效运行提供可靠保证。首先，政府部门应当收集各种相关信息，包括内部信息和外部信息，并对收集的信息进行筛选、核对、整合，以提高信息的有用性。其次，政府部门应当将内部控制相关信息在内部各管理级次、责任单位、业务环节之间，以及财政部门、供应商、中介机构、审计部门、监管部门和新闻媒体等有关单位之间进行沟通和反馈，及时发现问题并解决问题。最后，政府部门应当建立一套有效的机制提高信息的有用性和沟通的有效性，包括建立内部报告制度、建立反舞弊机制、建立岗位责任制、建立内部控制信息化系统。

首先，建立内部报告制度。内部报告是指政府部门为满足领导层的决策需要而编制的反映政府部门财务状况、资金使用情况和运行管理状况的信息文件。内部报告通过正式的信息沟通方式向组织成员传达与领导层决策相联系、为领导层提供决策、控制、评价、沟通所需要的各种信息，促使领导层做出与战略目标保持一致的决策；或者促使会计控制和管理控制的有效运作；或者为预算的执行情况分析或财政资金的使用效率和效果分析提供重要的信息基础(张先治，2010)。因此，内部报告的最大作用是将内部控制的相关信息整合成符合内部管理需求的信息，可以有效地提高信息沟通的效率和效果。

其次，建立反舞弊机制。政府部门应当建立反舞弊机制，坚持惩防并举、重在预防的原则，明确反舞弊工作的重点领域，关键环节和有关机构在反舞弊工作中的职责权限，规范舞弊案件的举报、调查、处理、报告和补救程序。根据著名的 Treadway Commission Report，反舞弊的四道防线分别是：一是书面及非书面的管理规章；二是政府部门的内部控制；三是内部审计职能；四是外部独立审计职能。这四道防线共同构成多方位、多层次的反舞弊体系，对政府部门的舞弊行为形成有效的“免疫系统”。另外，政府部门的反舞弊机制还可将预算委员会、党委纪检和监察部门纳入其中，建立符合我国国情的反舞弊体系。

再次，建立岗位责任制。岗位责任制是指根据各科室确定的总体职能、职责和职位说明书，将每个科室以及每个岗位的职责、任务、目标等内容具体化，并要求落实责任的制度。岗位责任制是机关效能建设的基本制度，是落实依法行政、依法履行职责，转变机关作风，提高工作效率的根本措施，是对处室以及机关工作人员进行年度绩效考评的主要依据。各级政府部门应当根据实际情况，合理有效地分解权力、落实职责，建立符合自身特点的岗位责任制，实现岗位权力与职责的有效匹配。

最后，建立内部控制的信息化系统。内部控制的信息化系统是指将内控理念、控制活动、控制手段等要素通过信息化的手段固化到信息系统，实现内部控制体系的系统化与常态化。一方面，信息化系统能够实现内控信息的程序化、标准化，极大地提高信息沟通的效率。另一方面，信息化系统可以有效地减少信息传递过程中人的因素的影响，提高信息沟通的效果。另外，内部控制的信息化系统可以实现政府部门的例外管理。例外管理是指对于例行经费支出等日常业务依据规范的控制程序与控制标准授权给下级管理人员进行管控，高级管理人员只保留对例外事项（即突发性、偶然性）的决策权限和审批程序。例外管理的最大优势是，将高级管理人员从日常琐事中释放出来，集中精力应对重要的或者突发性事项，提高风险管理的针对性和内部控制的有效性。

（五）内部监督

内部监督是政府部门对其内部控制的健全性、合理性和有效性进行监督检查与评估，形成书面报告并做出相应处理的过程。内部监督是内部控制得以有效实施的保障，具有十分重要的作用。在建立与实施内部控制的整个过程中，都离不开内部监督。内部监督帮助领导层预防、发现和整改内部控制设计和运行中存在的问题和薄弱环节，以便及时加以改进，确保内部控制系统能够有效运行。政府部门应当建立有效的内部监督制度，提高内部控制的效率和效果，实现内部控制的目标。具体来说，政府部门内部监督制度包括：内部控制评价制度、内部审计制度、党委纪检和监察制度、绩效考核制度。

首先，建立内部控制评价制度。内部控制评价是指领导层对内部控制有效性进行全面评价、形成评价结论、出具评价报告的过程。内部控制评价与内部控制的建立与实施，共同构成内部系统的有机循环。内部控制评价是通过评价、反馈、再评价，报告政府部门在内部控制建立与实施中存在的问题，并持续地进行自我完善的过程。政府部门通过内部控制评价查找、分析内部控制缺陷并有针对性地敦促落实整改，及时堵塞管理漏洞，防范偏离目标的各种风险，从设计和执行等全方位健全优化管控制度，促进政府部门内控体系的不断完善。

其次，建立内部审计制度。根据国际内部审计师协会的定义，内部审计是指“独立、客观的鉴证和咨询活动，以增加价值和改进经营”。内部审计制度是政府部门内部监督体系的重要组成部分，有效地内部审计制度可以及时发现并纠正内部控制缺陷，将政府部门的风险控制在可接受的范围内。正如国际内部审计师协会在其第 59 届年会上表述的那样：“内部审计是一项独立的、客观的确认和咨询活动，目的是改进单位工作质量和提高效益。它通过系统化、规范化的方法，评价和改进单位的风险管理、控制和管理的效率，从而实现经营目标。”政府部门内部审计制度应当由内部审计机构执行，内部审计机构直属于预算委员会。实际工作中，应当将内部审计制度与内部控制评价制度结合起来使用，充分发挥两者在内部监督方面的互补作用。

再次，建立党委纪检和监察制度。党委是部门内部的共产党组织，负责规划、领导、组织、管理政府部门的党务活动，具体包括：对党员进行教育和管理，督促党员履行义务；做好政府部门干部职工的思想政治工作，了解反映干部职工的意见；加强党内监督和党风廉政建设。纪检是指中国共产党纪律检查委员会领导的党内纪律检查，它的任务是检查党内违纪案件。纪检是严肃党的纪律，加强党风廉政建设，保证党的基本路线贯彻执行的重要手段。监察是指监察机关依法对监察对象履行职责方面贯彻执行国家法律法规决定命令中的问题的监督检查及违法失职行为的查处。纪检和监察的区别是两者的对象不同，纪检的对象是党组织和党员，监察的对象是国家行政机关和国家公务人员。另外，党委纪检和监察制度是政府部门内部控制区别企业内部控制的重要方面。

最后，建立绩效考核制度。绩效考核是指政府部门运用特定的标准，采取科学的方法，对承担职责的各级管理人员工作成绩做出价值评价的过程。绩效考核的重点是全面、客观、公正、准确地考核领导干部政治业务素质和履行职责的情况，加强对领导干部的管理与监督、激励与约束。建立健全科学的绩效考核制度，是推进干部工作科学化、民主化、制度化的重要举措，对于建设有活力有纪律的领导班子具有重要意义。另外，绩效考核可以和岗位责任制结合使用，充分发挥两者优势互补的作用。

六、我国政府部门内部控制的实施机制

目标、原则和要素是政府部门内部控制框架体系的核心，实施机制则是政府部门内部控制得以有效实施的关键。按照新制度经济学理论，任何一项完整的制度都应该包括正式制度、非正式制度及其实施机制（诺斯，1990）。政府部门内部控制框架体系作为政府部门内部控制制度的基础，也应当包括内部控制的实施机制，政府部门内部控制制度的有效实施有赖于这三者之间的有机配合。因此，构建政府部门内部控制框架体系需要将实施机制纳入其中，作为保证政府部门内部控制有效执行的重要手段。

实施机制是指针对正式内控制度的实施机制，是一种借助社会、组织或机构的力量对执行或违反正式内控制度的行为主体以各种形式予以奖励或惩处，从而使其得以实施的条件和手段的总称（缪艳娟，2010）。分析实施机制的概念，可以知道，实施机制的核心是对执行或违反正式内控制度施以的奖惩措施和手段。因此，如何制定有效的配套奖惩措施，是建立政府部门内部控制实施机制的核心。根据我国政府部门的特点，本文认为，我国政府部门内部控制的实施机制主要包括：立法机制、内部审计机制、信息披露机制和外部审计

机制。

在正式地论述如何构建这些实施机制之前，有必要先对这些实施机制之间的关系进行梳理。这些实施机制之间是相互联系、相互促进的，立法机制与其他三个机制之间的关系是统领与被统领的关系，立法机制类似于萨班斯法案，通过立法要求政府部门建立内部审计机制、信息披露机制和外部审计机制。内部审计机制、信息披露机制和外部审计机制之间也是相互联系、相互促进的。内部审计可以提高信息披露的质量，信息披露的强制要求可以加强内部审计的力度；内部审计能够提高外部审计的效率，外部审计能够进一步完善内部审计的工作；信息披露能够指明外部审计的重点，外部审计能进一步加强信息披露的质量。

（一）立法机制

立法机制是指通过立法的方式明确政府部门在建立和实施内部控制时应当遵守的基本要求的机制。立法机制是政府部门内部控制的重要实施机制，它通过立法的方式明确政府部门在建立和实施内部控制时必须要满足基本的要求。立法机制是提高政府部门内部控制执行力度的重要手段，更是建立其他实施机制的基础。根据我国政府部门的特点，本文认为，我国政府部门的立法机制主要包括两方面内容：一是建立政府部门内部控制规范体系，将内部控制提升至法律层面；二是建立相关法律制度，规定建立和实施内部控制的基本要求以及配套的实施机制。

第一，建立政府部门内部控制规范体系。从内容上来说，政府部门内部控制规范体系包括基本规范和配套指引。基本规范在政府部门内部控制规范体系中处于最高层次，起统驭作用，规定了内部控制的总体框架和基本要求，是制定配套指引和完善政府部门内部控制制度的依据。基本规范主要包括如下内容：政府部门内部控制的概念、目标、原则、要素和其他重要事项。配套指引是基本规范的具体化，包括应用指引、评价指引和审计指引。应用指引是指导政府部门建立和实施内部控制的依据。评价指引是指导政府部门评价其内部控制有效性的依据。审计指引是指导外部审计部门对政府部门内部控制进行审计的依据。从立法主体上来说，内部控制规范体系应当由财政部、审计署、组织部、中纪委和监察部五部委联合制定和发布。财政部是政府部门预算和财政资金的主管部门，审计署是政府部门预算和财政资金使用的监督部门，组织部是中共中央主管组织工作和干部工作的职能部门，中纪委负责中国共产党党内的纪律检查工作，监察部负责国家行政机关和国家公务人员的监督检查工作。这五个部门分别从不同角度对政府部门进行监督和检查，因此，政府部门内部控制规范体系应当由这五个部门联合制定和发布。

第二，建立相关法律制度，规定建立和实施内部控制的基本要求以及配套的实施机制。全国人民代表大会应当建立类似于萨班斯法案的法律制度，严格规定政府部门在建立和实施内部控制时应当遵循的基本要求以及配套的实施机制。从法律地位上来说，该法律的地位要高于政府部门内部控制规范体系。从内容上来说，该法律主要包括基本要求和执行机制两部分内容。基本要求主要包括以下方面：第一，明确政府部门内部控制的主管部门是财政部、审计署、组织部、中纪委和监察部，以提高政府部门内部控制的执行力度和实施效果；第二，政府部门应当按照内部控制规范体系的要求建立和实施内部控制，确保各政府部门的内部控制可比性；第三，政府部门的行政负责人和财务负责人要保证政府部门的预算报告、会计报告和内控报告等重要信息的真实性和完整性，以提高政府信息的透明度和社会公信力；第四，要求审计署加强对政府部门内部控制的监督检查力度，完善内部控制制度，确保内部控制的有效实施；第五，对积极有效执行内部控制规范的政府部门给予一定程度的物质奖励或精神鼓励，以提高政府部门建立和实施内部控制的积极性；第六，对不能有效执行内部控制规范的政府部门要予以惩罚，包括对政府部门的惩罚和对主要负责人、财务负责人的惩罚。执行机制主要包括：第一，建立内部审计机制，强化政府部门的内部监督，完善内部控制制度；第二，建立信息披露机制，加强社会的舆论监督，提高政府信息的透明度；第三，建立外部审计机制，加强政府部门的外部监督，提高政府部门的公信力。

（二）内部审计机制

内部审计机制是指内部审计部门通过一套系统、规范的方法评价和改进政府部门的风险管理、内部控制和预算管理的效果，以帮助政府部门实现其目标的机制。内部审计是相对于外部审计而言的，内部审计是一项独立、客观的鉴证和咨询活动，其目标在于增加价值并改进政府部门的管理。内部审计机制的主要机能是发现并改正政府部门的漏洞或者缺陷，确保政府部门健康可持续发展。可以说，内部审计机制是政府部门的免疫系统或者防火墙。

内部审计机制是改进政府部门内部控制的重要手段，也是提高政府部门管理效率和效果的重要途径，更是实现政府部门自我约束、自我监督的重要方式。根据我国政府部门的特点，本文认为，内部审计机制的主要内容包括：内部审计的内容、内部审计的组织形式和职责安排和内部审计的具体要求。

第一，明确内部审计的内容。明确内部审计的内容是建立和实施内部审计机制的前提和基础。根据我国政府部门的特点，本文认为，我国政府部门内部审计的内容主要包括：政府部门内部控制、政府部门财务信息以及政府部门的运行管理等。其中，内部控制部分地包括了财务信息和运行管理的内容。内部控制的审计重点是内部控制有效性。内部控制的有效性是指政府部门建立与实施内部控制对实现控制目标提供合理保证的程度，包括内部控制设计的有效性和内部控制运行的有效性。内部控制设计的有效性是指为实现控制目标所必需的内部控制要素都存在并且设计恰当。内部控制运行的有效性是指现有内部控制按照规定程序得到了正确执行。内部控制设计的有效性是内部控制运行的有效性的前期。财务信息的审计重点是财务信息的真实性和完整性。运行管理的审计重点是运行管理的效率和效果。

第二，明确内部审计的组织形式和职责安排。政府部门领导层是内部审计工作的领导部门，负责政府部门内部审计工作的总体规范和指导工作。内部审计部门是内部审计的具体实施部门，负责内部审计的具体组织实施工作，内部审计部门对领导层负责，领导层对内部审计承担最终责任。关于内部审计的职责安排，主要包括如下方面：领导层负责内部审计的总体指导安排，积极动员政府部门开展内部审计工作；内部审计部门按照领导层的部署负责组织实施内部审计工作，包括对内部控制、财务信息和运行管理等进行审计；财务部门和内部各相关部门要积极配合内部审计部门开展审计工作，包括按照要求提交财务报告、内部控制自我评价报告，协助内部审计人员开展必要的测试活动；政府部门所属单位也要积极配合内部审计部门逐级落实内部审计的工作。

第三，明确内部审计的基本要求。内部审计的基本要求是指政府部门开展内部审计工作应当遵循的具体要求，包括内部审计的依据、内部审计的权限、内部审计的时间和内部审计的原则等。内部审计的依据主要是中国内部审计准则、政府部门内部控制准则、行政单位会计制度等。内部审计的权限包括审查权和建议处理权，审查权是按照要求开展审计工作的权力，建议处理权是指对审计发现的问题可以提出解决建议的权力。但是，最终能否按照解决建议执行还要经过领导层的决策批准。内部审计的时间没有硬性要求，一般每年需要对会计报告、内部控制评价报告、预算报告和决算报告进行审计。内部审计的原则是内部审计必须遵循的基本准则，包括独立性、客观性、效益性和谨慎性。这里需要说明的是，内部审计的独立性是指内部审计部门对内部各部门及下属单位独立，而对领导层是不独立的，这是内部审计和外部审计的重要区别之一。

（三）信息披露机制

信息披露机制是指政府部门定期或者不定期按照规定的要求或标准向特定部门或者社会公众披露本部门特定信息，以便使相关部门和纳税人充分了解相关情况的机制。信息披露机制的实质是通过将社会关心的重要信息置于社会公众的监督之下，从而提高信息的真实性和可靠性。正如布兰代斯一百多年前所言“阳光是最好的消毒剂，灯光是最好的警察”。信息披露机制是提高政务信息和相关信息透明度，加强政府部门监管和社会舆论监督，改善政府部门社会形象，促进政府部门行政体制改革的重要手段。信息披露机制是政府部门建立和实施内部控制的重要机制，可以有效地提高政府部门内部控制效率和效果。信息披露机制的主要内容包括：信息披露的内容、信息披露机制组织形式、职责安排和信息披露的具体要求。

第一，明确信息披露的内容。明确信息披露的内容是建立和实施信息披露机制的前提和基础。根据政府部门的特点，结合国家相关法律法规，本文认为，政府部门信息披露的内容主要包括两部分：第一部分是政府信息公开条例规定的内容；第二部分是政府信息公开条例没有明确规定的重要内容。具体来说，第一部分主要包括行政法规、规章和规范性文件和财政预算、决算报告等。第二部分按照性质又可划分两类：第一类是与内部控制直接相关的信息，包括政府部门会计报告和内部控制自我评价报告等；第二类是中央政府强制要求披露的其他信息，如公开“三公经费”（出国（境）费、车辆购置及运行费、公务接待费）的2010年决算支出。这里需要注意的是，第一部分和第二部分的第二类内容虽然和内部控制不直接相关，但是对推动和完善政府部门内部控制的建立与实施至关重要，因此，也属于信息披露的重要内容。

第二，明确信息披露机制的组织形式和职责安排。政府部门领导层是信息披露工作的领导部门，负责政府部门信息披露的总体指导工作，另外，领导层对办公厅（室）和下属各部门各单位的信息披露工作负有监督的职责。领导层对政府部门信息披露承担最终的责任。领导层应当授权办公厅（室）负责信息披露的具体组织实施工作，包括组织各部门各单位的信息披露工作、分解落实各部门各单位的信息披露任务。法律法规部门负责制定行政法规、规章和规范性文件；预算委员会负责编制预算、决算报告，提供与预算相关的信息；财务部门负责编制会计报告和内部报告，提供与财务相关的信息；内部审计部门负责编制内部审计评价报告，提供与内部控制相关的信息。

第三，明确信息披露的基本要求。信息披露的基本要求是指政府部门对外披露的信息应当遵循的具体要求，包括信息披露的程度、信息披露的方式、信息披露的时间和信息披露的原则等。信息披露的程度是指信息披露的细度和精度，政府部门应当按照法律法规要求的细度和精度披露信息，不能以粗代细、以泛代精。信息披露的方式是指披露信息的载体，政府部门应当通过政府公报、政府网站、新闻发布会以及报刊、广播、电视等便于公众知晓的方式公开。信息披露的时间是指披露信息的最晚时间要求，政府部门应当在规定的时间内披露信息，保证信息披露的及时性和有用性。信息披露的原则是信息披露必须遵循的基本规则，包括相关性原则、可靠性原则、重要性原则和及时性原则。

（四）外部审计机制

外部审计机制是指外部审计机构依据有关财政收支、财务收支的法律、法规和国家其他有关规定进行审计评价，在法定职权范围内做出审计决定的机制。外部审计是相对于内部审计而言的，外部审计按照审计主体的不同分为政府审计和社会审计。政府审计的审计主体是国家各级审计机关；社会审计的主体是各类社会审计机构，主要是具有审计资质的会计师事务所。根据我国的国情，结合我国政府部门的特点，本文认为，我国应当建立以政府审计为主、社会审计为辅的外部审计机制。外部审计是对政府部门及其他公共机构财务报告的真实性、公允性，运用公共资源的经济性、效益性、效果性，以及提供公共服务的质量进行审计。外部审计是内部审计的重要互补，可以有效提高政府部门内部控制的执行力，是加强政府部门监管、提高政府部门公信力的重要手段。外部审计机制的主要内容包括：外部审计的内容、外部审计的组织形式、职责安排和外部审计的具体要求。

第一，明确外部审计的内容。明确外部审计的内容是建立和实施外部审计机制的前提和基础。我国应当建立以政府审计为主、社会审计为辅的外部审计机制。我国政府审计是依据宪法和审计法确定的，具有较高的法律地位和广泛的审计监督范围，因此，外部审计机制必须以政府审计为主。但是，由于政府审计资源非常有限而审计任务却非常繁重，同时社会审计在财务报表和内部控制审计等领域具有明显的优势，因此，外部审计机制又必须依托社会审计，形成政府审计和社会审计的优势互补。根据审计法的规定，政府审计的内容主要包括：政府部门的财政收支、预算的执行情况和决算以及预算外资金的管理和使用情况。根据前面的论述，社会审计作为政府审计的补充，应当发挥其特有的优势。因此，本文认为，社会审计的内容主要包括财务报表和内部控制等。

第二，明确外部审计的组织形式和职责安排。根据前面的论述，政府审计部门是外部审计机制的主导部门，政府审计部门在资源受限或者在内部控制等社会审计擅长的领域可以聘任社会审计机构进行审计，以充分发挥两者的优势互补。政府审计部门主管外部审计工作，负责对外部审计进行长期规划和总体指导，包括聘任社会审计机构承担部分政府审计职能。另外，政府审计部门对外部审计负有监督的职责，包括监督政府审计部门的工作和社会审计部门的工作。总而言之，政府审计部门对外部审计承担最终的责任。作为政府审计的补充，社会审计需要接受政府审计的聘任或者委托，才能对政府部门进行审计。为了提高政府部门内部控制执行的效率和效果，政府审计可以将内部控制等相关领域的审计交由社会审计负责，以充分发挥社会审计在该领域的专长。

第三，明确外部审计的基本要求。外部审计的基本要求是指外部审计应当遵循的具体要求，包括外部审计的依据、外部审计的权限和外部审计的原则等。政府审计的依据主要是审计法、审计法实施条例和国家审计准则，社会审计接受政府审计的委托也必须遵循上述法律法规。另外，社会审计的重点是内部控制和财务报告，因此，必须要遵循政府部门内部控制准则和行政单位会计制度。政府审计代表国家利益，对被审计单位的违法违纪问题既有审查权也有处理权，社会审计在接受政府审计委托的前提下能够行使审查权但无处理权。但是，政府审计可以根据社会审计的结果对违法违纪行为行使处理权。外部审计的原则是外部审计必须遵循的基本准则，包括合法性原则、独立性原则、客观性原则和效益性原则。

主要参考文献

[1] 中华人民共和国审计署:《审计机关内部控制测评准则》,2004。

[2] 中华人民共和国财政部:《企业内部控制规范讲解 2010》,北京,经济科学出版社,2010。

[3] 李连华:《内部控制理论结构:控制效率的思想基础与政策建议》,厦门,厦门大学出版社,2007。

[4] 方红星、王宏:《企业风险管理——整合框架》,大连,东北财经大学出版社,2005。

[5] 缪艳娟:《企业内部控制研究:制度视角》,大连,东北财经大学出版社,2009。

[6] 沈荣华:《行政权力制约机制》,北京,国家行政学院出版社,2006。

[7] 中华人民共和国审计署:《中国审计研究报告 2006》,北京,中国时代经济出版社,2007。

[8] 夏书章:《行政管理学》,北京,高等教育出版社,2008。

[9] 缪艳娟:《企业内控规范实施机制的新制度经济学分析》,载《会计研究》,2010(11),33~39页。

[10] 王光远:《中美政府内部控制发展回顾与评述——兼为〈联邦政府内部控制〉(中文版)序》,载《财会通讯》,2009(12),6~10页。

[11] 吴忠民:《关于公平、公正、平等的差异之辨析》,载《中共中央党校学报》,2003(4),15~20页。

[12] 陆树程、刘萍:《关于公平、公正、正义三个概念的哲学反思》,载《浙江学刊》,2010(2),198~203页。

[13] 张先治、刘媛媛:《企业内部报告框架构建研究》,载《会计研究》,2010(8),28~35页。

[14] OMB:Revisions to OMB Circular A-123,Management's Responsibility for Internal,2004。

[15] M. C. Jensen, W. H. Meckling,"Theory of the Firm:Managerial Behavior, Agency Costs and Ownership Structure",Journal of Financial Economics,1976(4),pp. 56-78.

[16] [美]爱德华·卡尼等:《联邦政府内部控制》,王光远等译,北京,中国时代经济出版社,2009。

内部报告对管理会计发展的影响研究[①]

张先治　季侃

（东北财经大学会计学院/中国内部控制研究中心　辽宁大连　116025）

摘　要　本文回顾了当前管理会计的定义、基本理论和框架内容，发现目前管理会计学至多可称为基于会计的管理，其本质、目标、内涵等并不符合会计学的基本特性。内部报告理论的提出可以更加明确管理会计是基于管理的会计这一本质，从而对管理会计的基本理论和框架内容都产生了重大的影响。而这必然会对重新定位管理会计学科，解决当前管理会计与成本会计、财务管理学科之间分工不明、内容交叉的问题有重要的启示，对管理会计学科的发展有重大的意义。在探讨了内部报告理论对于协调管理会计与相关学科关系的作用后，本文提出了相应的建议。

关键词　内部报告　管理会计　基本理论　框架内容　成本会计　财务管理

一、引言

20世纪50年代以来，管理会计取得了长足的发展。从发展历程来看，管理会计的每一次前进都体现了当时各种环境的客观要求。在知识经济时代和高度信息化的21世纪，生产和信息等各种技术高速发展，企业面临着更为激烈的国际、国内市场竞争环境，管理会计又应驶向何方？尤其是刚刚经历金融危机使我们更加清醒地认识到外部总体环境的不确定和经营环境的恶化会对企业造成巨大的甚至毁灭性的破坏。日趋复杂的环境要求管理会计必须为企业内部决策者提供更为全面的信息，必须有高质量的企业内部信息作为决策的保证。而内部报告无疑就是这种内部决策信息最集中和系统的反应。所谓内部报告，又称管理会计报告，它是相对于外部报告而言的。它是指企业为满足董事会、管理者及员工的决策与控制需要所编制的反映企业财务状况、经营成果和管理状况的信息文件（张先治，2009）。内部报告的提出，对管理会计的本质、基本理论、框架和内容都产生了重大影响，对管理会计学科的发展有着重要的意义。

---

①　本文为国家自然科学基金项目“基于会计相关性的内部报告理论研究与实践检验”（项目批准号：70972125）的阶段性成果。

二、管理会计理论相关文献回顾

管理会计实践最早出现在美国，但是理论的发展相对滞后。会计发展史表明，最早期的会计就是管理会计（胡玉明，1999），但是这种早期的管理会计并不是现代意义上的管理会计。直到1952年在伦敦举行的会计师国际代表大会上，会计学界正式提出了“管理会计”这一概念。在此之后，管理会计的定义、本质、研究对象、研究目标以及职能等基本理论逐渐完善起来。

（一）关于管理会计定义与本质

尽管管理会计的概念提出已久，然而关于管理会计的定义，学术界至今仍无一致的意见。目前，管理会计的定义主要有以下三种：第一种是比较狭义的定义，如1981年美国管理会计师协会为管理会计所下的定义为：“管理会计是一个对财务信息进行确认、计量、汇总、分析、编制、解释和传递的过程，这些加工过的信息在管理中被用于内部的计划、评价和控制，并保证合理地、负责地利用企业的各种资源。”第二种是比较广义的定义，如美国全美会计师协会管理会计实务委员会（1986）对管理会计的定义是：“管理会计是向管理当局提供用于企业内部计划、评价、控制以及确保企业资源的合理使用和经济管理责任的施行所需财务信息的确认、计量、归集、分析、编报、解释和传递的过程。管理会计还包括编制提供诸如股东、债权人、规章制定机构及税务当局等非管理集团使用的财务报告。”还有一种较为中义的定义，美国著名管理会计学家卡普兰等（1997）在《管理会计》（第2版）中这样定义：“管理会计是一个为组织的员工和各级管理者提供财务和非财务信息的过程。这个过程受组织内部所有人员对信息需求的驱动，并能引导他们做出各种经营和投资决策。”

与狭义的管理会计概念相比，广义的管理会计的内涵明显地扩大了很多，主要表现在：第一，管理会计不仅要为企业管理当局，各部门的管理人员，甚至是每一位员工提供所需要的信息，还要为股东和债权人等外部人员提供服务；第二，从内容上看，广义的管理会计涵盖范围非常大，既包括提供向外部投资者提供财务报告的财务会计，计算成本的成本会计，还包括进行决策的财务管理；第三，管理会计信息系统不仅可以处理并提供以货币单位计量的财务信息，还可以提供一些非财务信息。而卡普兰等（1997）的定义与狭义的管理会计相比，使用者的范围包括所有员工，提供信息的内容也包含非财务信息。与广义的管理会计相比，在涉及范围上还是主要以传统的管理会计为主，没有财务管理和成本会计的过多内容。

这些定义尽管对管理会计的研究范畴仍有争议，然而对管理会计的本质看法是一致的，即管理会计的存在是为了提供信息。然而，从当前管理会计的教材来看，无论是国内还是国外，虽然从表面看或名义上都符合会计的本质与内涵，但实质上都是强调利用会计信息进行预测、决策、规划与控制，而不是研究为进行预测、决策、规划与控制而如何提供会计信息。因此，现在的管理会计学实质上不是会计，它也不是会计信息系统的组成部分（张先治，2009）。而目前管理会计在本质上更多的是基于会计的管理，这实质上是偷换了管理会计的概念。

（二）关于管理会计的研究对象

关于管理会计研究对象，目前主要有以下几种代表性的观点：（1）现金流动；（2）价值差量；（3）经济活动和信息等。持第（1）种观点的学者认为管理会计的对象是企业的现金流动，这是因为他们认为会计的研究对象是资金的流动，管理会计作为会计的分支，其研究对象自然也是现金流动。而现金流动的确也贯穿于管理会计的各个环节中，如预测、决策、预算、控制、业绩考核与评价等。持第（2）种观点的学者认为管理会计的对象是价值差量，这主要是因为差量分析是现代管理会计的基本研究方法之一。持第（3）种观点的学者认为管理会计的对象是能反映和控制的经济活动及其发出的信息，这主要是因为他们认为会计的本质是一个信息系统，信息产生于企业的经济活动。因此，无论财务会计，还是管理会计，它们的研究对象都是一致的。

（三）关于管理会计的目标

在关于会计目标之争的过程中，国际学术界主要形成了两种不同的观点：受托责任观和决策有用观。目前，决策有用观更被普遍接受，即会计目标是提供对决策有用的信息，注重信息的相关性。而在我国，对此会计理论界主要有两种观点：一是认为会计是一种信息系统（葛家澍等，1998）；二是认为会计是一种管理活动（杨纪琬，1987）。张先治（2007）认为可后者的产生是与我国当时的会计教育中的学科划分、会计理论中的会计目标确定、会计实务中的会计职责界定有关。在我国当时学科划分中只有会计没有财务管理①的情况下，在会计理论研究中忽视会计目标研究，或将组织目标混同为会计目标的情况下，在会计实务中将财务与会计部门设置合二为一的情况下，这是完全可以理解和接受的。然而，在当前中国的经济环境下，会计信息系统论更符合会计的本质。因此，管理会计作为会计的分支，是一个管理会计信息系统，其目标是提供内部决策有用的信息。

（四）关于管理会计的职能

管理会计从其产生之后经历了不同阶段的发展，它的职能也因所在的时期

---

① 财务管理学科是教育部1998年调整本科专业时新设立的学科专业。

不同而有所不同。国内早期的管理会计著作一般认为20世纪20年代在社会化大生产和提高企业生产效率的背景下以泰罗的科学管理学说为基础形成和发展起来的标准成本系统，是管理会计的雏形。这一阶段管理会计的职能主要是提高生存效率，主要服务于企业成本管理。50年代以前以标准成本、预算控制、差异分析为主要内容的管理会计往往并不涉及有关企业决策层面的内容，而50年代以后，西方国家科技、经济得到迅猛发展，企业规模越来越大，面对的市场竞争也愈加激烈，此时客观要求管理会计能够满足战略层面的决策需要。事实上，在这段时间随着行为科学、决策理论、信息经济学等的不断发展并被引入管理会计，管理会计的作用更多地体现在其预测、决策职能。80年代以后，由于以卡普兰为代表的学者对管理会计相关性提出了质疑，引发了关于作业成本法研究的高潮。90年代中期以后，美国管理会计界出现的“第二次新潮”（Second New Ware），把主要精力转移到平衡计分卡、战略盈利性分析、价值链分析、经济增加值、非财务业绩等方面上来，视野更为广阔、内容也更为丰富了（余绪缨，2005），管理会计的职能也逐渐丰富起来。

（五）关于管理会计的框架和内容

从目前国内外主流管理会计教材来看，管理会计的主要框架大都是以介绍管理会计的产生、发展以及基本理论开始，然后是管理会计的具体内容。而对管理会计内容的划分有两种：一是分为完全成本会计、差异会计和管理控制会计；二是分为预测与决策会计、规划与控制会计和责任会计（阿特金森等，2009；威廉姆斯，2008；余绪缨，2005；潘飞等，2009；吴大军，2007）。从内容看，主要有成本性态、成本分析、预测决策、责任会计以及管理会计的一些新理论，如平衡计分卡、作业成本法、环境管理会计、战略管理会计等。但这些内容只是在讲述如何利用管理会计信息进行决策，并没有涉及如何生成这些用于决策的信息。

三、内部报告对管理会计理论的影响

由于早期的古典经济学关于企业“黑箱”性质的认识和后来的新古典经济学关于委托代理关系的认识，人们对于管理会计信息的内涵、特征及功能的认识一直处于迷惘状态，虽然各辟蹊径地研发出了各种各样的管理会计工具，但是就这些工具的应用离不开管理会计信息系统、管理会计信息系统的核心即内部报告等问题仍然没有解决。因此，内部报告理论的提出，可以更加明确管理会计的定义与本质，从而对管理会计基本理论、主要框架和具体内容产生了重大的影响。

（一）内部报告对管理会计定义与本质上的影响

内部报告是建立在管理会计相关性的基础上的。所谓会计的相关性是指会计提供的信息能够满足决策者的决策需要，根据信息使用者的不同，会计相关性可以分为财务会计信息相关性和管理会计信息相关性。财务会计信息相关性要求企业提供的会计信息应当与投资者等财务报告使用者的经济决策需要相关，有助于投资者等财务报告使用者对企业过去、现在或者未来的情况做出评价或者预测。而管理会计信息相关性则是站在内部工作人员需求的角度，侧重于内部决策的需求。企业作为价值创造实体，其经济活动是一个动态过程，企业管理的核心是管理决策和控制活动，价值管理需要持续、动态的管理和控制，需要通过种种财务的、非财务的信息来对其活动状态进行反映。内部报告作为一种重要的、正式的沟通媒介，通过在企业内部按照一定的方向传递，协调和沟通企业董事会、管理者和相关人员，满足企业决策与控制需要，从而使得企业内外部资源进行有效整合，并且和外部环境中存在的机遇相结合，实现企业战略目标的信息报告。因此，基于相关性的内部报告理论与体系构建，将有助于提高管理会计的相关性，更加明确管理会计的两个基本特征，即提供信息和服务于企业内部。而在前述三种管理会计的定义中，本文认为卡普兰教授所提出的较为中义的定义更恰当。

由于基于会计的管理不能反映出管理会计的基本特征，管理会计的本质也必然要发生变化。关于管理会计是一种会计还是一种管理的问题，首先应从会计的本质谈起。如果将会计本质确定为是一种会计管理活动，那么现在的管理会计无论是基于管理的会计，还是基于会计的管理，都应理解为是会计。但是，如果将会计本质理解为一个会计信息系统，那么，只有基于管理的会计才能称为管理会计，基于会计的管理就不是管理会计。企业内部报告的形成，是建立在对复杂和全面的相关内部信息提炼加工的基础之上的，而这些相关内部信息的提供客观要求管理会计系统的建立。试想，如果管理会计的目标是利用相关信息进行预测、决策、规划、控制以及考核等活动，那么提供这些信息又会是谁的职能？因此，内部报告的提出和体系的建立更有助于明确管理会计的本质问题，即作为会计学重要分支的管理会计应是能为组织内部管理者提供所需要的决策有用会计信息的系统，它应是基于管理的会计（张先治，2009）！

（二）内部报告对管理会计研究对象的影响

内部报告的提出，对管理会计的内涵产生了深远的影响。从内部报告涉及内容的范畴看，除了提供财务信息与数量信息外，内部报告还提供一些非财务信息和非数量信息。它不仅注重历史信息，同时也关注现在和未来的信息。从理论上讲，只要与公司的经营管理决策相关的内容，都应纳入它的范畴，都是管理会计的研究对象。内部报告应同时包含短期与长期，静态与动态，微观与宏观，具体与综合的各种与内部管理者决策相关的信息。内部利益相关者，无论是高级管理层，还是中层，甚至可能是员工，都可以从内部报告这一最集中的管理会计信息资源中获取有益于自身进行战略、管理和各种作业层面的决策。因此，内部报告对管理会计信息系统提出了非常高的要求，它应能够更迅速地适应企业动态的经营管理环境的变化，从而极大地拓宽了管理会计的视野，大大促进了管理会计的价值思维及体系边界的扩展。管理会计边界由相对静止（即认为管理会计的边界是明确、清晰与固定的）向逐渐变化的动态发展（即认为管理会计的边界是随环境条件而变化，呈现出模糊性）（余恕莲、吴革，2005），对当前的管理会计有着本质的影响。因此，从管理会计的研究对象和研究范畴的角度讲，服务于内部报告的管理会计更应该是一个广义的概念，本文更倾向于前文所述的关于管理会计研究对象的三种观点中的第（3）种，即能够反映和控制的经济活动及其发出的信息。

（三）内部报告对管理会计目标的影响

管理会计作为一个信息系统，它的目标就是向使用者提供决策有用的信息。然而，需要明确的是管理会计的服务对象是谁，即究竟要向何种使用者提供信息。内部报告作为管理会计信息系统的最系统和最全面地反映，它与管理会计在服务对象上具有一致性。而内部报告只服务于内部管理人员还是同时也向诸如股东、债权人等外部利益相关者提供服务？如果内部报告的服务对象涉及如股东、债权人等外部利益相关者，则会造成内部报告对外部报告在内容上的涵盖，从而模糊了管理会计与财务会计的界限。从这个角度讲，我们所说的会计本质上就是管理会计，这样造成管理会计的范畴过度宽泛。财务会计产生于现代公司制度和资本市场的发展以及企业所有权和经营权逐渐分离的背景下。由于股东不能了解公司的经营和财务状况，为了适应股东的信息需求，财务报告应运而生，从而促使了财务会计的产生与发展。管理会计所需要的资料，很大一部分来源于财务会计，并根据财务会计资料进行一定的加工整理。尽管管理会计与财务会计并不是相互独立，没有联系的，但两者在会计主体、服务对象、基本职能、核算依据、方法及程序等方面都存在着差别。如果将两者强行融合在一起，反而不利于会计学科的发展。因此，本文对内部报告服务对象的范围界定为内部使用者，没有考虑外部使用者。然而，与传统的仅仅满足于内部管理者的决策需求不同，内部报告作为最系统、最全面的内部信息，它应满足所有的内部利益相关者的信息需求，不仅包含董事会、经理层等高级管理者，还应包含企业中层乃至每一名员工。

（四）内部报告对管理会计职能的影响

要界定会计的目标与职能，首先必须认识到会计的职能是由会计的本质所规定的，而职能又是会计所能达到目标的前提，有了职能才能实现目标（黄志忠，1997）。由于会计是一个提供有助于决策的信息系统，会计的职能就是为了实现这一目标而定的。一般认为，反映和监督是会计的基本职能，而反映又是首要职能。那么反映又是如何实现的，对于财务会计信息系统来说，通过输入经济交易和事项，最终形成一个综合性的信息载体——财务报告。然后，通过向外部发布财务报告，实现财务会计向投资者、债权人等利益相关者提供决策有用信息的目标。从这个角度讲，可以认为财务会计的直接职能就是编制财务报告。而内部报告作为根据企业内部经营管理需要编制的并为企业内部决策与控制提供信息保证的各种报表、附注及相关辅助资料的集中反映，它在管理会计中的地位应与财务报告在财务会计中的地位相似。因此，管理会计最直接的职能应是编制内部报告，而不是利用内部报告上的信息进行决策，如评价、考核等。

（五）内部报告对管理会计框架和内容的影响

总体来看，目前主流教材中关于管理会计的框架是合理的，符合企业内部进行决策的信息需求。如前文所述，其所存在的问题主要是内容上的不合理，因为这些内容只是在讲述如何利用管理会计信息进行决策，而没有交代所使用的管理会计信息是如何产生的。这实际上还是关于管理会计的本质问题，即管理会计究竟是基于管理的会计还是基于会计的管理。基于会计的管理，简称为会计管理，这一概念是我国著名会计学家杨纪琬和阎达五在20世纪80年代提出的，并得到了很多学者的响应。在当时的计划经济体制以及没有财务管理的背景下，“会计管理”这个概念无论从理论或实践来看，都有更大的概括性，应用“会计管理”概念要比套用西方“管理会计”的概念，于理于事更为有利（杨继良，1983）。而在当前我国的经济环境下，过度考虑会计的监督职能，而对会计的核算职能没有给予过多的重视，在很大程度上会使得管理会计侵犯财务管理的职能。内部报告理论的提出，使得管理会计有了更加明确的目标，即通过其直接职能——编制内部报告，向内部人员提供决策有用的信息。因此，管理会计的整个框架以及框架下的具体内容都应围绕这一目标展开。管理会计教材的内容应把主要精力用于讲解如何产生并得到管理会计信息，进而编制内部报告，而不是讲述如何利用管理会计信息进行决策。

四、基于内部报告的管理会计与相关学科发展的协调

管理会计、财务管理和成本会计是会计学专业里三门核心课程，但是目前这三个学科存在着分工不明、内容交叉的现象。长此以往，这必然不利于各个学科的发展，而解决这一问题的关键在于明确管理会计和其他相关学科的本质特征有何不同。

（一）当前管理会计发展中存在的问题

由于对管理会计本质的认识不恰当，这导致管理会计与其他相关学科存在着较为严重的内容交叉现象。尽管管理会计和财务会计的联系密切，但由于目标和职能不同，在双方教材中也能进行区分。真正在内容上与管理会计存在重合的是成本会计与财务管理。

1. 管理会计与成本会计

管理会计与成本会计同根共源。19世纪末以来，英国的工业革命带来了生产力的急速发展，企业规模不断扩大，“所得”与“所费”的观念逐渐引起经营者和外部股东的重视。成本会计便是在这种背景下产生的，这一时期成本会计以成本核算为主。随着企业规模的进一步扩大，这种单纯的事后成本核算暴露出很多问题，这加强了企业对现代管理制度的需求。泰罗科学管理被广泛应用后，成本会计引进了标准成本法和预算控制，这也被学术界普遍认为是管理会计的雏形。由此可见，现代管理会计是在成本会计的基础上发展起来的，两个学科在内容上必然存在重叠的部分。从我国当前成本会计教材的内容看，主要有成本核算、成本分析以及作业成本、质量成本、战略成本等成本会计的新方向，其中关于成本会计的核算（产品成本的核算，如品种法、分批法、分步法等；期间费用的核算，如管理费用、营业费用和财务费用的核算）是成本会计教材的主要内容。管理会计的教材则普遍都是从成本性态、成本分析展开的，从一定程度上讲，管理会计是成本会计的延伸。目前，我国大多数院校会计学专业同时开设成本会计与管理会计，而成本会计与管理会计之间内容重复势必会造成极大的教育资源浪费。

2. 管理会计与财务管理

管理会计与财务管理也存在着内容交叉的问题。管理会计与财务管理均以资金运动或价值运动为研究对象，其具体范畴涵盖资产、负债、所有者权益、收入、费用和利润六大会计要素，并且均以定量分析为主要研究方法。相同的内容，采用相同的方法，由此导致的交叉重复无法避免（牛彦秀，2002）。而当前财务管理（或公司理财）教材的内容主要包括财务管理基本概念（时间价值、风险报酬、证券估价、资本成本和资本结构等），筹资、投资、收益管理，价值评估（王化成，2010；姚益龙，2010），有的教材也涉及预算、财务分析等内容（陈玉菁、宋良荣，2008）。预算、投资决策等内容属于管理会计和财务管理交叉的部分。

（二）基于内部报告的管理会计有助于管理会计与相关学科的协调

内部报告理论的提出，更加明确管理会计的相关性是其根本质量特征，是区分于其他学科的重要标志。这不仅为协调管理会计和相关学科奠定了理论基础，也为完善和发展会计学科体系提供了新思路。

1. 关于管理会计学科的定位问题

如前文所述，现在的管理会计实质上不是会计，它也不是会计信息系统的组成部分，它与会计学基础无关，这种管理会计显然不是会计学本质、目标和内涵所界定和反映的。作为会计学重要分支的管理会计应是基于管理的会计。管理会计的本质、目标、内涵和方法等都要符合会计学的基本特性。因此，管理会计改革与完善的方向应是将管理会计置于会计学大框架下进行研究，将围绕管理会计本质和目标进行的管理会计的确认、计量、记录和报告作为管理会计的基本内容和基本方法。提供内部报告应是管理会计目标与方法所决定的，正如同财务会计要提供财务会计报告一样。

2. 内部报告对管理会计与成本会计内容交叉的协调

关于成本会计与管理会计的关系一直在学术界存在很大争议。有的将成本会计与管理会计合二为一称为成本管理会计；有的名称是成本会计，内容与管理会计相关无几；有的名称为管理会计，内容又包含大量成本会计。当然，还有的将成本会计与管理会计完全独立，严格划分边界。如何协调管理会计和成本会计学科之间的冲突？面对这个问题，主要有两条思路：一是取消成本会计，将其纳入管理会计体系；二是将管理会计中的成本会计分离出来，使之成为一个独立的学科。将会计体系划分为财务会计和管理会计已成为学术界的共识，如果将成本会计作为一个独立学科，那么它的目标应与财务会计和管理会计有着本质的不同。从目标来看，财务会计的目标主要是向外部利益相关者提供有助于其做出决策的信息，管理会计则是向内部利益相关者提供有助于其做出决策的信息。而成本会计的目标主要是提供企业有关成本费用的信息，这些信息是利润核算、利润表编制的基础，也是内部管理层经营决策的依据，它与财务会计或管理会计的目标具有相似性。

前文已经对管理会计课程的定位进行了探讨。在明确了管理会计课程定位的基础上，成本会计课程的目标定位有三个：一是基于财务会计报告的要求进行相应的财务成本核算和报告；二是基于内部报告和决策、控制的要求进行管理成本核算与报告；三是基于企业管理的要求，进行成本预测、成本决策、成本控制、成本分析和成本考核。成本会计的这三个目标可能在其他课程中会得到某种程度的实现，但从成本核算与管理的全面性、系统性及科学性角度考虑，独立的成本会计是必要的和可操作的。

3. 内部报告对管理会计与财务管理内容重合的协调

关于管理会计和财务管理，从两者的目标看，管理会计是向内部利益相关者提供决策相关的信息，而财务管理的目标则是实现股东或是相关者的利益最大化，两者的目标明显不同。管理会计的对象是能反映和控制的经济活动及其信息，也有的学者认为是现金流动，财务管理的研究对象也是资金流动。虽然两者的研究对象相似，但两者侧重点有所不同，尤其是在对内部报告的需求与日俱增的背景下，管理会计更侧重于经营管理活动，为经营决策提供相关的信息，并不对资金运动进行直接管理。而财务管理侧重于企业的资本经营活动，对资金运动进行直接管理，通过对资金的筹集管理、资金投放管理和资金的收入与分配管理实现企业理财目标。造成两个学科内容重合的原因是没有认识到管理会计的本质，把管理会计视为基于会计的管理，从而将管理会计伸向了财务管理的领域。因此，在协调两者的内容交叉问题时，处理原则是管理会计应以为内部报告系统提供信息支持，满足内部利益相关者决策需求为主线，财务管理则应以资金运动过程中所涉及的筹集、投资和资金的收入与分配活动为主线。两者的框架可以出现交叉，但是内容不能重合，两者的联系是管理会计提供用于财务管理的信息。

五、结语

会计的本质是一个信息系统，决策有用性是会计的最根本质量特征，财务会计和管理会计是会计的两个重要组成部分。然而，本文在回顾了当前管理会计的定义、基本理论和框架内容后，发现目前管理会计至多可称为基于会计的管理，其本质、目标、内涵等并不像财务会计那样符合会计学的基本特性。内部报告理论的提出可以更加明确管理会计是基于管理的会计这一本质，从而对管理会计基本理论和框架具体内容都产生了重大的影响。而这必然会重新定位管理会计课程，解决当前管理会计与成本会计、财务管理学科之间分工不明、内容交叉的问题，对管理会计学科的发展有着重大的意义。

尽管内部报告反映了时代的要求，在管理会计研究和实践工作中，内部报告在管理会计中的地位远远没有像财务报告在财务会计中的地位那样得到重视。企业内部普遍存在的一些内部报表，如成本费用分析表、控制表、销售收入预测表，并不是作为一个内部报告系统的某一部分而存在的，难以发挥信息系统的优势。如何将这些零散的、非系统的现存内部资料纳入内部报告系统，根据内部报告的需要进行相关信息的编制，这对管理会计理论的创新提出了要求，但这种创新不能背离管理会计目标，特别是管理会计的相关性。从企业内部经营管理需求看会计相关性，就是要为管理者提供内部决策、控制、评价、沟通所需要的各种信息，特别是会计信息，而这为内部报告体系与内容创新指明了方向。

主要参考文献

[1] 张先治:《基于会计相关性的企业内部报告地位与价值》,载《会计研究》,2009(12),65~69页。

[2] 胡玉明:《二十世纪管理会计的发展及其未来展望》,载《外国经济与管理》,1999(5),3~7页。

[3] 张先治:《财务学科定位与发展研究——基于会计学科定位的思考》,载《会计研究》,2007(6),48～54页。

[4] 黄志忠:《从会计本质看会计目标与会计职能》,载《会计研究》,1997(6),33～36页。

[5] 杨继良:《会计管理与管理会计》,载《会计研究》,1983(10),23～28页。

[6] 牛彦秀:《管理会计、成本会计、财务管理内容交叉问题的探讨》,载《会计研究》,2002(6),40～41页。

[7] 葛家澍、刘峰:《会计学导论》,上海,立信会计出版社,1998。

[8] 杨纪琬:《中国现代会计手册》,北京,中国财政经济出版社,1987。

[9] [美]托马斯·约翰逊、罗伯特·卡普兰:《相关性遗失——管理会计兴衰史》,金马工作室译,北京,清华大学出版社,2004。

[10] [美]安东尼·A. 阿特金森:《管理会计》(第5版),北京,清华大学出版社,2009。

[11] [美]威廉姆斯:《会计:企业决策的基础(管理会计分册)》(第14版),赵银德等译,北京,机械工业出版社,2008。

[12] 余绪缨:《管理会计学》,北京,中国人民大学出版社,2005。

[13] 潘飞、陈振婷:《管理会计》,上海,上海财经大学出版社,2009。

[14] 吴大军:《管理会计》,大连,东北财经大学出版社,2007。

[15] 王化成:《财务管理》(第3版),北京,中国人民大学出版社,2010。

[16] 姚益龙:《现代公司理财》,北京,机械工业出版社,2010。

[17] 陈玉菁、宋良荣:《财务管理》(第2版),北京,清华大学出版社,2008。

[18] 余绪缨.:《管理与管理会计理论研究中的几点新认识》,第五届会计与财务问题国际研讨会——当代管理会计新发展,2005。

[19] 余恕莲、吴革:《管理会计的本质属性、边界及发展》,第五届会计与财务问题国际研讨会——当代管理会计新发展,2005。

制度背景、公司价值与社会责任成本①——来自沪深300指数上市公司的经验证据

万寿义　刘正阳

（东北财经大学会计学院　辽宁大连　116025）

摘　要　本文基于《内部控制应用指引第4号——社会责任》，根据利益相关者理论和产权理论，将社会责任成本信息评价指标分为3个层次，构建了企业社会责任成本信息评价体系。以382家沪深300指数上市公司2008—2009年的数据为样本，从样本总体和分行业两个角度，研究了企业社会责任成本与公司价值的相关关系，结果表明：当期是否发生安全生产支出、销售费用支出率、纳税贡献率与公司价值显著正相关，当期是否发生环保支出、欠款未偿付率与公司价值显著负相关，而其他评价指标代表的企业社会责任成本对公司价值的影响并不显著；各行业回归差异较大，应充分考虑不同行业社会责任履行的差异。本文的研究成果为监管机构制定相关政策、上市公司完善社会责任报告和投资者优化投资决策提供了新的经验证据。

关键词　公司价值　社会责任成本　利益相关者　契约　评价指标　相关性

一、研究动机与制度背景

伴随着中国三鹿奶粉、英国石油公司墨西哥湾漏油等一系列违规事件发生，企业社会责任日益成为各方关注的焦点。在社会责任会计研究中，有关社会责任成本的研究更加紧迫和切合实际。这不仅因为理论和实践已经反复证明，企业履行社会责任对于促进社会经济发展具有重要作用，而且伴随着工业化的进程一些上市公司已经以不同形式（如在年报附注中涉及、单独出具社会责任报告），在不同程度上披露了社会责任成本信息。这使得我们有必要对社会责任成本问题展开研究，以便更好地为企业披露社会责任成本信息提供理论支撑和规范指引，同时也为理论界研究企业履行社会责任与实现公司价值最

---

① 基金项目：本文是辽宁省社会科学规划基金项目“企业社会责任成本控制研究”（L080DJY119）的阶段性成果。作者感谢参加第六届公司治理国际研讨会的代表，特别感谢南开大学周建教授、华东政法大学胡贵毅老师和日本札幌大学汪志平老师对本文提出的宝贵建议。

大化的关系问题提供更多经验数据。

近年来，我国政府十分关注企业履行社会责任，针对企业社会责任信息披露，陆续出台了一系列规定（详见表1）。2006年1月1日，全国人民代表大会常务委员会修订的《中华人民共和国公司法》（以下简称《公司法》）要求企业承担社会责任。2006年9月25日，深圳证券交易所正式公布了《上市公司社会责任指引》（以下简称《指引》），对企业披露社会责任信息进行了规范，并鼓励企业自愿披露《社会责任报告》①，但是《指引》对企业社会责任报告披露的内容和格式没有详细的规范。因此，不难发现目前上市公司社会责任报告以文字描述为主的占居多数，量化信息披露较少，且格式不统一。关于社会责任，最具体规范应当是2010年4月26日财政部等五部委联合发布的《企业内部控制配套指引》，该指引将社会责任单独作为一个应用指引，即《内部控制应用指引——第4号社会责任》（以下简称《内控指引第4号——社会责任》）。《内控指引第4号——社会责任》的发布，预示着各利益群体对社会责任的关注进一步提高。

在这样的制度背景下，加上近年来很多上市公司以不同形式披露社会责任会计信息，为研究上市公司社会责任成本会计的实证问题提供了良好契机。基于此，本文利用沪深300指数非金融保险类上市公司2008—2009年年度报告和社会责任报告中披露的社会责任成本信息，立足于《内控指引第4号——社会责任》，基于利益相关者理论和产权理论，对社会责任成本信息评价体系的构建提出了自身见解，并对我国上市公司价值与社会责任成本的相关性进行了研究。这一问题的深入研究，对于探求社会责任成本信息评价体系的建立，并研究企业发生社会责任成本是否影响公司价值，具有重要的理论意义和现实意义。

表1　**与企业社会责任履行相关的规定和报告**

时间及发布机构	规定名称	具体要求/内容	适用范围
2006年1月1日 全国人民代表大会常务委员会	《中华人民共和国公司法》	《公司法》修订案正式施行，要求企业承担社会责任	境内企业
2006年9月25日 深圳证券交易所	《上市公司社会责任指引》	《指引》要求，上市公司在经营活动中应当遵纪守法，遵守商业道德，维护消费者的合法权益，保障劳动者的健康和安全，并积极承担保护环境和节约资源的责任，参与社会捐献、赞助等各种社会公益事业。鼓励企业在披露年报的同时自愿披露《社会责任报告》	上市公司

① 部分企业披露的是《可持续发展报告》，本文认为其等同于《社会责任报告》。

续表

时间及发布机构	规定名称	具体要求/内容	适用范围
2010年4月26日 财政部、证监会、审计署、银监会、保监会	《企业内部控制应用指引——第4号社会责任》	《企业内部控制应用指引——第4号社会责任》详细规范了企业在安全生产、产品质量等多个方面应当承担的社会责任，要求企业充分重视社会责任，切实做好相应的社会责任工作。要求企业在《内部控制评价报告》中详细披露企业履行的社会责任，并聘请事务所出具相应的审计报告	2011年1月1日起在境内外同时上市的公司实施，2012年1月1日起在深沪两所主办上市公司实施，择机要求中小板和创业板企业实施，鼓励非上市大中型企业提前实施
2010年9月15日 环保部	《上市公司环境信息披露指南》 （征求意见稿）	为满足公众的环境知情权，敦促上市公司积极履行保护环境的社会责任，《指南》要求，16类重污染行业上市公司应当发布年度环境报告，定期披露污染物排放情况等方面的环境信息；发生突发环境事件的上市公司，应当在事件发生1日内发布临时环境报告，披露环境事件的发生时间、地点、主要污染物质和数量、事件对环境影响情况和人员伤害情况（如有），以及已采取的应急处理措施等	在沪深两市A股市场的上市公司，具体包括火电、钢铁、水泥、电解铝、煤炭、织金、化工、石化、建材、造纸、酿造、制药、发酵、纺织、制革和采矿业

二、文献综述

国外学者研究公司价值与社会责任成本相关性问题始于20世纪70年代，但是由于受到社会责任成本数据可获得性的限制以及计量方法的不同，截至目前尚未形成统一的结论。Moskowitz（1972）、Bowman等（1975）和Cochran P. 等（1984）是坚持正相关的典型代表，Moskowitz对样本公司的社会责任表现进行赋值后进行回归，结果表明企业履行社会责任越多，股票平均回报率越高，两者成正比关系。Bowman等以美国食品行业为样本，通过计算企业社会责任指数，研究了社会责任信息披露与企业价值的关系，发现企业两者正相关。而Cochran P. 等研究也发现企业履行社会责任越多，公司价值越大，但是Vance（1975）选取了Moskowitz研究样本的一个子样本和纽约证券交易所上市的部分公司作为研究样本，将两者对照后，得出了负相关的结论。与此同时，Holman和Walter R.（1985）也研究发现企业承担过多的社会责任，增加了企业负担，支付过多的成本，企业利润会下降，进而导致公司价值下降。另外，国外学者也有支持企业社会责任与公司价值不存在相关性的例子，如Mc Williams等（2001）通过研究发现两者之间不存在相关性。

近年来，我国学者也对公司价值与社会责任成本相关性问题展开了广泛地研究，但由于起步较晚，研究成果较少。陈玉清和马丽丽（2005）对上市公司履行社会责任所引起的市场反应进行研究，发现两者相关性强，但不同行业之间价值相关性有所不同。李正（2006）以2003年沪市521家上市公司为研究样本，发现企业当期承担的社会责任越多，企业的价值越低。姚海鑫等（2007）研究了企业社会责任对股东财富的影响，发现企业履行社会责任有利于增加股东财富。温素彬和方苑（2008）研究发现，企业社会责任表现对公司当前财务业绩影响为负；但从长远看，对财务绩效影响为正。王建琼和何静谊（2009）通过研究制造业企业，发现企业的社会责任表现与经济绩效相关性较弱。陈煦江（2009）利用沪深两市2003—2006年的面板数据研究企业社会责任表现对企业价值的影响，发现两者之间存在或正或负的相关关系。朱雅琴和姚海鑫（2010）进行大样本回归分析发现，社会责任各评价指标与企业价值之间存在不同的相关关系，如对政府和职工的社会责任与企业价值正相关，而对投资者的社会责任与公司价值负相关等。

总体上来讲，目前国内外现有文献的研究结论并不统一，这可能源于以下几个方面的原因：第一，行业之间承担的社会责任存在很大差异；第二，企业社会责任成本信息评价标准尚未建立，研究者的评价标准并不一致；第三，反映企业社会责任履行状况的因素难以量化；第四，关于公司价值的计算方法存在诸多争议，不同指标计算出来的结果有很大不同。

基于此，本文在研究思路和方法上与现有文献有明显差别，本文首先对可量化的社会责任成本信息进行等级划分，建立起更加完善的社会责任成本信息评价体系；然后对我国上市公司社会责任成本信息评价指标与公司价值的关系进行了分析。

三、理论分析与研究假设

现代经济学试图从利益相关者理论和产权理论解释企业社会责任与公司价值相关性这一命题。利益相关者理论认为在现代社会中，公司既要谋求股东利益最大化，也应当最大限度的实现员工、顾客、债权人、供应商、政府和社区等其他利益相关者的利益；公司的权利来源于所有利益相关者的授权，因此公司经营者不仅要向股东负责，还要对其他利益相关者负责，以实现公司价值与社会责任协同发展。利益相关者理论充分体现了不同利益群体对企业社会责任的关注，并从不同的角度阐述了社会责任与公司价值之间的关系。产权理论认为，企业为了维持其生产经营活动，需要与不同要素所有者建立不同的契约，企业就是各种契约的结合体，这些契约包括与投资者建立的股份合同、与供应商和顾客建立的购销合同、与债权人建立的贷款合同、与税务机关形成的纳税合同等。企业履行与社会责任相关的各项契约关系，不仅有利于降低企业业务风险（Bryan W. Husted，2005），同时对于实现企业价值具有重要意义。为了保证这些契约产权有效持续运行并实现企业自身的价值，就必须对生产要素的所有者进行补偿。这些补偿表现在多方面，包括对投资者的股利支付、对员工的薪酬和福利支付、对债权人的利息支付以及对国家税收的支付等。

基于上述理论和既有的研究成果，结合《指引》① 和《企业内部控制应用指引——第4号社会责任》② 中对社会责任的定义，本文将影响公司价值的企业社会责任成本信息进行了一定划分，由于社会责任成本衡量难度较大、数据难以取得，本文采用比率评价指标对企业各方面社会责任成本支付进行度量，具体分为三级，即一级社会责任成本信息评价指标、二级社会责任成本信息评价指标、三级社会责任成本信息评价指标，以此构建了社会责任成本信息评价体系（详细划分见表2）。首先，企业对职工报酬的支付责任、对消费者的产品保障责任、为生产产品而支付的各项环保代价以及资源节约程度应该是企业在任何时候所必须履行的责任。因此，我们将与这些责任相关的指标划为一级评价指标，即最高层次的评价指标。二级社会责任成本信息评价指标体现的是企业对社会和国家的一种回报。由于企业受其当年的经营状况（如亏损）的影响，不可能每年都为国家缴税、捐赠和按期偿还债务。因此，我们将对社会贡献指标中的捐赠支出、对国家纳税的支出以及偿还债权人债务的支出划为二级评价指标。在对三级社会责任成本信息评价指标的界定过程中，本文认为在利益相关者理论中股东尤其是控股股东是企业最重要的利益相关者，供应商也是企业各项契约中最紧凑的一个环节，但是供应商和股东与企业经营状况直接相关，当企业经营状况欠佳时，可能不分红、不支付欠款，这些侧重于企业本身问题的指标与社会责任相关度较弱。因此，从社会责任层面上讲，应该是企业最外层的社会责任，我们将对股东获利率和欠款偿付率划分为三级评价指标。

根据上述划分，本文将影响公司价值的各项社会责任成本逐一进行分析、梳理，并按照对应的社会责任成本信息评价指标提出了研究假设：

1. 一级社会责任成本信息评价指标

利益相关者理论要求企业不应只关注股东的利益，还应当关注员工、顾客、环境、社区等利益相关者。作为企业生产成本的主要组成部分，员工是企业首先应当重视的利益相关者，员工利益的补偿是履行劳动契约的重要体现，对公司价值的实现具有重要意义。这种补偿主要体现在职工的收入是否按期支付、工作场所是否做到安全生产等。同时，企业积极改善与员工的关系，能够大幅度的降低企业的权益成本（Sadok El Ghoul 等，2011），实现企业的价值。

① 2006年9月25日，深圳证券交易所正式公布的《指引》中第2条规定：“本指引所称的上市公司社会责任是指上市公司对国家和社会的发展、自然环境和资源。”

② 2010年4月26日，财政部、证监会、审计署、银监会、保监会联合发布的《企业内部控制应用指引——第4号社会责任》中“所称的社会责任是指企业在经营发展过程中应当履行的社会职责和义务，主要包括安全生产、产品质量、环境保护、资源节约、促进就业、员工权益保护等”。

产权理论认为，企业与顾客之间是契约的结合体。企业要实现自身的价值不应该仅局限于眼前利益，而应当充分履行这种契约以实现长远利益。销售费用支出的多少，表明企业主动承担了多少产品售前和售后的责任，是企业履行对顾客责任的具体体现。企业为维护消费者利益付出的越多，越容易得到顾客的青睐（朱雅琴等，2010），越有利于实现企业的价值。

利益相关者理论认为，企业在满足自身发展的同时，如果积极回报社会（包括环境保护、资源节约、社区贡献），不仅可以树立良好企业形象（朱雅琴等，2010），而且有利于降低企业权益资本并赢得普遍赞誉（Brammer 等，2005；Sadok El Ghoul 等，2011），进而提升自身价值。据上述分析，我们提出假设 1：

假设 1—1：薪金支付率越高，公司价值就越大；

假设 1—2：当期发生安全生产费用支出的企业，公司价值就越大；

假设 1—3：企业与产品质量相关的销售费用支出越高，公司价值就越大；

假设 1—4：当期节能降耗的企业，公司价值就越大；

假设 1—5：当期为社区做出贡献的企业，公司价值就越大；

假设 1—6：当期积极环保的企业，公司价值就越大。

2. 二级社会责任成本信息评价指标

税收是国家财政收入的主要来源，国家财政通过税收获取资金，进行基础设施建设等，为企业发展创造了良好的生产环境。企业积极纳税，既有利于获得更多的国家政策支持（朱雅琴等，2010），也有利于实现企业价值。

从产权理论和利益相关者理论来看，企业与债权人之间既是利益相关者中一对重要关系组合，同时两者之间又存在不可回避的契约链条。在市场经济条件下，企业规模的扩大，仅仅靠股东投资和内部资金积累是不够的（朱雅琴等，2010），大量债务融资也是企业发展不可或缺的重要因素，但是经营环境的不确定性以及企业面临的各种财务风险直接影响了企业与债权人契约的履行。Allen Goss 等（2010）发现社会责任好的企业可以借入利息较低的长期贷款，而履行社会责任较差的企业往往只能借入高利息的短期贷款。因此，企业履行维护好与债权人的关系，有利于企业价值的实现。

与对债权人的责任不同，在相关利益者链条中企业对社会弱势群体的捐助，既体现了企业社会责任，也体现了企业的伦理和道德。企业积极的慈善活动会使企业获得普遍的赞誉，使企业获得更多的收益（Brammer 等，2005）。企业当期捐献越多，企业被媒体曝光度越大，就越有利于实现自身价值。据此，我们提出假设 2：

假设 2—1：企业纳税贡献率越高，公司价值就越大；

假设 2—2：企业利息保障倍数越高，企业债务安全边界越高，公司价值就越大；

假设 2—3：企业社会捐献赞助率越高，公司价值就越大。

3. 三级社会责任成本信息评价指标

公司股东特别是控股股东对企业的直接投资，是企业营运资本的主要来源。现金股利分配的多少，直接影响了股东对企业投资的积极性（万寿义等，2010）。企业股东获利率越高，股东越发积极地关注企业发展，越有利于企业价值的实现，但与其他利益相关者相比，股东利益是企业主动要承担的责任，因此本文把与股东有关的社会责任成本支出划为三级评价指标。对供应商的责任也是企业发展中重要关注的关系，企业与供应商之间保持良好的伙伴关系，有利于企业缓解供应链上的各种潜在问题，实现企业原材料供应的良性循环，从而推动公司价值的提高。据此，我们提出假设3：

假设3—1：企业股东获利率越高，公司价值就越大；

假设3—2：企业欠款未偿付率越低，公司价值就越大。

四、研究设计

1. 样本选择与数据来源

本研究选取了2008—2009年沪深300指数上市公司作为研究样本，样本筛选程序如下：（1）由于金融保险类行业业务处理的特殊性，剔除了被中国证监会分类为金融保险行业的30家上市公司；（2）剔除了研究期间没有对外发布社会责任报告或相关数据缺失的158家上市公司。最终选定同时发布年度报告和社会责任报告的样本公司为382家，其中中国中冶（601618）2009年社会责任报告为英文版。

有关上市公司捐献金额、环保支出、安全生产费支出、节能降耗、社区贡献和赞助费等数据，均根据上市公司对外公布的社会责任报告逐一手工采集取得。其余数据均取自国泰安研究服务中心提供的上市公司年报数据库和Wind中国金融数据库。所用的上市公司年报来自于巨潮资讯网，社会责任报告来自于巨潮资讯网和企业社会责任中国网。

2. 变量界定

（1）公司价值

关于“公司价值”一词最初由Modigliani和Miller（1958）提出，但公司价值的计算方法至今存在争议。本文采用了计算公司价值最普遍的方法——Tobin's Q值，这与李正（2006）、温素彬等（2008）、陈煦江（2009）等计算方法相同。

Tobin's Q =企业总资本的市场价值÷期末企业总资产

=（股权市值+净债务市值）÷期末企业总资产

（2）企业社会责任成本评价指标

基于研究假设，本文选取的解释变量及定义见表2。在控制变量中，加入资产总额的自然对数，用以限定公司规模对公司价值的影响。加入社会责任报告所属年度，主要是上市公司每年承担的社会责任不同可能对公司价值的影响存在差异。

表2 变量定义表

<table>
<tr><th colspan="3">变量名称</th><th>变量代码</th><th>变量计算</th><th>级别</th></tr>
<tr><td>解释变量</td><td colspan="2">公司价值</td><td>Tobin's Q</td><td>Tobin's Q＝企业总资本的市场价值÷期末企业总资产＝（股权市值+净债务市值）÷期末企业总资产</td><td></td></tr>
<tr><td rowspan="11">被解释变量</td><td rowspan="2">对员工的责任</td><td>薪金支付率</td><td>GOVR</td><td>支付给职工及为职工支付的现金÷主营业务收入</td><td rowspan="7">一级指标 CSR_1</td></tr>
<tr><td>是否发生安全生产费支出</td><td>SAC</td><td>存在安全生产费支出的为 1，否则为 0</td></tr>
<tr><td>对顾客的责任</td><td>销售费用支出率</td><td>SER</td><td>销售费用÷主营业务收入</td></tr>
<tr><td rowspan="4">对社会的责任</td><td>是否当期节能降耗</td><td>ECRE</td><td>虚拟变量，若有资源节约记为 1，否则为 0</td></tr>
<tr><td>是否有社区贡献</td><td>COM</td><td>虚拟变量，存在对社区的贡献记为 1，否则为 0</td></tr>
<tr><td>是否发生环保支出</td><td>EP</td><td>虚拟变量，存在为 1，不存在为 0</td></tr>
<tr><td>社会捐献赞助率</td><td>SD</td><td>（捐赠支出+赞助费）÷税前利润</td></tr>
<tr><td>对债权人的责任</td><td>利息保障倍数</td><td>LXBS</td><td>息税前利润/利息</td><td rowspan="2">二级指标 CSR_2</td></tr>
<tr><td>对政府的责任</td><td>纳税贡献率</td><td>TAXR</td><td>（支付的各项税费－收到的税费返还）÷资产总额</td></tr>
<tr><td>对投资者的责任</td><td>股东获利率</td><td>SR</td><td>（分配股利、利润支付的现金）÷净利润总额</td><td rowspan="2">三级指标 CSR_3</td></tr>
<tr><td>对供应商的责任</td><td>欠款未偿付率</td><td>PAR</td><td>（应付账款＋应付票据＋预收账款）÷资产总额</td></tr>
<tr><td rowspan="2">控制变量</td><td colspan="2">公司规模</td><td>SIZE</td><td>公司总资产的自然对数</td><td rowspan="2"></td></tr>
<tr><td colspan="2">年度</td><td>YEAR</td><td>虚拟变量，2008 年为 0，2009 年为 1</td></tr>
</table>

3. 模型设计

为了研究企业发生的社会责任成本对公司价值的影响，本文建立如下模型：

$$(Tobin'sQ)_i=\beta_0+\beta_1 GOVR+\beta_2 SAC+\beta_3 SER+\beta_4 ECRE+\beta_5 COM+\beta_6 EP+\beta_7 SD+\beta_8 LXBS+\beta_9 TAXR+\beta_{10} SR+\beta_{11} PAR+\beta_{12} SIZE+\beta_{13} YEAR_i+u_i \quad (1)$$

同时考虑到不同层次指标之间的关联程度，本文按前述社会责任成本信息评价体系的三个层次，又构建了如下模型：

$$(Tobin'sQ)_i=\beta_0+\beta_1 GOVR+\beta_2 SAC+\beta_3 SER+\beta_4 ECRE+\beta_5 COM+\beta_6 EP+\beta_7 SIZE+\beta_8 YEAR_i+u_i \quad (2)$$

$$(Tobin'sQ)_i=\beta_0+\beta_1 SD+\beta_2 LXBS+\beta_3 TAXR+\beta_4 SR+\beta_5 PAR+\beta_6 SIZE+\beta_7 YEAR_i+u_i \quad (3)$$

$$(Tobin'sQ)_i=\beta_0+\beta_1 SR+\beta_2 PAR+\beta_3 SIZE+\beta_4 YEAR_i+u_i \quad (4)$$

上述所有模型中，i 的取值范围为 0 或 1，i=0 时为 2008 年，i=1 时为 2009 年。

五、实证检验

1. 描述性统计

(1) 关于社会责任报告的描述性统计

从披露社会责任报告的数量看，沪深 300 指数上市公司对外披露社会责任报告的数量逐年增加，2008 年对外披露报告 183 家，2009 年对外披露报告 199 家，详细信息见表 3。从是否单独公布社会责任报告看，在沪深两市交易的公司公布社会责任报告方式有所不同。在深圳证券交易所进行交易的公司基本上都是单独对外公布社会责任报告，而在上海证券交易所进行交易的公司多在年报中附加，详细信息见表 4、表 5。

表 3　**2008—2009 年社会责任报告对外披露数量**

	深圳证券交易所	上海证券交易所
2008 年	68	115
2009 年	75	124

表 4　**2008 年社会责任报告对外公布的位置**

	单独对外公布	作为年报一部分	其他
深圳证券交易所	67	0	1
上海证券交易所	0	110	5

注：其他指的是除单独对外公布或者作为年报一部分对外公布的情况，不包括同时以上述两种方式对外公布的情形。

表 5　**2009 年社会责任报告对外公布的位置**

	单独对外公布	作为年报一部分	其他
深圳证券交易所	75	0	0
上海证券交易所	3	121	0

沪深300指数非金融保险类上市公司股票交易在深圳证券交易所进行的公司有83家，在上海证券交易进行的公司有187家。从表3中我们可以发现：2008年在深圳证券交易所进行交易的上市公司对外披露社会责任报告的数量占深圳证券交易所83家上市公司的81.93%，而在上海证券交易所上市的公司对外披露社会责任报告的数量占上海证券交易所187家上市公司的61.50%；2009年分别占全部公司的90.36%、66.31%。从比例上看，在上海证券交易所交易的300指数公司对外披露的社会责任报告显著小于在深交所上市的300指数公司。从表4和表5中可以看出：自2009年开始，上市公司社会责任报告开始在更加显著的位置披露，以此来反映公司对社会责任的重视程度。总体上讲，我国上市公司特别是沪深300指数公司的社会责任意识正在逐渐加强。

（2）全部样本公司各变量描述性统计

结合表6，从具体指标分析可以看出：①样本公司的公司价值相差较大；②安全生产支出、社区贡献的平均水平为20%，这表明上市公司在这方面的社会责任意识偏低；③社会捐赠贡献率的平均水平仅为2%，这表明上市公司对社会弱势群体关注很低；④利息保障倍数最大值4 719.468，最小值-715.175，标准差高达251.299，这种差异说明债权人权益的保障程度有巨大差异，部分公司债务契约履行程度较差；⑤股东获利率最大值与最小值之间相差632.668，表明样本公司股东获利水平存在较大的差距，这可能会影响公司股价走势，进而影响到公司价值；⑥其他指标整体表现良好。

表6　**全部样本公司各变量描述性统计**

	样本量	最小值	最大值	中位数	平均值	标准差
Tobin's Q	382	0.582	9.965	1.174	1.610	0.998
GOVR	382	0.007	0.495	0.064	0.080	0.613
SAC	382	0.000	1.000	0.000	0.223	0.417
SER	382	0.000	0.451	0.022	0.042	0.060
ECRE	382	0.000	1.000	1.000	0.622	0.486
COM	382	0.000	1.000	0.000	0.234	0.424
EP	382	0.000	1.000	1.000	0.643	0.480
SD	382	-0.964	1.700	0.004	0.022	0.146
LXBS	382	-715.175	4 719.468	5.343	25.403	251.299
TAXR	382	-0.038	0.272	0.037	0.052	0.045
SR	382	-3.036	629.632	0.580	3.139	32.919
PAR	382	0.003	0.793	0.132	0.188	0.153
SIZE	382	20.903	28.003	23.358	23.561	1.168

2. 回归分析

(1) 样本总体回归分析

本文选用 SPSS16.0 软件对各解释变量进行多重共线性检验，各解释变量的 Tolerance① 值均大于 0.75，VIF 远小于 10，表明各解释变量之间不存在严重的多重共线性。在不存在多重共线性的情况下，我们代入估计模型，进行回归分析，结果见表 7。模型 1 的回归结果表明：

①安全生产支出、销售费用支出率、纳税贡献率与公司价值显著正相关，与假设 1—2、1—3、2—1 一致。这说明各利益相关者对企业当期安全生产的保障、对消费者权益的保护和对政府的责任非常关注，企业履行上述社会责任越好，公司价值就越高。

②欠款未偿付率与公司价值显著负相关，与假设 3—2 一致，这说明企业如果未能履行对供应商的责任，流动负债比例越大，公司价值就越低。

③企业当期发生的环保支出越多，公司价值就越低，这与研究假设1—6相悖，这可能是因为企业当期的环保支出多发生在企业违反环境规定并接收处罚后，是对环境破坏及相关利益者的一种补偿性支付。这种支出过多，表明企业当期破坏环境较大，投资者做出负面反应，股价下跌，公司价值就降低。

④除上述指标以外，其他变量在统计水平上均不显著，但是我们可以通过回归系数的符号透视出各评价指标代表的公司社会责任成本对公司价值的影响，进一步分析如下：是否节能降耗、是否有社区贡献、社会捐赠赞助率的系数为正，这表明公司当期节能降耗、对社区做出贡献、进行社会捐赠越多，公司社会形象更好，公司价值越大。同时，薪金支付率、利息保障倍数、股东获利率的系数为负，与假设不一致，这暗含了企业当期发生上述社会责任成本不利于企业当期价值的实现，但是可能有利于企业长期价值的实现。

⑤从模型整体结果上看，一级社会责任成本信息评价指标的显著性好于二级和三级指标，这说明社会责任成本信息评价体系构建是合理的。

从模型 2 到模型 4 中可以看出，除欠款未偿付率对公司价值的影响不再显著外，模型其他各变量反应程度并未有变化，前述各结论依然成立。欠款未偿付率可能因为不再受到其他变量的影响而不再显著，但是预期符号并未发生改变，欠款过多依然对公司价值具有负面影响。

模型 1 到模型 4 调整后的 R^2 均超过 34%，且模型 1 调整后的 R^2 达到 38%，这表明各模型整体拟合度较高，本文对影响公司价值的社会责任成本因素考虑比较全面，进一步表明本文构建的社会责任成本信息评价体系是合理的，但是不可否认仍然有影响公司价值的因素（如公司治理特征等）未考虑。

① 限于文章篇幅容忍度和 VIF 并没有列示。

表7　多元回归结果

	模型1 系数 （t值）	模型2 系数 （t值）	模型3 系数 （t值）	模型4 系数 （t值）
截距	10.3821 *** （11.2800）	10.8907 *** （11.7604）	10.4371 *** （12.5017）	10.7604 *** （12.7229）
GOVR	−0.9283 （−1.2655）	−0.6123 （−0.8604）		
SAC	0.2015 ** （1.9500）	0.2283 ** （2.1962）		
SER	2.2191 *** （2.9815）	2.6233 *** （3.5806）		
ECRE	0.0654 （0.7333）	0.0976 （1.0822）		
COM	0.0655 （0.6674）	0.0718 （0.7184）		
EP	−0.2322 *** −2.6162）	−0.1779 ** （−1.9954）		
SD	0.2385 （0.8615）		0.2229 （0.7932）	
LXBS	−0.0001 （−0.5720）		−0.0001 （−0.5427）	
TAXR	3.2534 *** （3.4475）		3.9331 *** （4.2729）	
SR	−0.0018 （−1.4843）			−0.0017 （−1.3201）
PAR	−0.5668 ** （−2.0130）			−0.3935 （−1.4235）
SIZE	−0.3905 *** （−9.8712）	−0.4131 *** （−10.4058）	−0.4008 *** （−11.3581）	−0.4019 *** （−11.0859）
YEAR	0.7666 *** （9.3371）	0.7228 *** （8.7313）	0.7862 *** （9.5269）	0.7666 *** （9.1517）
F值	19.2786 ***	27.9538 ***	44.4017 ***	49.9667 ***
Adjusted-R^2	0.3847	0.3620	0.3635	0.3401
D-W	1.5422	1.6190	1.5330	1.4940

注：＊＊＊、＊＊、＊分别表示在1%、5%、10%的置信水平上显著。

（2）按照行业回归分析

我们按照中国证监会《上市公司行业分类指引》（2001）对样本公司按行业进行划分并归类，进行回归分析①，研究发现食品饮料类样本公司的拟合度最好，其全部社会责任成本信息评价指标在5%的置信水平上显著影响公司价值，其拟合度高达100%。金属、非金属类样本公司的薪金支付率和股东获利率分别在1%和5%的置信水平上显著影响公司价值，交通运输、仓储业样本公司的欠款未偿付率和纳税贡献率分别在1%和5%的置信水平上显著影响公司价值。其他行业样本公司社会责任成本信息评价指标对公司价值的影响较弱，其中对制造业中石油、化学、塑胶、塑料类上市公司公司价值的影响仅有8.329%，这可能是分行业回归时，各行业样本量太少造成的。

虽然受样本量制约，大部分行业回归结果表明社会责任成本对公司价值的影响不太显著，但从结果中依然可以得出如下结论：本文构建的社会责任成本信息评价体系能够反映企业社会责任成本对公司价值的影响，同时不同行业回归结果差异较大，具体分析时应当充分考虑行业差异。

（3）稳健性检验

考虑到股权分置改革对我国资本市场的影响②，本文将MVE/BVE作为被解释变量替代Tobin's Q，进行稳健性检验。公司市场价值（MVE）的计算采用了杨丹等（2008）提出的修正方法，即MVE=P×TS+P×NTS×f。其中，f为每股限售股的价格与每股流通股价格之比，即限售股的价格P=f×流通股的价格。TS、NTS分别为流通股股数、限售股股数，BVE为公司账面价值。P为流通股的价格，对于流通股股价的计算，本文采取最接近于年报资产负债表日（包括12月31日）起，前推30个股票交易日股价平均数（万寿义等，2010）。

在计算f值③时，笔者运用EVIEWS5.0④统计软件，采用了最大似然估计方法，利用非线性模型：MVE/BVE=（a/BVE+b+c*ROE）/（1-NTR*(1-f)），分别求得2008年和2009年的限售股对流通股的折价比率为0.686和0.549，进而求得样本公司的MVE/BVE，以此对公司价值Tobin's Q进行替代，重新进行全样本回归（结果见表8）。

---

① 限于文章篇幅，具体数据没有列出。

② 股权分置问题是我国特殊制度背景下的制度安排，它导致上市公司同时存在流通股和非流通股（杨丹等，2008），致使股票市场中流通股和非流通股股价并不相等。作为目前各种计算公司价值方法不可回避的考虑因素，流通股和非流通股股价不同导致了公司价值计算结果的扭曲。虽然目前已进入后股权分置改革时代，但限售股依然存在，流通股与限售股股价依然存在差别，因此有必要采取方法消除这种影响。

③ 本文选用当年全部在沪深上市的公司作为样本，对f值进行计算。根据样本情况，进行了如下剔除：A. 考虑到金融保险行业的特殊性，剔除了金融保险类的公司；B. 剔除了那些资料不全或者根本无法找到资料的上市公司；C. 剔除存在其他极端情况的上市公司。最终用于计算f值的样本共2 721个，其中2008年1 119个、2009年1 602个。

④ 除此外，本文其余各回归均采用SPSS16.0。

表8 Tobin's Q 被替代为 MVE/BVE 后的回归结果

	模型5 系数 (t值)	模型6 系数 (t值)	模型7 系数 (t值)	模型8 系数 (t值)
截距	16.1298*** (6.2679)	16.6542*** (6.4943)	16.0771*** (6.9259)	17.5401*** (7.5606)
GOVR	0.1888 (0.0921)	−1.1727 (−0.5951)		
SAC	0.5680** (1.9657)	0.6237** (2.1664)		
SER	4.3224** (2.0771)	5.9951*** (2.9550)		
ECRE	0.0136 (0.0547)	0.0176 (0.0704)		
COM	0.1856 (0.6761)	0.2186 (0.7902)		
EP	−0.5144** (−2.0732)	−0.4785** (−1.9381)		
SD	0.3158 (0.4081)		0.3652 (0.4673)	
LXBS	−0.0002 (−0.3771)		−0.0001 (−0.2235)	
TAXR	6.6922*** (2.5363)		8.0241*** (3.1352)	
SR	−0.0034 (−0.9796)			−0.0030 (−0.8531)
PAR	1.4522* (1.8446)			1.5984** (2.1078)
SIZE	−0.6293*** (−5.6896)	−0.6250*** (−5.6859)	−0.6193*** (−6.3127)	−0.6741*** (−6.7783)
YEAR	1.4299*** (6.2291)	1.3917*** (6.0708)	1.5336*** (6.6836)	1.4523*** (6.3206)
F值	8.1582***	11.6348***	17.4771***	20.5654***
Adjusted-R^2	0.1967	0.1829	0.1782	0.1708
D-W	2.1073	2.1062	2.0875	2.0621

注：***、**、*分别表示在1%、5%、10%的置信水平上显著。

通过表8可以看出，在模型5和模型8中欠款未偿付率对公司价值的影响虽然表现出一定的显著性，但是与模型1和模型4回归结果的系数符号正好相反。这可能是Tobin's Q的计算既需要考虑股权市场价值，同时也要考虑企业净债务价值；MVE/BVE的值完全通过计算股权市场价值得到；而欠款未偿付率在计算中运用了公司资产负债表中流动负债的账面价值，对Tobin's Q产生了影响，导致与先前结论有所不同。除此之外，研究结果没有发生实质性改变，本文的结论是稳定的。

此外，本文还进行如下稳健性检验①：（1）用资产总额年初与年末的平均数替代资产总额年末数；（2）加入控制变量国有股股东持股比例；（3）加入控制变量是否属于上证治理板块和公司上市地点。上述稳健性检验的研究结果表明，本文的结论没有发生实质性改变。

六、结论与政策建议

1. 研究结论

（1）从社会责任信息披露的内容看，目前我国上市公司通过社会责任报告和年报对外披露的社会责任信息，大都是基于非会计基础，量化信息较少，即便有少数量化信息也多被文字广泛覆盖，严重影响了信息使用者使用，这也使得本文部分变量以虚拟变量体现。

（2）从样本总体回归结果看，企业履行对顾客、政府和供应商等利益相关者的社会责任产生的成本支出会对公司价值产生显著影响，具体体现在被媒体经常曝光的产品质量、企业纳税、环保支出、是否有巨额欠款等方面。而这些信息多在年报中涉及，这也侧面反映出目前我国资本市场对社会责任报告关注较少、资本市场的有效性不强以及信息使用者对社会责任信息的需求有限等问题。

（3）从分行业的回归结果看，属于食品、饮料类行业的企业产生的社会责任成本对公司价值影响较高，模型拟合度近乎100%，这说明自石家庄三鹿集团股份有限公司三聚氰胺事件后，各利益相关者对食品行业的社会责任成本信息关注度普遍增强，该行业企业社会责任的履行程度会影响到公司价值的实现，而对其他行业的关注相对较低，对公司价值的影响较小。从这一点不难发现，我国信息使用者对企业社会责任成本信息的关注多集中于事后，对社会责任成本信息的事前关注程度较弱。

2. 研究局限和政策建议

本文研究存在三方面的局限：首先，本文研究样本是沪深300指数非金融保险类上市公司中披露社会责任报告的公司，研究的外部有效性有所削弱，影

① 限于文章篇幅，检验结果并未列出。

响了研究结论的普遍意义；其次，由于受社会责任信息量化的限制，本研究中部分变量为虚拟变量，未必能够深入检验这部分变量代表的社会责任成本对公司价值的影响。最后，由于数据收集能力有限，研究不能完全涵盖可能影响公司价值的所有社会责任成本信息。

尽管如此，本文的经验证据对于上市公司的如何有效披露社会责任成本信息，以及信息使用者和监管者如何加强上市公司社会责任监督仍有借鉴意义。因此，本文提出以下几点政策建议：

（1）逐步完善我国相关法律制度，加强实际监管力度。企业履行社会责任，其监管涉及国家多个部门，如国家税务总局、环保部、国家食品药品监督管理局、中国人民银行及其各大商业银行等。各部门之间应当相互协作，定期对大型企业进行安全排查，发现问题及时制定解决措施，加强对上市公司食品安全、环境保护、及时纳税和信息披露等方面的监管。财政部等五部委联合发布的《企业内部控制配套指引》是制度安排中很好的典范，虽然企业如何得到有效的贯彻尚需时间的观察，但是这种制度安排本身的合理性已经得到了一定的证明。笔者认为，除了要求企业建立良好的内部控制制度并接受事务所审计外，国家还可以要求国有控股企业并鼓励民营企业建立随时接受上级检查的协调小组，对于各种可能发生的事故进行有效监督检查。这种做法虽然表面上增加了监督成本，但是实际上却降低了事故发生后的后续治理成本，如处罚成本、整治成本以及其他相关的成本。国家及地方各部门相互协调，对企业各方面进行及时监督，对于问题企业加大处罚成本，使其处罚成本大于不法行为获取的收益，增大企业潜在损失。

（2）相关部门应规范社会责任报告披露形式，要求企业加强在会计基础上披露社会责任成本信息，防止信息失真。自 2006 年深圳证券交易所公布《上市公司社会责任指引》并鼓励企业披露社会责任报告以来，报告披露数量逐年增加，但增长缓慢，并且以叙述性报告为主，社会责任报告多流于形式。财政部应继续联合国家相关部门建立成本会计准则，健全社会责任信息披露的规则、准则和指南，以指导企业编制社会责任报告，如联合环保部构建环境会计信息披露的相关指引、准则和指南等。同时，也可以构建成本会计准则，并将社会责任成本准则作为成本会计准则的一个具体准则。准则应当明确企业披露的内容，如环境成本、产品售后服务成本等，并要求企业在按照会计准则披露相关信息的同时，在社会责任报告或是环境报告中按照收付实现制披露企业当期发生的社会责任成本或环境成本，以方便利益相关者获取必要信息，全面了解上市公司社会责任的履行状况，以此提升利益相关者决策的准确性，促进社会责任履行好的公司的价值获得提升。

（3）上市公司应当进一步完善社会责任报告，增强货币性社会责任成本信息披露，对于社会责任报告中的具体内容，如果可以量化，上市公司应当公布量化信息。除年度社会责任报告外，上市公司应当不定期及时披露各种社会责任公告，使利益相关者了解到企业除主要经营活动外的其他活动信息。笔者认为，现阶段能够货币化并能够提升企业价值的信息主要包括：企业用于当期产品质量检测的费用和为消费者进行售后服务的支出、企业当期事前环境保护支出、企业进行员工培训的支出、响应国家政策增加就业岗位的支出和企业对外捐赠支出。除上述信息外，企业可货币化的社会责任成本还包括产学研支出、职工生产环境的改善支出、企业按期偿还债务的利息支出以及为社区服务的支出等，以此进一步提升上市公司价值。

主要参考文献

[1] Moskowitz, M., Choosing Socially Responsible Stocks, Business and Society Review, 1972 (1), pp. 29-42.

[2] Bowman, E. and Haire, M., A Strategic Posture Towards CSR, California Management Review, 1975, 18(2), pp. 49-58.

[3] Cochran P. and Wood, R., Corporate Social Responsibility and Stock Market Performance, Academy of Management Journal, 1984(27), pp. 42-56.

[4] Vance S. C., Are Society Responsible Corporations Good Investment Risks? Management Review, 1975(8), pp. 19-24.

[5] Holman, Walter R., New, J. R. andol, and Singer Daniel, The Impact of Corporate Social Responsiveness on Shareholder Wealth, Research in Corporate Social Performance and Policy, 1985 (7).

[6] McWilliams A., Siegel D., Corporate Social Responsibility: A Theory of the Firm Perspective, The Academy of Management Review, 2001(1).

[7] 陈玉清、马丽丽:《我国上市公司社会责任会计信息市场反映实证分析》,载《会计研究》,2005(11),6~81页。

[8] 李正:《企业社会责任与企业价值相关性研究——来自沪市上市公司的经验证据》,载《中国工业经济》,2006(2),77~83页。

[9] 姚海鑫、陆智强、李红玉:《企业社会责任对股东财富影响的实证研究》,载《东北大学学报(社会科学版)》,2007,9(4),315~320页。

[10] 温素彬、方苑:《企业社会责任与财务绩效关系的实证研究》,载《中国工业经济》,2008(10),150~159页。

[11] 王建琼、何静谊:《公司治理、企业经济绩效与企业社会责任》,载《经济经纬》,2009(2),83~86页。

[12] 陈煦江:《企业社会责任对企业价值的影响——基于沪深股市的面板证据》,载《科学·经济·社会》,2009,27(2),81~86页。

[13] 朱雅琴、姚海鑫:《企业社会责任与企业价值关系的实证研究》,载《财经问题研究》,2010(2),102~106页。

[14] Bryan W. Husted, Risk Management, Real Options, and Corporate Social Responsibility, Journal of Business Ethics, 2005, 8(2), pp. 175-183.

[15] Sadok El Ghoul, Omrane Guedhami, Chuck C. Y. Kwok, Dev R. Mishra Does Corporate

Social Responsibility Affect the Cost of Capital Journal of Banking and Finance, 2011(2), pp. 1-19.

[16] Stephen Brammer and Andrew Millington, Corporate Reputation and Philanthropy: An Empirical Analysis, Journal of Business Ethics, 2005(1), pp. 29-44.

[17] Allen Goss, Gordon S. Roberts, The Impact of Corporate Social Responsibility on the Cost of Bank Loans, Journal of Banking and Finance, 2010(5), pp. 1-17.

[18] 万寿义、刘正阳:《从产权视角看我国上市公司现金股利分配》,载《兰州学刊》,2010(7),68～71页。

[19] 杨丹、魏韫新、叶建明:《股份分置改革对中国资本市场实证研究的影响及模型修正》,载《经济研究》,2008(8),73～86页。

[20] 万寿义、刘正阳:《大股东收益对公司价值影响的研究——基于上市公司2005至2008年的经验数据》,载《财政监督》,2010(1),15～19页。

[21] 沈洪涛:《顺势应时 建设和谐企业——解读深圳证券交易所〈上市公司社会责任指引〉》,载《财务与会计》,2006(12),14～16页。

[22] 刘长翠、孔晓婷:《社会责任会计信息披露的实证研究》,载《会计研究》,2006(10),36～43页。

[23] 万寿义、张佳伟:《企业社会责任会计信息披露问题研究》,载《现代管理科学》,2010(6),20～22页。

[24] 林万祥:《成本论》,北京,中国财政经济出版社,2001。

我国政府会计研究的回顾与评价

张琦[1]　王森林[1]　张娟[2]

（1. 中南财经政法大学政府会计研究所　湖北武汉　430073；
2. 财政部会计司　北京　100820）

摘　要　20世纪80年代以来，国外政府会计进行了一系列的改革。国外的学者为政府会计改革的有序推进，进行了大量卓有成效的研究。目前，我国政府会计研究已取得了较丰富的成果，但仍未形成完善的理论体系和实践模式。因此，有必要对我国近年来的政府会计理论研究情况和成果进行回顾与评价，为未来政府会计的研究提出值得关注的重点和方向。

关键词　政府会计　研究　回顾　评价

20世纪80年代以来，新西兰、澳大利亚、美国、英国和西班牙等国一系列的政府会计改革引起了全球会计界的广泛关注。为了改革的有序进行，国外学者对政府会计的理论问题进行了深入的研究。国外的改革经验和研究成果都为我国政府会计的研究创造了良好的契机。在财政部和中国会计学会的大力推动下，我国政府会计研究也取得了一系列的成果。本文拟以回顾和评价近年来我国政府会计研究成果为基础，对我国政府会计研究的现状和未来提出一些基本想法。

一、1994年至2009年各会计期刊发表政府会计论文情况分析

本文选择了1994年至2009年我国公开发行的会计期刊上发表的政府会计方面论文为研究对象，得出了以下分析结果①。

（一）各种期刊刊登文章的数量结构分析

17种会计类核心期刊发表政府会计类研究论文的数量结构见表1②：

① 本文所收集的442篇文章主要是通过中国全文期刊网检索而来的，由于中国全文期刊网的起点时间是1994年，而且经过对《会计研究》、《财会通讯》、《财会月刊》等期刊1994年以前的载文情况进行检索，基本上没有发现有关政府会计方面的文章，所以本文选择1994年为研究起点。在检索论文时，本文采用了篇名、摘要或关键词的联合检索，输入的关键词分别是政府会计和预算会计。

② 这17种会计类核心期刊分别是《会计研究》、《四川会计》、《上海会计》、《广西会计》、《财会通讯》、《财会月刊》、《财务与会计》、《财会研究》、《财经理论与实践》、《当代财经》、《审计理论与实践》、《审计研究》、《审计与经济研究》、《中国农业会计》、《中国审计》、《财贸经济》及《山西财经大学学报》。此处的顺序是按照北京大学图书馆主编的《中文核心期刊要目总览》（3版，18页，北京大学出版社，2000）排列的。

表 1　各种期刊刊登政府会计相关文章的数量结构分析表

期刊名称	《会计研究》	《上海会计》①	《财会研究》	《财务与会计》	《中国农业会计》	《广西会计》	《财会通讯》	
数量	43	16	22	27	13	6	51	
比重(%)	16.6	6.18	8.49	10.42	5.02	2.32	19.69	—
期刊名称	《四川会计》	《当代财经》	《财会月刊》	《审计与经济研究》	《财贸研究》	《财经理论与实践》	《山西财经大学学报》	合计
数量	4	5	61	4	3	3	1	259
比重(%)	1.54	1.93	23.55	1.54	1.16	1.16	0.40	100.00

从表 1 中我们可以看出，自 1994 年至 2009 年我国核心期刊上发表的政府会计方面的论文总体篇数不多，为 259 篇。17 种会计类核心期刊十几年刊发政府会计方面的文章占前 4 位的分别是《财会月刊》、《财会通讯》、《会计研究》、《财务与会计》，占文章总数的 70% 以上，而其他核心刊物发表的政府会计方面论文较少（其中，《审计研究》和《中国审计》2 个刊物发表的政府会计方面论文为 0，故未在表 1 中列示）。这说明我国的政府会计研究起步较晚，学术领域的研究氛围不够浓厚，导致我国政府会计研究相对发展缓慢。

（二）各种期刊刊登文章的年限分布情况分析

会计类期刊在不同年份内发表政府会计类研究论文的数量结构见表 2：

表 2　各种期刊刊登政府会计相关文章的年限分布情况分析表

年限		1994 至 1999 年	2000 年	2001 年	2002 年	2003 年	2004 年	2005 年	2006 年	2007 年	2008 年	2009 年	合计
数量	核心	40	6	9	19	21	25	23	27	25	28	36	259
	非核心	272	34	27	43	68	71	83	120	164	175	181	1 238
	小计	312	40	36	62	89	96	106	147	189	203	217	1 497
比重（%）		20.84	2.67	2.40	4.14	5.95	6.41	7.08	9.82	12.63	13.56	14.50	100.00

从表 2 中反映的统计结果，可以看出，自 1994 年以来有关政府会计的论文数量总体上呈增长趋势，但是在 2000 年前后有关政府会计的论文数量呈下降趋势，本文认为主要原因在于此段时间我国致力于企业会计制度的建设，国家政策导向企业会计研究，学者也更多的关注企业会计的相关研究。从 2002 年有关政府会计的论文数量开始上升，并从 2006 年开始大幅度增长。本文认为主要有以下几个原因：一是 2006 年我国颁布《企业会计准则》实现企业会计的国际趋同，标志着我国企业会计规范体系走向成熟，而政府会计的研究相

① 《上海会计》自 2004 年起转为内部刊物，现《上海会计》编辑部的全部资源已转到《新会计》，并经国家新闻出版总署批准于 2009 年正式公开发行。

对滞后，不能满足建立绩效政府、服务政府与透明政府的需要①，因此在政府政策引导下，学术界也更加关注政府会计研究。二是国外政府会计理论体系的建立并逐渐成熟，以及政府会计改革的不断推进，为我国政府会计的研究提供了有利的契机。三是财政部、中国会计学会将我国政府会计研究和政府会计改革提上议事日程。2004 年与 2008 年中国会计学会先后推出了两批政府会计研究课题。2009 年 8 月，财政部会计司在中南财经政法大学召开了“政府会计改革研讨会”，并同时推出了《医院会计制度》（征求意见稿）与《高等学校会计制度》（征求意见稿），正式拉开了我国政府会计改革的序幕。财政部部长谢旭人在 2010 年全国财政工作会议上也直接提出推进政府会计改革是当前财政工作的重点。理论界与实务界的上述举措有力地推进了我国近年来的政府会计理论研究。

二、近年来我国政府会计研究的理论成果

从现有文献分析，近年来，我国政府会计的研究成果主要体现在以下十个方面：

（一）我国现有预算会计体系的缺陷

无论是学术研究还是实践改革都是为了让现有的不完美尽可能的完美化，当然政府会计改革及政府会计理论研究也不例外，都是因为现有的政府会计制度和理论体系存在缺陷，并且已经不能满足现实需要。因此，我们有必要首先研究现存的问题，在此基础上开展进一步的后续研究。

我国现行预算会计体系是以修正的收付实现制为基础，记录和反映政府预算收支状况及合规性，以适应国家宏观经济管理和上级财政部门及本级政府部门对财政管理的需要，包括财政总预算会计、行政单位会计、事业单位会计、国家预算和各级总预算执行的国库会计、基建拨贷款会计和收入征解会计、预算外资金会计等。无疑现有预算会计体系在提供宏观经济管理和政府财政管理信息方面发挥着重要作用，但是也存在着严重的缺陷：

张兴国（2008）认为现有预算会计体系存在四大缺陷：一是预算会计体系不协调，表现为财政总预算会计与行政事业单位会计不协调，财政总预算会计与新的资金管理会计制度不协调，制度缺乏灵活性和适应性。二是预算会计核算基础存在弊端，导致同一会计期间政府权力和责任不相匹配，无法准确反映政府负债状况，不能客观公正地反映政府在各个会计期间提供公共产品和服务的实际耗费与效率水平，不利于对政府活动的效率效果进行评价和监督，也不利于政府内部的效率改进。三是预算会计核算内容不全面，存货没有作为资

① 详见新华社 2007 年 10 月报道的《胡锦涛在党的十七大的报告》。

产确认，对固定资产核算和反映不全面，对政府债权、股权核算和反映不完整。四是预算会计信息披露与形势发展不适应，披露的范围过于狭窄，内容过于简单，信息不公允[1]。张琦、程晓佳（2008）认为，现有预算会计体系的局限性有：一是现有会计系统不同于西方国家的政府会计，无法全面反映政府整体的财务状况与运营情况。二是现有会计系统也非真正意义上的预算会计，难以完全发挥预算管理的作用。三是现有会计系统按照组织机构分别设置会计制度，缺乏完整统一的体系，所披露的信息具有片段性[2]。

（二）政府会计的界定及特点

1. 政府会计的界定

何嘉萍（2002）、张霞（2003）、李强等（2005）认为我国政府（预算）会计①，是指各级政府、使用预算拨款的各级行政单位、各类事业单位核算和监督各项财政性资金运动、单位预算资金运动的过程与结果以及有关经营收支情况的专业会计[3][4][5]。哈尔滨、景宏军、王蕴波（2008）将预算会计定义为：用于确认、计量、记录预算批准和预算执行整个过程中所发生的经济活动或事项，报告预算拨款和拨款使用情况的信息系统；将政府会计定义为：反映、核算和监督政府单位及其构成实体在使用财政资金和公共资源过程中财务收支活动的会计管理系统。认为政府会计反映的是政府管理国家公共事务、运用公共资源及受托责任履行的情况，它从功能上可以划分为四个部分：政府财务会计、政府管理会计、政府成本会计和政府预算会计[6]。陈劲松等（2008）提出政府预算会计应当反映立法机构批准的预算及政府执行该预算的情况及结果，通过设立一套自我平衡的预算账户体系，运用会计的程序和方法，对预算及预算收支执行情况进行确认、计量和记录，以加强预算的会计控制，并通过预算与实际执行情况的比较分析，定期向政府行政长官、立法机构及其他相关部门报告预算执行情况的会计信息，借以评价和考核政府执行预算收支的财务责任[7]。

2. 政府会计的特点

杨绮（2000）、张国康等（2003）通过比较美国政府会计，认为我国政府会计具有以下特点：在适用范围方面，我国预算会计不适用于国有企业，但财政总预算将事业单位纳入预算范畴[8][9]；李定清、刘东（2003）认为在政府会计体系方面，我国中央政府和各级地方政府会计是一个有机整体，它们共同组成政府会计体系；在政府会计模式方面，我国政府会计是预算会计模式[10]。宋衍蘅、陈晓（2002）指出不同政府会计模式之间差异产生的原因：法律体系不同；议会与政府之间的关系不同；联邦（中央）政府与地方政府的关系不同[11]。

在我国非企业会计体系的构建方面，很多学者做了探讨。阎达五、赵西卜

---

① 由于我国理论界尚未对政府会计的含义给出明确的表述，因此一般学者对其核算范围进行界定是以预算会计的概念为媒介进行的。

(2003)，赵建勇（2001）等认为非企业会计体系分为政府会计及非盈利组织会计[12][13]；段爱玲（2003）把企业会计体系以外的预算会计体系分为政府会计和事业单位会计[14]；王庆龙（2004）则把非企业会计体系分为非营利组织会计（分为民办非营利组织和公立非营利组织会计，即事业单位会计两种）和政府会计（分为行政单位会计和财政总预算会计，其中财政总预算会计为核心部分）[15]；路军伟、李建发（2006）认为应当以是否掌握和使用公共资源以及是否承担公共受托责任作为判定政府单位的两项重要标准，并据此重新构建我国的政府会计体系[16]。

（三）政府会计概念框架的构建

詹雷、王成（2004）认为政府会计概念框架不同于企业会计概念框架，表现为：政府不存在剩余索取权的股东，缺少界定清晰的所有者权益；政府的产出是公共物品或自然垄断产品；政府经营目标比企业经营目标复杂得多；政府的利益相关者众多；政府资产并非带来未来的经济利益；政府的许多资产不是通过交换性、互利性交易取得；政府职责相对固定；政府服务接受者和政府收入提供者之间不存在对应关系；政府活动缺乏企业所面临的制约力量；政府预算必须公开[17]。

李定清（2002）指出了我国政府会计概念框架的构建环境表现为："统一领导、分级管理"的预算管理；"一级政权、一级事权、一级预算"的国家政权结构；政府公共财政框架逐步建立；国库单一账户制度的逐步实施；政府采购制度的逐步推广等方面[18]。裴荣、郝东洋（2004）进一步指出了构建政府会计准则概念框架的重要性：有助于具体规范间的相互协调；增强准则的可理解性；有助于政府会计准则发展和演化的连续性[19]。贝洪俊（2005）提出政府会计概念框架的内容包括：政府会计目标、政府会计假设、政府会计信息质量特征、政府会计要素、政府会计确认基础、政府会计准则制定模式，并且将我国政府会计概念框架分为了三个层次：会计基本假设、会计对象和会计目标；会计要素、会计信息质量特征；会计要素的确认、计量、记录与报告[20]。陈志斌（2009）在剖析、类聚相关改革模型的基础上，依据权变理论，提炼、总结和构建了一个包括了触发器、结构变量、实施、实践与反馈等四个子模块的政府会计概念框架整体分析模型[21]。王雍君、梁丽等（2007）认为将现行依托"组织类别"转向依托"支出周期"概念构造新型的政府会计框架[22][23]。

（四）政府会计目标

1. 政府会计目标的特点及界定

王湛（2003）通过比较政府会计和企业会计，指出政府受托责任源于民主社会制度的建立[24]。因此，于国旺（2004）提出政府会计目标的特殊性在于，它以公共受托责任为基础[25]。陈立齐、李建发（2003）认为，政府会计的目标有三个层次：基本目标是检查、防范舞弊和贪污，保护公共财政资金的安全；中级目标是促进健全的财务管理；最高层次的目标是帮助政府履行公共受托责任[26]。而贝洪俊（2004）将政府会计目标分为全面目标、基本目标和具体目标。全面目标是指帮助政府履行受托责任；基本目标是促进政府单位建立健全财务管理机制；具体目标是保证公共财政资源用于限定用途[27]。陈小悦、陈璇（2005）指出政府会计目标在于实现政府履行职责的高经济透明度[28]。陈劲松、彭珏、石道金（2008）认为政府会计的最终目标是解除政府公共受托责任，但是应该根据政府会计改革基础选择分为三个阶段：修正的收付实现制、修正的权责发生制、应计制三个阶段逐步提高公共受托责任的解除水平[29]。张琦、程晓佳（2008）认为我国现阶段政府会计改革的目标应兼顾两个方面：一是财务管理目标。该目标下政府会计信息主要体现为各种财务信息，包括政府公共资金的使用效率（主要是全面成本核算系统的建立）、对政府资产的管理水平（包括存量信息、流量信息与耗费信息）、政府承担债务的规模与结构以及偿还能力等；二是预算管理目标。政府预算是一种强制性的法定预算，它强调立法机构对政府资金使用的控制[2]。

2. 我国政府会计目标的特殊性及内容

赵建勇（1998）我国政府会计目标的特点表现为：第一，我国是人民民主专政的社会主义国家，人民群众需要充分了解和分析评价政府及其成员的责任履行情况；第二，我国是公有制经济为基础的社会主义国家，政府代表国家行使国有资产的所有权，有义务提供国有资产保值和增值情况的报告；第三，我国绝大部分非营利组织都是国有的，它们提供服务的数量和质量也构成政府的受托责任[30]。因此，陈志斌（2003）、北京市预算会计研究会《政府会计课题组》（2006）等认为，我国政府会计目标应该包括以下几个方面的内容：符合预算法的要求，提供与预算相关的信息；反映国家资源的总存量、流量以及变化情况，反映国有资产的总量以及受托保管和经营中的保值增值财务信息，反映国家财政和财务状况的会计信息；界定政府的受托责任，提供政府及公共部门的业绩信息；提供帮助政府机构内部管理与控制，以及立法机构或审计部门监督和检查政府及其机构的有关信息[31][32]。

（五）政府会计基础

1. 两种会计基础的比较与选择

大多数学者认为，在政府会计基础的选择上，权责发生制要优于收付实现制。

张继珍、刘宁（2003），李从菊（2002），杨朝晖（2004），刘炳江（2009）等认为收付实现制作为政府会计传统模式的原因是，政府只需要对公共资源的使用负责，而不需对资源的使用结果负责。收付实现制对于确保合规性是有优势的，但政府会计采用收付实现制基础存在以下问题：（1）收付实现制基础上编制的财务报表反映的受托责任较窄，不利于绩效管理和考核，易为管理当局操纵；（2）财政支出只包括以现金实际支付的部分，不反映那些当期已发生，但尚未用现金支付的部分；（3）预算已经安排，但由于各种原因，当年无法支出而作为年终节余处理，从而使年终节余“虚增”；（4）收付实现制无法反映某些政府承诺和长期决策的全部成本，无法反映固定资产净值情况[1][33][34][35][36]。

现代预算管理强调的绩效导向是权责发生制改革的原因，其优势表现为：（1）刘炳江（2009），王先元（2002），陈继初（2003），邢俊英（2006）认为，权责发生制能真实反映政府资产耗费和负债的积累情况，促进政府转变职能，节约政府行政成本，有利于提高政府行政的透明度，也是对政府负债风险控制目标的必然选择[36][37][38][39]；（2）张丽秀（2003）认为，权责发生制具有能提供成本信息，有利于与私立单位进行信息比较等优势，有助于改进公共服务的质量和效率，增强政府竞争力[40]；（3）陈胜群、陈工孟、高宁（2002），孔龙、徐在起（2009）认为，权责发生制可以提供衡量财政长期支持能力方面的信息，优化政府的长期决策；可以使得管理者更重视政府机构的效率、效果等绩效问题；更加适应新公共管理环境下拓展公众受托责任的要求[41][42]。

然而，刘炳江（2009），张茅（2003），弥跃旭（2003）认为，权责发生制也存在一些固有的缺陷：权责发生制会计的实施成本较高；在实务中存在估计的主观性问题；会计信息的客观性和可比性受到影响；现金流量方面信息不足；会计信息的透明度可能因权责发生制较为复杂的原则和假设而受到影响[36][43][44]。

2. 我国政府会计的选择

陈继初（2003）指出了权责发生制引入的可能性：社会主义市场经济体制的完善和发展；西方国家政府会计改革提供了有益的借鉴；经济国际化推动了政府会计的国际化；研究政府会计改革的学者越来越多[38]，但学者们对政府会计引入权责发生制的程度有不同看法。陈立齐、李建发（2003），郝东洋（2005）指出，权责发生制可以分为低度、中度、强度和完全四个层次。权责发生制强度越高，风险就越大，需要解决的计量问题就越多，结果将会更加主观。我国政府会计权责发生制改革应采取一种循序渐进式和对称的方法[26][46]。王丹芳（2002），刘淑蓉（2002）等在比较权责发生制和收付实现制的基础上指出，修正的权责发生制更适合我国政府会计的现状[45][47]。但周立宁（2000）认为，我国政府会计改革应根据经济业务的不同性质，采用不同的确认标准，并提出修正的收付实现制的思想[48]。徐镇绥（2006）提出，我国政府会计现阶段不宜采用权责发生制会计基础，因为如果会计与预算使用不同的会计基础，会使管理不当和财政失灵现象更为严重；经济转轨的特点也决定了我国政府会计基础暂不适宜采用权责发生制，我国预算体系和政府会计目前的重点仍是保证财政资金的“合规性”。同时，在现行的预算管理模式和政府会计核算体系下，权责发生制的长处难以得到有效发挥，因此在会计基础选择上，政府会计仍应实行以收付实现制为基础、以权责发生制为适度补充的“修正的收付实现制”[49]。

（六）政府会计要素

王彦、王建英、赵西卜（2009）认为，从对会计要素的认定以及划分的惯例看，报表上的项目类别是否能被称为会计要素，取决于它们是否在日常账户中按照一定的会计基础进行记录，只有按照一定会计基础进行确认和计量的项目才会被视为会计要素，否则不被视为会计要素[50]。

贝洪俊（2004）认为，在资产要素方面，绝大部分国有资产不是通过交易取得的，所以历史成本没有意义，而市场价格虽然可验证，但又很难获得[27]。詹雷、王成（2004）指出，政府会计中资产的特点是强调能带来未来的服务潜能[17]。刘曼（2004）在比较中美资产要素界定后指出，我国政府会计的资产被定义为经济资源，而美国政府基金表述为财务资源[51]。杨绮（2000）认为这是因为，我国政府会计定义的资产范围较广，包括流动资产、固定资产、无形资产等，而美国只将需要用以偿还流动负债的政府基金资产（只有流动资产）表述为财务资源[52]。因此程晓佳（2004）建议，将资产分为金融资产和非金融资产，对于金融资产，应报告全部金融资产和比较信息，披露金融资产的计量方法及对金融资产的限制等[53]，并且张琦（2006）提出，在引入应计制和绩效评价的要求下政府资产的确认主要应关注非金融资产的适当确认与披露问题[54]。

在负债要素方面，政府会计中的负债不易于在中央政府契约或法定义务与其政治承诺和对大众福利的社会责任之间划清界限。关于负债的分类，程晓佳（2004）指出负债可以分为公共债务和其他负债[53]。而詹雷、王成（2004）则认为，政府负债应包括直接显性负债、间接负债和隐性负债。由于我国行政单位是独立核算的会计和报告主体，因此存在政府内部的负债。政府财务报告应报告全部负债、债务规模及比较信息、披露负债计量方法、未确认的或有负债以及债务拖欠本利等[17]。

李定清、刘东（2003）认为在资产与负债的差额表述方面，我国政府会计要素包括净资产要素。而美国的政务基金用基金余额表述资产与负债的差额，权益基金则用基金权益表示，而信贷基金中仅包括资产和负债[55]。詹雷、王成（2004），赵建勇（2004），刘淑蓉（2002）指出，政府会计净资产含义不明确，只是一个资产减去负债的节余项、调整项[17][56][45]。

在收入与支出方面①，政府提供公共物品，没有人愿意为之付费，所以只能通过税收来筹集资金，这个特征切断了履行服务与收入确认之间的联系，使

① 美国权益基金使用“费用”要素，而不使用“支出”要素（赵建勇，2004）。

得收入很难与支出配比。程晓佳（2004）对收入和支出进行了分类。收入可以分为交换性交易收入和非交换性交易收入。而支出可以分为承担以非市场基础向社会提供部分商品和服务责任而发生的支出，以及通过转移支付对收入和财富进行再分配而发生的支出。周立宁（2000）认为，我国将支出定义为财政资金的再分配，而美国将其定义为，财务资金的减少或者使用[48]。赵建勇（2004）指出，政府会计中通常将“收入和其他财务资源的流入”以及“支出和其他财务资源的流出”合并在一起考虑[56]。

（七）政府会计假设

我国政府会计制度未明确会计信息产生和会计报表编制所基于的会计假设。

张志宁（2004）阐述了关于会计主体假设，认为政府或政府单位是对外承担受托责任的“组织主体”，各类基金是限定资源用途的“基金主体”[57]。何嘉萍（2002）认为，我国总预算会计的会计主体是各级政府而非财政机关，行政单位会计主体是行政单位，事业单位会计主体是事业单位[58]。而詹雷、王成（2004）则认为，我国的会计报告主体是各级财政部门或单位，而确定会计主体的标准是预算单位[17]。通过比较美国政府会计，张连江等（2003），郝东洋（2005）认为，记账主体与财务报告主体概念的适当分离[59]。贝洪俊（2005）指出，政府会计应该是三重主体并存：基金报告主体、政府部门或单位报告主体、政府报告主体[20]。张连江、吕炜（2003）建议，我国政府会计核算主体也以基金为单位划分。在报告主体方面，我国政府可以分为三个层次：第一层次为基本政府，即各级政府；第二层次为政府的组成单位或直属单位，如现行预算会计体系中的行政事业单位；第三层次为政府的相关单位，包括国有独资企业、政府参股企业、政府公用事业单位[59]。叶龙、冯兆大（2006）根据公共财政理论与代理理论提出我国政府会计的政府主体和基金主体的“双主体”模式[60]。张国兴（2008）认为，对于我国政府会计主体的确立，借鉴国际上的经验，提出两点设想：一是引进“基金会计”概念。这一概念中的基金与我国预算会计中的基金不同，它是指具有特定目的和用途的资金。二是实行“双主体”：报告主体和记账主体[1]。张琦、程晓佳（2008）认为，我国的政府财务会计主体的确定需要考虑两个原则：一是该主体是否承担政府职能；二是该主体是否占用公共资源。按照上述原则，我国政府财务会计主体除包括政府行政单位外，还包括履行部分政府职能并使用财政资金的事业单位[2]。王娟、朱海英（2008）认为，除国有企业外，应当以“掌握和使用公共资源以及承担公共受托责任”作为判定“政府单位”的两项重要标准，来确认政府会计主体[61]。

关于持续经营假设，张志宁（2004）认为，该假设在政府会计理论中应做出适当的修正，即政府的公共活动具有连续性，而基金财务收支活动则具有暂时性[57]。赵建勇（2001）则认为，持续经营通常只与政府会计中的权益基金相关。关于会计分期假设，赵建勇指出对于政务基金而言，该假设是在一个预算期间内财务资源的实际流动及其预算比较相关的概念，而不是一个与利润的确定相关的概念[13]。关于货币计量假设，学者们大多没有涉及，张志宁（2004）认为，货币计量假设在政府组织具有适用性[57]。

（八）政府财务报告与政府会计信息披露

1. 我国政府财务报告与信息披露的现状与特点

李建发、肖华（2004）认为，政府财务报告应该是一种通用的、全面而系统地反映政府财务状况和运行情况的规范化的信息披露方式[63]。杨绮（2000）指出，我国现行的政府财务报告体系主要由资产负债表、收入支出表和必要的附表、收支情况说明书等组成。该财务报告体系提供预算数与实际数相比较的信息、财政周转等方面的信息，行政事业单位提供有关财务状况和收支情况等方面的信息。而这些信息的使用者主要包括各级政府和上级财政部门以及预算单位自己[52]。

詹雷、王成（2004）指出，我国政府财务报告体系的特点是：面临竞争性信息来源；需要财务信息与非财务信息的结合[17]。王娟、朱海英（2008）认为，相对于美国政府财务报告体系而言，我国政府财务报告体系存在以下缺陷：一是我国不重视期中财务报告的报送，不利于政府预算资金的营运分析与管理；二是会计报告的种类较少，报表体系不完善；三是报告编制方法单一，我国各级政府之间主要是以汇总方式编制会计报告而不是以合并方式编制；四是我国仅按照财政部门和上级单位下达的有关决算规定编制的会计报表；五是我国现行政府预算会计不能反映政府资金的运用[61]。因此，有些学者将我国政府会计信息披露不充分的原因归纳为：我国实行的是预算会计制度，尚未建立真正的政府会计；我国政府机构庞大，职能范围广泛，相应的财务活动涉及面广；财政职能薄弱；审计监督机制不完善。

2. 我国政府财务报告与信息披露的改进建议

通过比较美国政府财务报告体系，学者们建议从以下几方面改进我国政府财务报告体系和会计信息披露机制：（1）我国政府财务报告可以从政府层面报告到可选择的双重视角报告（个别基金和政府整体报告）。（2）改革和完善政府会计制度，从主要满足政府内部使用者的需要，转向同样重视政府外部使用者的需要，除提供预算收支状况的信息外，还提供政府财务状况和绩效评价方面的信息。（3）明确政府财务报告原则。编制政府财务报告应当遵循全面性、可靠性、相关性、一致性、可比性、可理解性、有用性等原则。（4）巩固财政部门在政府会计信息披露中的权威地位。（5）提高会计基础工作，改进审计监督，确保政府会计信息的真实性。（6）年度财务报告应该经权威鉴证机构审计核定。（7）建立政府财务报告对外公布制度。

李建发、肖华（2004）指出，我国政府财务报告应提供以下信息：政府公共部门的财务状况和财务活动结果、成本费用，以及受托业绩[63]。程晓佳（2004）在研究政府会计改革与财政透明度时指出，政府财务报告的内容至少应当包括：政府财政活动的所有信息；其他公共部门的准财政活动；中央政府的或有负债对财政的影响，以及税收支出的定量信息；披露包括中央政府的全部负债、金融资产、非金融资产的所有信息；政府财政报告的合并信息；政府绩效报告。因此，改革后的政府会计信息披露体系可由政府财务报告、分项财务报告、统一财务报表、附注及非财务信息组成[53]。贝洪俊（2004）进一步建议，政府财务报告除了提供财务报表外，还应提供管理层阐述与分析、要求披露的补充信息等[64]。黄世忠、刘用铨、王平（2004）指出，政府会计信息披露应转换观念，强调适当披露[65]。王庆东、常丽（2007）认为，我国政府财务报告改进应该树立双重导向观，即兼顾外部信息使用者的需求和内部控制以及宏观经济管理的需要[66]。张雪芬（2008）认为，从我国目前各方面对政府财务信息的需求来看，应选择以政府为主体编制政府财务报告。它包括两个报表体系和综合文字说明：一个报表体系是财务报表体系（基于修正的权责发生制），包括资产负债表、财务运行绩效表和现金流量表；另一个报表体系是预算报表体系（基于收付实现制），包括预算收支执行情况报表及一些附表。综合文字说明部分包含宏观经济环境分析、政府财务状况和管理绩效分析、经济发展趋势分析、财务报表以外应予披露的附加信息等内容[67]。

（九）政府会计规范

李定清、刘东（2003）对中美政府会计进行了比较研究，指出：在政府会计规范方面，美国由联邦政府与州和地方政府两套会计规范构成，而我国政府会计规范由国家颁布的《会计法》、《预算法》和财政部制定的《财政总预算会计制度》及《行政单位会计制度》组成。美国政府会计规范是准则型，而我国是制度型；美国的规范制定机构是独立的民间组织，属于“社会公认型”，我国是国家政府机构制定，属于“法规型”；美国规范侧重对外财务报告准则的规范，我国侧重具体业务规范[55]。石金明（1994）提议，将政府会计规范归纳为“两个准则层，三个准则群”，即基本准则（基本准则群）和具体准则（通用业务准则群和特殊业务准则群）[68]。王湛（2003）建议，以政府部门为核心构建、完善政府会计法律体系，包括三个层次。北京市预算会计研究会政府会计课题组（2006）指出，我国政府会计规范体系为：第一层次是《会计法》，第二层次包括《预算法》、《预算会计法》和《政府财务会计法》，第三层次包括预算会计准则或制度、政府财务会计准则或制度，即我国政府会计的规范形式为准则加制度模式[69]。尹艳芙（2008）建议，从“制度规范”模式转向“准则规范”模式[70]。

（十）政府会计改革

1. 国外政府会计改革的经验及教训

李雄飞（2003）指出了 OECD 国家权责发生制预算和政府会计改革的成效是：（1）财政状况得到了控制，财政支出明显减少。（2）以权责发生制为基础的产出及绩效管理，使政府工作效率有了明显提高，公共服务得到改善。（3）在权责发生制基础上提供的政府会计信息，使政府财政收支的透明度得到提高。（4）权责发生制预算和会计能全面、真实反映政府的财务状况，提高了政府防范风险的能力[71]。陈立齐（2004）分析了美国政府会计改革也实现了四个重大变化：从基金报表上升到政府层面报表；从短期状况扩大到长期状况；从收付实现制转移到权责发生制；会计从遵从预算变成评价预算[72]。

但国外政府会计改革过程中仍存在一些亟待解决的问题。黄世忠、刘用铨、王平（2004）指出，美国联邦政府会计改革中存在的十大缺陷，包括联邦政府财务报告的编制以及内容的完整性存在问题，联邦政府财务管理系统存在致命的信息安全缺陷，重大内部控制存在的薄弱环节等[65]。李雄飞（2003）也指出了政府会计改革中的难点：（1）改革过程中，会计层面的问题较易解决，但预算层面较为复杂。（2）最主要和最艰巨的工作是对政府所拥有的资产进行评估，按评估价值登记入账，编制期初资产负债表。（3）对政府雇员养老金、福利及各种补助和因此带来的负债的确认较困难[71]。

非营利组织会计问题研究课题组（2001），财政部会计司考察团（2004），陈璐璐（2007）等通过比较研究美、英、法等国政府会计改革，有以下方面值得我国借鉴：（1）政府会计规范逐渐靠近企业会计规范。（2）政府会计规范的制定和发布具有连续性和完整性，并区别于预算会计规范。（3）政府会计规范可以容纳、借用一些其他规范方面的内容。（4）推行政府会计改革宜循序渐进，稳步推进。（5）政府会计改革应重视政府会计管理信息系统建设。（6）推进政府会计改革需要转变观念，提高素质。（7）政府会计改革应以公共管理、公共财政、政府治理等领域的改革为前提，在试点地区与试点部门进行，在总结经验的前提下再全面推行。（8）由于政府会计的特殊性，政府会计改革不能照搬国外的模式，也不能套用企业会计模式，而应该植根于一国的政治经济环境[73][74][75]。

2. 我国政府会计的现状及改革思路

郑彩凤、赵福山（2003），王雍君、蔡燕青（2003）认为，我国政府会计缺乏一个整合的会计体系，存在的主要问题有：会计核算的确认基础不适应公共财政管理的需要；会计核算的内容无法反映公共财政管理的全貌；现有的会计核算方法不满足政府采购的需要；无力提供绩效方面的信息[76][77]。因此，政府会计改革势在必行。王淑杰（2004）认为，财政赤字压力大，财政绩效难以考核，以及政府会计透明度不高等是国内外政府会计权责发生制改革的原因[78]。金希萍（2007）认为就我国而言，建立公共财政，实行部门预算，建立政府采购，国库集中支付和国库单一账户制度都是财政预算管理体制改革的重大举措，这些直接影响着政府会计与财务报告的内容与方法，要求政府会计制度、核算方法做出相应改革，并且我国市场经济环境已经发生了巨大变化，政府职能的转换、公共财政体制的改革、政府收支分类科目的变化，政府绩效评价制度的建设以及政府监督的加强等，对反映政府经济活动的政府会计信息提出了更高要求，从而需要积极推进政府会计改革[79]。

在我国政府会计改革目的方面，陈志斌（2003），贝洪俊（2004）等指出，新型的政府会计体系应突出受托责任和绩效管理[80]。在我国政府会计改革的总体部署方面，大多数学者认为，我国处于市场经济不断完善和深化的转轨时期，政府会计核算基础改革不可能一蹴而就，只能根据财政管理体制改革不断推进的程度，分项目渐进实行权责发生制，逐步扩展以适应财政管理体制的要求。政府会计核算涉及政治、经济，在改革过程中要权衡成本收益。李雄飞（2003）进一步指出，我国政府会计的改革应采取“先会计后预算”逐步深入，“由局部到整体”逐步扩大的战略[71]。宋衍蘅、陈晓（2002）指出，在我国政府会计改革的具体措施方面，几乎所有学者都指出，政府会计应引入权责发生制核算基础，完善政府会计信息体系，增加政府会计信息的透明度[81]。同时，刘玉廷（2004）提出，建立起一套完整的政府会计标准和政府财务报告制度也是当务之急[82]。张琦（2007）建议，在我国政府会计改革的学术支持方面，应加强政府会计的研究：把握研究重点，特别是自然资源的确认、计量和报告等难点问题；重新定义政府会计要素，引入成本概念，正确看待成本改革问题；改革报告主体等[83]。

三、我国政府会计研究现状的评价

根据前述的简要回顾与分析，可以看出，近十年来我国政府会计研究状况上呈现出以下五方面的基本特点：

（一）政府会计基本理论研究已初具规模

我国政府会计改革和政府会计准则建设，应当理论先行。学者们广泛研究了政府会计目标、政府会计要素、政府会计确认基础和政府会计假设等政府会计理论框架构建中的重要问题，以及这些问题在我国的特殊性和适用性，取得较大的成果，为我国政府会计改革奠定良好的基础。

（二）积极借鉴国外经验和企业会计研究成果

绝大部分学者在进行政府会计研究时采用了比较研究方法，包括政府会计的中外比较、政府会计与企业会计比较等。通过与企业的比较研究，学者们归纳出政府会计与企业会计的异同点，如政府会计目标的公共受托责任特征等；通过与国外政府会计的比较研究，学者们探讨了政府会计理论在我国特殊社会经济环境中的适用性，为我国政府会计理论框架的建立奠定基础，也为我国政府会计改革提供了可鉴之处。

（三）研究成果尚缺乏实践指导性

从目前的研究内容上看，一部分学者较为关注政府会计的基本理论问题，如政府会计的目标、要素、基本假设等，而另一部分学者主要介绍国外政府会计的改革经验，但具体如何在我国政府会计实践中运用和借鉴这些理论和国外改革经验，大多学者并未作深入的研究。例如，绝大部分学者都赞成我国政府会计在现阶段应向修正的权责发生制基础过渡，但究竟如何过渡，哪些项目应首先过渡，权责发生制在政府财务报告中运用的程度，我国的政府会计信息使用者有哪些，他们的信息需求对我国政府会计目标的定位和权责发生制改革有哪些影响等具体问题都未涉及。大部分文章还停留在对权责发生制和收付实现制的理论比较上，未将理论研究与我国财政和预算改革的实践以及信息使用者的实际需求联系起来。

（四）研究内容缺乏系统性

目前我国政府会计的研究内容涉及面广，但缺乏对单个问题的深入和系统研究。从文章的标题来看，大量的文章是以“政府会计诸项比较”、“中美政府会计理论框架比较”等涵盖面较广的标题命名来进行研究的。针对某一特定问题，如我国政府会计目标的定位、政府会计确认基础研究等专项系统的研究成果较少。大部分学者的研究仅停留在一两篇文章上，缺乏对政府会计长期深入的研究。另外，现有文章的研究方法过于单一，多是描述性和分析性研究，实证研究的成果较少，在本文选取的442个样本中仅2篇，不到全部文章总数的1%[84][85]。

（五）研究力量仍相对薄弱

在财政部和中国会计学会的促进和支持下，越来越多的学者们加入政府会计理论的研究行列，但我国政府会计的研究力量相对企业会计而言仍相对薄弱，10余年来在核心期刊上发表的政府会计文章仅200多篇，这与我国企业会计蓬勃发展并取得丰硕成果的现状相比是极不对称的。因此，长期致力于政府会计研究的学者人数还有待提高。

主要参考文献

[1] 张国兴:《关于构建我国政府会计体系问题的研究》,载《会计研究》,2008(3),11～

18页。

[2] 张琦、程晓佳:《政府财务会计与预算会计的适度分离与协调:一种适合我国的改革路径》,载《会计研究》,2008(11),35~41页。

[3] 李强、王智宁、叶新凤:《政府会计的中美差异比较》,载《财会通讯(学术版)》,2005(3),60~62页。

[4] 张霞:《中美政府会计比较及其启示》,载《财会通讯》,2003(8),29~30页。

[5] 何嘉萍:《中美政府会计比较》,载《上海会计》,2002(8),3~5页。

[6] 景宏军、王蕴波:《论我国预算会计的定位》,载《财会月刊》,2008(2),6~8页。

[7] 陈劲松、彭珏、石道金:《我国政府会计组成体系构建》,载《财会通讯》,2008(4),6~8页。

[8] 杨绮:《中美政府会计诸项比较》,载《会计之友》,2000(11),20~21页。

[9] 张国康、程晓苏:《中美政府会计比较》,载《重庆工商大学学报》,2003(6),4~6页。

[10] 李定清、刘东:《中美政府会计比较研究》,载《经济师》,2003(8),199~200页。

[11] 宋衍蘅、陈晓:《西方国家政府会计的比较及其借鉴》,载《会计研究》,2002(9),58~62页。

[12] 阎达五、赵西卜:《关于我国企业会计准则和事业单位会计准则合一问题的思考》,载《当代财经》,2003(3),85~88页。

[13] 赵建勇:《试论中国预算会计体系》,载《财经研究》,2001(6),60~64页。

[14] 段爱玲:《重塑我国预算会计体系的思考》,载《事业财会》,2003(4),2~3页。

[15] 王庆龙:《论我国非企业会计组成体系的构建》,载《会计研究》,2004(4),3~9页。

[16] 路军伟、李建发:《政府会计改革的公共受托责任视角解析》,载《会计研究》,2006(12),14~19页。

[17] 詹雷、王成:《政府特征与政府会计概念框架》,载《中南财经政法大学学报》,2004(6),98~102页。

[18] 李定清:《论政府会计准则理论结构》,载《商业研究》,2002(12),13~14页。

[19] 裴荣、郝东洋:《论我国政府会计准则概念框架的构建》,载《财会月刊》,2004(9),9~10页。

[20] 贝洪俊:《关于建立我国政府会计概念框架的设想》,载《财会通讯(学术版)》,2005(2),22~25页。

[21] 陈志斌:《政府会计概念框架整体分析模型》,载《会计研究》,2009(2),19~27页。

[22] 王雍君:《支出周期:构造政府预算会计框架的逻辑起点》,载《会计研究》,2007(5),3~9页。

[23] 梁丽、敖德萨:《我国政府会计改革的思考》,载《财会通讯》,2007(2),70~72页。

[24] 王湛:《政府会计改革应借鉴企业会计发展的经验》,载《内蒙古财经学院学报》,2003(3),108~111页。

[25] 于国旺:《试论公共受托责任与政府会计目标》,载《事业财会》,2004(5),7~8页。

[26] 陈立齐、李建发:《国际政府会计准则及其发展评述》,载《会计研究》,2003(9),49~52页。

[27] 贝洪俊:《政府会计目标层次构建》,载《财会月刊》,2004(7),15~16页。

[28] 陈小悦、陈璇:《政府会计目标及其相关问题的理论探讨》,载《会计研究》,2005(11),61~65页。

[29] 陈劲松、石道金、彭珏:《论我国政府财务会计目标的定位》,载《财会月刊》,2008(10),3~4页。

[30] 赵建勇:《政府会计目标的国际比较》,载《财经研究》,1998(2),53~61页。

[31] 陈志斌:《公共受托责任:政治效应、经济效率与有效的政府会计》,载《会计研究》,2003(6),36~39页。

[32] 北京市预算会计研究会《政府会计课题组》:《关于建立中国政府会计准则的研究报告》,载《会计研究》,2006(3),34~44页。

[33] 张继珍、刘宁:《政府会计改革:从现金制到应计制》,载《内蒙古财经学院学报》,2003(2),89~91页。

[34] 李从菊:《浅谈政府会计核算基础改革》,载《财会研究》,2002(8),40~41页。

[35] 杨朝晖:《改进政府会计与预算的研究》,载《福建农林大学学报》,2004(7),62~65页。

[36] 刘炳江:《关于政府会计权责发生制改革的若干思考》,载《财会月刊》,2009(2),10~11页。

[37] 王先元:《关于政府会计向权责发生制转换的思考》,载《时代财会》,2002(3),59~60页。

[38] 陈继初:《论政府会计引入权责发生制的必要性和可能性》,载《事业财会》,2003(3),77~79页。

[39] 邢俊英:《政府负债风险控制:影响政府会计改革的重要因素》,载《会计研究》,2006(9),64~68页。

[40] 张丽秀:《初探政府会计方法之选择》,载《山西财税》,2003(7),14~15页。

[41] 陈胜群、陈工孟、高宁:《政府会计基础比较研究——传统的收付实现制与崛起的权责发生制孰优孰劣》,载《会计研究》,2002(5),34~39页。

[42] 孔龙、徐在起:《我国政府会计引入权责发生制会计基础的思考》,载《财会研究》,2009(6),31~33页。

[43] 张茅:《浅议政府会计基础的改革方向:权责发生制》,载《上海会计》,2003(4),50~51页。

[44] 弥跃旭:《我国政府会计引入权责发生制的思考》,载《甘肃科技纵横》,2003(4),20~21页。

[45] 刘淑蓉:《中美政府会计要素比较》,载《北方经贸》,2002(10),94~95页。

[46] 郝东洋:《谈我国政府会计概念结构中的几个理论问题》,载《商丘师范学院学报》,2005(2),90~91页。

[47] 王丹芳:《权责发生制在政府会计中的运用研究》,载《广西财政高等专科学校学报》,2002(6),30~32页。

[48] 周立宁:《谈谈我国政府会计的确认基础》,载《财会通讯》,2000(1),40~42页。

[49] 徐镇绥:《试论政府会计改革中会计基础选择问题》,载《会计研究》,2006(12),20~24页。

[50] 王彦、王建英、赵西卜:《政府会计中构建二元结构会计要素的研究》,载《会计研究》,2009(4),24~30页。

[51] 刘曼:《中国预算会计与美国政府会计资产要素的比较》,载《云南财贸学院学报》,2004(1),68~70页。

[52] 程晓佳:《财政透明度与政府会计改革》,载《会计研究》,2004(9),22~27页。

[53] 张琦:《论绩效评价导向政府会计体系的构建》,载《会计研究》,2006(4),3~8页。

[54] 赵建勇:《政府会计的显著特征——兼谈政府会计教育》,载《会计研究》,2004(9),11~15页。

[55] 张志宁:《四大基本假设对政府会计的适应性》,载《经济论坛》,2004(6),123~124页。

[56] 何嘉萍:《中美政府会计比较》,载《上海会计》,2002(8),3~5页。

[57] 张连江、吕炜:《论政府会计的记账主体与报告主体》,载《四川会计》,2003(7),9~11页。

[58] 叶龙、冯兆大:《我国政府会计模式构建过程中主体界定问题初探》,载《会计研究》,2006(9),69~75页。

[59] 王娟、朱海英:《从公共受托责任角度看政府会计改革》,载《财会月刊》,2008(7),20~22页。

[60] 李相志、罗付珍:《我国政府会计体系改革探讨》,载《财会月刊》,2009(1),23~24页。

[61] 李建发、肖华:《公共财务管理与政府财务报告改革》,载《会计研究》,2004(9),7~10页。

[62] 贝洪俊:《会计制度变迁的利益冲突与协调》,载《财会月刊》,2004(1),13页。

[63] 黄世忠、刘用铨、王平:《美国联邦政府会计难点热点问题及其启示——基于联邦政府审计报告的分析》,载《会计研究》,2004(11),13~18页。

[64] 王庆东、常丽:《政府财务报告改革导向及其实现机制探索》,载《会计研究》,2007(3),88~90页。

[65] 张雪芬:《推动政府会计改革的若干思考》,载《财会月刊》,2008(1),19页。

[66] 金石明:《我国预算会计准则的框架构想》,载《财会通讯》,1994(9),18页。

[67] 尹艳芙:《预算会计体系研究》,载《财会月刊》,2008(3),89~91页。

[68] 李雄飞:《OECD国家权责发生制预算和政府会计改革探析》,载《企业经济》,2003(2),31~33页。

[69] 陈立齐:《美国政府会计的原则和重大变化简介》,载《会计研究》,2004(11),28~30页。

[70] 非营利组织会计问题研究课题组:《美国的政府会计规范及其借鉴》,载《会计研究》,2001(4),36~42页。

[71] 财政部会计司考察团:《英、法非营利组织和政府会计准则考察报告》,载《会计研究》,2004(11),81~83页。

[72] 陈璐璐:《英国政府会计管理与改革情况及对我国的启示》,载《会计研究》,2007(12),24~30页。

[73] 郑彩凤、赵福山:《改进政府会计核算的几条思路》,载《财会月刊》,2003(12),22页。

[74] 王雍君、蔡燕青:《以国库会计为重心构造政府会计》,载《中央财经大学学报》,2003(5),72~75页。

[75] 王淑杰:《改革我国政府会计基础的思考》,载《财会月刊》,2004(4),21~22页。

[76] 金希萍:《公共财政管理与政府会计目标》,载《财会通讯》,2007(9),123~124页。

[77] 贝洪俊:《新公共管理:基于绩效导向的政府会计系统》,载《财会研究》,2004(5),26~28页。

[78] 刘玉廷:《我国政府会计改革的若干问题》,载《会计研究》,2004(9),3~6页。

[79] 张琦:《新西兰政府会计改革及启示》,载《财会通讯》,2007(8),77~78页。

[80] 陈工孟、邓德强、周齐武:《我国预算会计改革可行性的问卷调查研究》,载《会计研究》,2005(5),59~65页。

[81] 张琦、张象至、程晓佳:《政府会计基础选择、利益相关者动机与制度环境的影响》,载《会计研究》,2009(7),35~42页。

安全漏洞、内部控制与审计风险[①]
——基于审计风险模型与制度经济学的证据

曾建光　罗炜　伍利娜　王立彦

（北京大学光华管理学院　北京　100871）

摘　要　美国总统奥巴马认为，21 世纪的经济繁荣取决于信息安全。本文根据审计风险模型和制度经济学的原理考察了威胁信息安全的首要因素的安全漏洞，对于我国资本市场的影响。学者研究发现：在其他条件相同的情况下，危急型安全漏洞或者高危型安全漏洞发生的频度与审计风险呈显著正相关，而中危型安全漏洞或低危型安全漏洞发生的频度与审计风险呈显著负相关。在其他条件相同的情况下，对于非“五大”而言，危急型安全漏洞或者高危型安全漏洞发生的频度与审计风险溢价呈显著正相关；而对于非“五大”而言，中危型安全漏洞或低危型安全漏洞发生的频度与审计溢价呈显著负相关。

关键词　安全漏洞　内部控制　审计风险　信息风险　制度经济学

一、引言

随着企业信息化的逐步深入以及 Internet 的飞速发展，企业的日常运营的支撑越来越依赖于 IT 系统的正常运行，同时，企业采用的信息系统也越来越多，其规模和覆盖面也不断扩大，复杂度也越来越高，当我们享受信息技术经济、高效、智能的工具性的同时，也体会到了或有所耳闻当安全隐患发生时，所可能造成的问题。信息技术存在的安全漏洞是导致这些问题的关键因素。因此，IT（information technology）风险已成为公司管理层、监管部门等重点关注的对象，IT 内部控制也已成为企业内部控制的主要组成部分。由于计算机及其信息系统的安全漏洞对于企业内部控制的威胁，导致企业的控制风险（control risk）以及固有风险（inherent risk）和（或）信息风险（information risk）的增加，在面对这些风险增加的情况下，审计师为了控制整体的审计风险必然会降低检查风险（detection risk），从而最终影响审计风险。基于此，本

---

①　本文得到国家自然科学基金项目的资助“ERP 系统实施与企业绩效增长关系研究”，项目批准号：70772006）。

文根据审计风险模型和制度经济学的原理，通过考察计算机及其信息系统的安全漏洞对于企业内部控制质量的影响，而企业内部控制质量的变化势必影响企业的控制风险以及固有风险和（或）信息风险，进而影响审计师的检查风险，最终导致审计风险的变化。

安全漏洞是 Internet 时代的一种客观存在，已成为信息安全管理工程师与攻击者双方博弈的对象。新华网 2010 年 10 月 3 日报道，一种利用 Microsoft 漏洞的新型病毒（Stuxnet）能够通过移动存储介质和局域网进行传播，并利用西门子控制系统中存在的漏洞，感染数据采集与监视控制系统。该系统广泛用于能源、交通、水利等，一旦遭受病毒侵害，则可能造成钢铁、电力、能源、化工等重要行业的企业运行异常，或者造成商业秘密失窃，甚至停工停产等严重事故①。又据中国新闻网 2010 年 10 月 13 日报道，微软向全球用户发布了 16 个月度安全补丁，用于修复 Office、浏览器、Windows 等系列的操作系统的多处漏洞，Windows 用户如果不及时修补，那么在浏览网页、听音乐、运行 Office 等情况下，很可能会遭受木马病毒的远程攻击，导致隐私数据遭到恶意程序的篡改或窃取。由此可知，随着 Internet 的迅猛发展，基于 Internet 的企业级的 Web 应用和服务也变得越来越多，安全漏洞变得越来越与企业的运营息息相关。

美国总统奥巴马就提出：21 世纪的经济繁荣取决于信息安全，如果对信息安全漏洞掉以轻心，美国就会重蹈德军密码机在第二次世界大战中被英军破译的覆辙（杨谷，2009）。因为信息系统中的一个微小漏洞都可能导致重大的人员伤亡和财产损失，甚至导致国家安全问题，如导弹发射控制系统，飞机导航系统、证券系统等。公安部网络安全保卫局副局长顾坚在 2010 年第四届中美互联网论坛上发言也指出："我国每 10 台接入互联网的计算机中有 8 台曾受到'僵尸网络'的控制，且绝大多数僵尸网络的控制端位于境外，我国平均每天有近 200 个政府网站被入侵，其中超过 80% 的攻击来自境外。"②

Krsul（1998）认为，一个软件漏洞是存在于系统规范说明书、设计阶段、开发阶段或配置过程中的一个错误实例，它的执行违反了安全策略。安全漏洞是指信息技术、信息产品、信息系统在设计、实现、配置、运行等过程中，由操作实体有意或无意所产生的缺陷。（中国国家安全漏洞库，2010）。本文所说的安全漏洞，主要指计算机相关设备及其信息系统中由于技术原因而造成的安全问题，这种安全问题可能存在于构成信息系统的软件、硬件等中，如存在于 CPU、BIOS、操作系统和数据库等中。

不管安全漏洞是因为设计，还是系统过程开发中、运行中抑或维护阶段甚

---

① 新华网，2010 年 09 月 29 日，中国 600 万个人计算机用户遭"超级工厂"病毒攻击，http://news.xinhuanet.com/tech/2010-09/29/c_12619868.htm，2010-12-12。

② 人民网，2010，公安部网络安全保卫局副局长顾坚，http://media.people.com.cn/GB/22114/207332/207334/13169398.html，2010-11-09。

至是测试阶段的失误造成的，还是人为有意设置的，都会威胁到计算机及其相关信息系统的安全性。这些漏洞以不同的形式存在于计算机及其相关信息系统的各个层次和环节之中，而且随着信息系统的不同（包括版本、系统等的不同）而不同；这些漏洞一旦被恶意主体发觉并利用，就可能损害计算机及其相关信息系统的安全性，进而影响甚至破坏、中断计算机及其相关信息系统的正常服务（张涛，吴冲，2008）。

2008年5月22日，财政部、证监会、审计署、银监会和保监会五部委联合制定并发布的《企业内部控制基本规范》第7条规定："企业应当运用信息技术加强内部控制，建立与经营管理相适应的信息系统，促进内部控制流程与信息系统的有机结合，实现对业务和事项的自动控制，减少或消除人为操纵因素。"《企业内部控制基本规范》的这条规定，着重于信息技术在信息处理方面的优点，而忽视了由于信息技术的采用所导致的信息安全隐患，由此造成偏离内部控制的目标。故在2010年4月26日颁布的《企业内部控制应用指引》第18号——信息系统中的第三章第十三条中就规定："企业应当综合利用防火墙、路由器等网络设备，漏洞扫描、入侵检测等软件技术以及远程访问安全策略等手段，加强网络安全，防范来自网络的攻击和非法侵入。"因此，为了更有效地发挥信息技术的优点，避免由于信息技术的负面作用给企业带来不必要的损失，如商业秘密的泄露等，我们必须加强企业内部控制，对安全漏洞的危害性保持足够的重视。

基于以上分析，在日益发达的互联网技术以及移动互联网技术的今天，每个企业都无法生存在不采用信息技术的真空中。信息技术为企业提供了良好的发展平台，已融入到企业的生产、研发、运营和管理等各项活动中，同时又由于信息平台存在安全漏洞的问题，势必对企业的内部控制提出更高要求。当企业的内部控制不仅仅受到传统的企业内部环境的影响，而且还受到来自Internet上的攻击威胁时，安全漏洞对于我国企业的影响又是如何呢？

本文以2005—2009年中国国家安全漏洞数据库统计的危急型、高危型、中危型和低危型四类安全漏洞为研究对象。学者研究发现：危急型和高危型的安全漏洞发生频度越高，审计风险越小，信息风险越大；而中危型和低危型的安全漏洞发生频度越高，审计风险越大，信息风险越小；安全漏洞的发生频率对于审计风险没有显著影响，但是提高了信息风险，却降低了IT企业的信息风险。本文的研究为处于信息化生态环境下的企业内部控制，应该引入防范嵌入在软件中的漏洞风险的内部控制架构（陈志斌，2007）提供了一个实证检验，本文的研究也为《企业内部控制应用指引》的实施提供了一个实证证据，同时本文的研究也为Hogan和Wilkins（2008）提出的可能的结论解释，采用中国资本市场的数据提供了一个明确的解释，即当审计师面对固有风险和控制风险增大时，虽然面临的法律风险提高，但是审计师并没有显著提高其努力程度，Hogan和Wilkins（2008）发现的审计费用的提高，很可能就是对风险的溢价。

本文可能的贡献主要体现在五个方面：第一，首次引入安全漏洞考察 IT 技术的缺陷对于公司内部控制的影响，同时，融合了企业的内部环境与企业的外部环境的交互作用，并不单纯地就内部控制论企业的内部环境，丰富了内部控制方面的文献；第二，首次尝试了信息安全性的度量问题，为 IT 治理和 IT 内控的安全性尝试提供了一种测度方法；第三，在审计风险的影响因素中，首次引入 IT 技术，并把 IT 技术的安全性作为内生影响因素进行考察；第四，为处于信息化生态环境下的企业内部控制，应该引入防范软件中内控机制漏洞风险的架构（陈志斌，2007）提供了一个实证证据；第五，本文的研究为 Hogan 和 Wilkins（2008）提出了可能的结论解释，本文的研究在一定程度上证伪了 Chen et al.（2010）的研究结论。

本文安排如下：第二部分是理论分析与文献回顾；第三部分是研究假设与研究设计；第四部分是样本选择与描述统计；第五部分是检验结果；第六部分是研究结论与不足。

二、理论分析与文献回顾

根据美国审计准则公告第 47 号（Statement on Auditing Standards（SAS）No. 47）（American Institute of Certified Public Accountants（AICPA），1983）文件的表述，审计风险模型如模型（1）所示：

审计风险（audit risk）= 固有风险×控制风险×检查风险　　(1)

模型（1）中的审计风险，根据国际审计准则第 200 号（ISA 200）的定义为："财务报表中存在重大错报而审计师发表了不恰当的审计意见的风险。"固有风险和控制风险是审计师基于对客户的评估得到的，而检查风险是指审计师面对高固有风险和控制风险时，通过增加测试降低检查风险，从而达到控制整体审计风险的目标。

已有的关于审计工作计划的研究，对于审计师面对高固有风险和控制风险时是否会增加测试来降低检查风险并没有得到一致的研究结论。Mock 和 Wright（1999）采用实务中的应收账款审计业务的数据，研究发现，在实务中并没有证据表明客户风险与审计计划存在关联性，也即在实务中，审计工作计划并不会随着风险的变化而变化（Bedard，1989）。Hackenbrack 和 Knechel（1997）和 Felix et al.（2001）研究发现，审计师的努力只会随着固有风险的变化而调整而不会随着控制风险的变化进行调整。这些已有的研究都是基于 2002 年之前的数据。

随着 2002 年美国 Sarbanes - Oxley 法案的颁布实施，Hogan 和 Wilkins（2008）采用审计费用和应计盈余质量分别作为审计师的努力程度和信息风险的代理变量，研究发现，当内部控制存在缺陷时，审计费用平均高出 35%；

当内部控制存在最严重的缺陷时，审计师付出的努力也最多，自然审计费用也最高；内部控制存在缺陷的公司较其他公司具有更高的固有风险和信息风险；同时作者也认为导致审计费用的提高不排除是对内部控制风险的溢价而非审计师付出的努力的增加。根据 Hogan 和 Wilkins（2008）的研究，我们可知，在内部控制存在缺陷时，不论审计师是否会增加努力，都会导致审计风险的变化；如果审计师付出了足够的努力导致检查风险的降低，那么审计风险会降低；如果审计师付出的努力不够，那么审计风险会显著增加。基于此，我们可以认为内部控制存在缺陷时，会影响审计风险的大小。

发现财报中重大错漏的概率并报告发现的错漏的概率表示的是审计师的检查风险。发现财报中重大错漏的概率是审计师团队执业素质的体现，报告发现的错漏的概率则是审计师团队独立性的体现，为了更好地提高审计质量，必须同时提高发现财报中重大错漏的概率和报告发现的错漏的概率，而不能有所偏颇。

发现财报中重大错漏的概率的前提是，企业存在错漏的概率。企业存在错漏的概率又是由企业内部控制构建的错漏的概率以及企业外部环境对于内部控制构建的破坏威胁的联合概率分布函数，这种对于内部控制构建的破坏威胁，在信息技术被企业普遍采用的信息时代主要来自于客观存在的安全漏洞。也就是说，企业外部环境，尤其是日新月异的 Internet 技术，增加了企业的内部控制风险和 IT 风险。随着现代企业外部环境与内部环境界限的透明性，模糊性和脆弱性的增加，要求内部控制具有足够的灵活性、动态性和健壮性，为了更好地提高审计质量，除了需要提高发现财报中重大错漏的概率和报告发现的错漏的概率，还必须同时提高发现企业外部环境对于内部控制构建的潜在的破坏威胁的应对能力以及内部控制应对外来威胁的响应及时性，而不能有所偏颇。

根据 COSO 内部控制架构的五要素模型，在“信息与沟通”要素部分把信息系统置于战略的高度进行了阐述，该框架要求：必须将信息系统的规划、设计和实施与企业的整体战略形成有机的统一体。信息系统的战略作用体现在无缝集成财务和业务的管理控制系统之中，这样有助于业务流的实时控制、记录与跟踪。对于参照 COSO 架构建立的内部控制系统，由于在“信息与沟通”要素部分采用了 IT 技术，而 IT 技术的致命缺陷就是安全漏洞，而且这种漏洞是有潜伏期的，管理人员很难预知安全漏洞什么时候被利用，甚至管理人员对于安全漏洞被恶意利用还浑然不知。此外，该框架对如何构建该信息系统并没有作进一步探讨（吴炎太等，2009），这样使得企业在参照 COSO 架构建立内部控制系统时，在“信息与沟通”要素部分容易出现更多的安全漏洞。因此，“信息与沟通”要素部分出现问题，很有可能导致公司员工职责执行的低效率，也可能导致在信息与沟通的过程中，公司重要信息的泄密，甚至公司的资产的安全性无法得到保证。总之，安全漏洞对于 COSO 架构的影响主要体现在“信息与沟通”的要素上，一旦 COSO 架构的载体受到安全漏洞的威胁，COSO

内部控制的效率和有效性就受到威胁，为实现或达成企业目标所必需的条件就难以得到满足，企业也就无法为财务报告的可靠性提供合理保证，也就提高了企业的固有风险和控制风险。

在 COBIT 框架中，企业需要借助可以控制的 IT 资源，获取所需的信息，以实现企业目标。此外，由于 COBIT 是一个通用的信息系统控制标准，主要是一个建立内部控制的指导思想，但缺乏足够的实践指引，与信息系统的实践过程联系不够紧密或不够具体（吴炎太等，2009），这个问题容易导致在信息系统的实践过程中造成不必要的安全隐患。也就是说，在 COBIT 框架中，IT 技术是实现企业目标的载体和工具。伴随 IT 资源而生的安全漏洞是对 COBIT 框架中 IT 准则的天然威胁。安全漏洞直接威胁到 IT 资源的可用性、完整性、保密性以及可靠性。当违反了 COBIT 框架中的 IT 准则，内部控制的有效性就无法得到保证，当内部控制形同虚设，企业的固有风险和控制风险也就增加了。

我国 2008 年颁布的《企业内部控制基本规范》第 7 条规定："企业应当运用信息技术加强内部控制，建立与经营管理相适应的信息系统，促进内部控制流程与信息系统的有机结合，实现对业务和事项的自动控制，减少或消除人为操纵因素。"2010 年颁布的《企业内部控制应用指引》第 18 号——信息系统中的第三章第十三条规定："企业应当综合利用防火墙、路由器等网络设备，漏洞扫描、入侵检测等软件技术以及远程访问安全策略等手段，加强网络安全，防范来自网络的攻击和非法侵入。"《企业内部控制应用指引》从信息系统的开发、运行维护与变更、信息系统安全性等方面提出了明确的要求，但是，该指引没有给出漏洞扫描的目标，频度以及发现了安全漏洞后的处理措施等，而且该指引从 2011 年 1 月 1 日起首先在境内外同时上市的公司施行，2012 年 1 月 1 日起扩大到在上海证券交易所、深圳证券交易所主板上市的公司施行。因此，对于没有按照上述准则建立的内部控制系统，其受到安全漏洞的威胁更大。

总之，潜在的安全漏洞对计算机及其相关系统的安全性造成潜在的威胁，也即安全漏洞被发现并被人利用后直接对计算机及其相关系统的保密性、完整性及可用性等方面都会造成负面影响，影响了企业日常运营以及企业内部控制的效率，增加了企业的固定风险和控制风险，也增加了企业在财务报表中发生重大错漏的概率，增加了审计人员无法发现这种重大错漏的概率，从而影响了审计质量，同时也影响了投资者对于企业风险的评估，导致投资决策的风险增大。

在美国，随着 2002 年 SOX 法案的颁布与实施，该法案的 404 条款除了要求上市公司在年报中披露管理层对内部控制的评价之外，还要求外部审计师对管理层关于内部控制的结论进行评价，出具审计意见。

内部控制对审计风险的影响，现有的文献主要是从披露的内部控制缺陷进行研究。为了考察内部控制缺陷的问题，首先需要考察导致这些内部控制缺陷的各种因素。现有的文献主要从经济因素方面进行考察。Ashbaugh-Skaife et al.（2007）采用SOX法案302条款实施之后且在404条款实施之前的上市公司在年报中自愿披露的内部控制缺陷的数据，研究发现，相对那些没有披露内部控制缺陷的企业，披露了内部控制缺陷的企业具有更大的会计风险，更多的报表重述以及在披露内部控制缺陷之前，有更多的审计师离职等。Doyle et al.（2007a）则采用SOX法案302条款和404条款都实施之后，采用的数据是SEC要求强制披露的内部控制的实质性缺陷的上市公司的数据，研究发现，披露内部控制缺陷的公司一般都是一些成立时间不长的比较小的公司，这些公司的财务状况一般也较差，业务也较复杂但高速增长或者正在进行业务重组；在这些公司中，内部控制稍差些的公司是成立时间不长，财务状况较差的比较小的公司；而内部控制稍好些的公司财务状况较好，但是采用复杂，多变的多元化经营模式；作者认为，决定内部控制缺陷的因素不能一概而论，需要根据各个公司面临的具体的内部控制问题进行具体分析。Leone（2007）认为，Ashbaugh-Skaife et al.（2007）和Doyle et al.（2007a）首次把公司的特征与内部控制缺陷联系起来，他们都通过考察在年报中披露了内部控制中的重要缺陷或者内部控制的实质性缺陷的上市公司，研究发现影响内部控制信息披露的风险因素包括公司组织结构的复杂性、存在重要的组织变革以及公司在构建内部控制系统方面的投资力度，作者认为这三种因素具有较强的说服力。

总之，上述考察导致内部控制质量的各种经济因素的文献表明，企业的内部控制缺陷导致了企业的固有风险和控制风险的增加，但是鲜有文献考察技术的因素对于内部控制缺陷的影响。

还有一些文献从内部控制缺陷对盈余质量的影响来考察内部控制缺陷的经济后果。Ge和McVay（2005）研究发现，披露了内部控制存在实质性缺陷的公司最普遍的会计问题就在于可操控性应计方面。Bedard（2006）研究发现，按照SOX法案302条款披露的内部控制缺陷的公司较其他公司，在披露的当年有更多的可操控性应计利润，但是按照404条款披露的内部控制缺陷的公司较其他公司，在披露的当年可操控性应计利润得到了降低。Mitehell（2007）研究发现，存在重大内部控制缺陷的公司往往累计盈利能力较低且负债水平较高。Tang和Xu（2007）研究发现，披露了内部控制存在实质性缺陷的公司较其他公司的运营绩效和股票回报都较差。Doyle et al.（2007b）研究发现，按照SOX法案302条款披露了内部控制实质性缺陷的公司相对于其他公司的盈余质量更差，而按照404条款披露的内部控制实质性缺陷与盈余质量没有显著相关性。Ashbaugh-Skaife et al.（2008）通过考察内部控制缺陷以及对于这些缺陷的修复对于盈余质量的影响，研究发现披露了内部控制缺陷的公司相对于其他公司的盈余管理程度更大。Chan et al.（2008）研究发现，按照SOX法案404条款披露的内部控制实质性缺陷的公司较其他公司有更多的盈余管理。

Prawitt et al.（2008）研究发现，内部审计功能（internal audit function，IAF）质量越高，可操控性总应计利润的绝对值越低，也即盈余管理程度越少。Feng et al.（2009）通过考察SOX法案404条款实施后2004—2006年的样本，内部控制质量对管理层盈余预测的精确度的影响，研究发现，那些报告了内部控制缺陷的公司，管理层盈余预测的精度和质量都显著偏低。Altamuro 和 Beatty（2010）采用在美国上市的银行为样本，研究发现，FDICIA的内部控制强制披露要求有助于提高银行业的贷款损失准备金的合理性、盈余的可持续性和现金流的可预测性。这些证据表明，内部控制的质量之所以能够对盈余质量起到作用，是由于较以前增加了额外的监督机制，比如审计师、董事会以及机构投资者。譬如，Doyle et al.（2007b）和Hogan 和 Wilkins（2008）认为，审计师的实质性测试能够作为内部控制的一种代替，能够部分地减轻内部控制实质性缺陷对于盈余质量的负面影响。

总之，上述考察导致内部控制质量的经济后果的文献表明，内部控制的质量影响了盈余质量，即内部控制的质量越差，信息风险越高。

还有一些文献考察内部控制缺陷对于审计师行为等的影响。Ashbaugh-Skaife et al.（2007）采用302条款实施之后且在SOX法案404条款实施之前的上市公司在年报中自愿披露的内部控制缺陷的数据，研究发现，导致这些公司主动发现并自愿披露内部控制缺陷，是因为这些公司更偏好聘请知名的会计师事务所。Ashbaugh-Skaife et al.（2008）通过考察内部控制缺陷以及对于这些缺陷的修复对于盈余质量的影响，研究发现，经过审计师确认已改正的内部控制缺陷的公司较没有改正的公司，其盈余质量有较大的提高。Raghunandan 和 Rama（2006）研究发现，存在内部控制缺陷的公司由于审计师需要付出更多的努力和审计师法律风险的提高导致了审计费用的提高。Hogan 和 Wilkins（2008）研究发现，披露了内部控制存在实质性缺陷的公司较其他公司具有更高的固有风险和信息风险，根据审计风险模型，审计师为了达到预期的审计风险水平，可能需要付出更多的努力，也即需要收取更高的审计费用；作者还认为审计这种费用的提高，不一定是由于审计师需要付出更多的努力，也有可能是一种风险溢价，但是作者并没有给出实证检验。Yan（2007）研究发现，由于内部控制缺陷的增加不仅导致了较高的审计风险，还会导致审计师变更的频率。Li（2007）研究发现，由于内部控制缺陷的增加导致了增加会计错误发生的概率以及审计师发现这种错误的难度的增加，审计师为了控制审计风险，其需要增加工作范围和大量的工作量，从而导致审计延迟的增加，实质性内部控制缺陷造成的审计延迟较重大内部控制缺陷更长。此外，Li（2007）和Yan（2007）进一步考察了实质性内部控制缺陷与审计师变更之间的关系，研究发现：已经（或预期将）发现存在实质性内部控制缺陷的公司，审计师主动辞职的概率较高，在这种情况下，“四大”事务所更不可能成为其继任审计师；已经（或预期将）收到负面内部控制审计意见的公司，主动辞退审计师的概率较高，但辞退之后，公司获得的非标审计意见的概率更大，这表明无法通过更换审计师来实现审计意见购买。Li（2007）还考察了客户重要性在SOX法案颁布前后对于审计师独立性的影响变化，研究发现，在SOX法案颁布之前，客户重要性对审计师独立性没有显著影响；而在SOX法案颁布之后，客户重要性对审计师的独立性具有显著正影响。

总之，上述文献考察的是内部控制质量对于审计师行为等影响，这些文献表明，企业的内部控制缺陷导致了企业的固有风险和控制风险的增加，审计师为了达到预期的审计风险，增加了测试计划，目的是达到控制审计风险的目标。

以上文献考察的都是基于美国的制度背景之下。模型（1）的定义是来自于美国审计准则的公告，隐含的制度背景是成熟的资本市场，特别是SEC的强大的监管能力，以及比较完善的、执行力很强的美国司法制度，因此，审计师非常在意自已的声誉，也就是说，审计师对于其面临的风险会理性地进行控制，比如，面对较大风险时，审计师会选择主动辞职（Li，2007，Yan，2007），或者被辞退（Yan，2007），或者增加风险溢价（Hogan 和 Wilkins，2008）等。而在像我国这样的新兴资本市场，由于保护投资者的制度环境较弱（LaPorta et al.，1997，LaPorta et al.，1999，LaPorta et al.，2000），因此，我们在使用模型（1）考察我国资本市场的行为时，需要充分考虑制度背景因素。也即根据模型（1），可扩展为审计师风险模型，如模型（2）：

$$\begin{aligned}\underset{(\text{Auditor Risk})}{\text{审计师风险}} &= \text{审计风险} \times \text{制度风险} \\ &= \begin{matrix}\text{审计}\\\text{风险}\end{matrix} \times \begin{matrix}\text{审计失败被}\\\text{识别的风险}\end{matrix} \times \begin{matrix}\text{惩罚的}\\\text{力度}\end{matrix} \times \begin{matrix}\text{惩罚的}\\\text{执行力}\end{matrix} \qquad (2)（陈正林，2006）\end{aligned}$$

模型（2）其实也体现了审计质量就是发现会计报表重大错漏的概率以及报告该错漏的概率的联合分布函数（DeAngelo，1981）的思想。模型（2）中的审计风险反映的是审计师的执业能力的技术风险，而制度风险反映的是由于审计师的技术风险导致的审计失败被识别出来的概率以及审计失败被识别后的惩罚制度及其执行力；从模型（2）可知，当制度风险很大时，审计师必然会主动降低审计风险，从而提高了审计质量；若制度风险很小，审计师就没有激励去降低审计风险，从而降低了审计质量，也即识别制度和惩罚制度的有效性决定了审计师的行为（陈正林，2006）。在美国，特别是在SOX法案颁布实施之后，审计师面临的制度风险陡增，而且在美国这样的成熟资本市场，拥有大量的、专业的机构投资者、分析师等，从而极大地增加了审计失败被识别的风险，审计师为了降低审计师风险，必然会努力控制审计风险。模型对于以上研究美国制度背景下的文献，具有很好的解释力。也就是说，在美国这样成熟的司法和资本市场的制度背景下，模型（2）和模型（1）才具有一致性，特别是在SOX法案颁布实施之后。而要考察我国资本市场，模型（2）才是具有较好的解释力的模型。

“银广夏”等事件的爆发，直接导致了2002年1月15日，最高人民法院颁布实施《最高人民法院关于受理证券市场因虚假陈述引发的民事侵权纠纷案件有关问题的通知》。接着在2003年1月9日最高人民法院发布，自2003年2月1日起施行的司法解释——《最高人民法院关于审理证券市场因虚假陈述引发的民事赔偿案件的若干规定》。这项法律的出台，要求法院受理和审理因虚假陈述引发的证券市场上的民事侵权纠纷案件，在一定程度上，对审计师的不作为具有较大的威慑力。2007年6月15日，最高人民法院又颁布实施了专门针对审计师的司法解释——《关于审理涉及会计师事务所在审计业务活动中民事侵权赔偿案件的若干规定》。这个司法解释的出台，在一定程度上进一步加大了主张者举证的难度，也就是说，这个司法解释的实施的成本更大。虽然该法律允许普通投资者对审计师的不当行为提起民事诉讼，但由于过高的成本和偏低的收益，导致审计师被真正提起诉讼的概率偏低，再者，尽管在我国非标审计意见的出具频率比以往有了很大的提高（Defond et al.，2000），但是，并没有改变，由于低风险的司法制度环境在相当程度上造成了我国上市公司审计质量总体偏低的怪相（刘峰，许菲，2002）。

在投资者保护较差的中国（Allen et al.，2005），审计市场的整体审计质量较差（Wang et al.，2008，杨德明等，2009）。这是由于在我国制度风险较小，导致审计师风险也较小，而审计师作为一个理性经济人，没有激励去吃苦不讨好地努力提高审计质量；除非审计风险过大，审计师为了维持个人的声誉以及惧于法律的威慑力，他才会努力去降低审计风险，这也是我国会计职业界实际所承受的法律风险仍然较低（刘峰、许菲，2002）的原因之一。这表明，模型（2）也适用于我国资本市场。

研究我国内部控制的文献较少。李艳姣（2009）通过考察2007年深市A股上市公司，研究发现，内部控制缺陷与审计收费不存在显著相关性。方红星等（2009）通过考察我国沪市非金融上市公司2003—2005年年度报告中自愿披露的内部控制信息，研究发现，上市公司是否自愿披露内部控制信息与非标审计意见类型显著负相关；在影响上市公司内部控制信息自愿披露的因素中，外部审计没有显著影响。李享（2009）通过分析我国强制性披露内部控制信息的文献后，研究发现，在我国内部控制自评报告、审核意见的披露属于公司自愿的选择性行为，也就是说外部审计师在面对内部控制缺陷时，存在一定的审计意见购买行为。杨德明和胡婷（2010）通过考察我国A股上市公司2007—2008年的数据，研究发现，在我国，内部控制与外部审计之间存在一定的替代效应，而且这种替代效应与审计费用呈显著正向关系。财政部驻河北省财政监察专员办事处课题组（2005）研究也发现，在我国市场需求主体对高质量的审计产品缺乏内在需求。Wang et al.（2008）研究发现，我国审计市场总体上并不需要，甚至排斥高质量的审计。杨德明等（2009）认为，我国审计市场尚不太成熟，审计质量并不太高。辛清泉和黄琨（2009）发现，在中天勤事件之后，事务所为了避免客户的大量流失，审计师更可能妥协于客户压力，在其他条件不变的情况下，出具非标意见的概率因此下降。杨德明和胡婷（2010）的研究表明，在审计费用缺乏的公司，审计师一旦发现内部控制质量较高，大幅度削减实质性测试的概率大大增加；反之，在审计费用比较充裕的公司，审计师即使发现内部控制质量较高，大幅度削减实质性测试的可能也不大。

通过研究我国内部控制以及审计市场的文献，我们可知，在我国不论是否要求强制性披露内部控制缺陷，都存在着较大的审计意见购买的可能，也就是说内部控制质量对于审计师出具审计意见没有显著影响。我国的情况与 Li（2007）和 Yan（2007）的研究结论不一致，表明在我国由于制度风险过低，审计师并没有对内部控制缺陷问题导致的控制风险，固有风险（信息风险）进行足够的，充分的相应的审计风险的调整，因此，在我国，由于识别制度和处罚制度的共同失灵是造成我国审计质量不高的根本原因（陈正林，2006）。从这些研究我国内部控制以及审计市场的文献，进一步检验了模型（2）在我国资本市场上的适用性。

此外，Chen et al.（2010）通过考察我国 1995—2004 年期间的上市公司，研究发现在 2001 年之后，由于我国制度环境更加有利于投资者，因此，对于签字审计师来说，客户重要性越大，越有可能出具非标的审计意见，而对于事务所来说，客户重要性对于出具非标的审计意见没有显著影响。Chen et al.（2010）研究结论的问题在于：忽视了中国的特殊制度背景，即在中国审计市场上，签字审计师很少是真正进行审计的审计师，很多是部门经理或者是事务所的合伙人，所以用签字审计师来考察客户重要性存在极大的偏误，这也许就是作者没有发现事务所客户重要性对于审计意见的显著性的原因之一。Chen et al.（2010）在文章的结尾处为新兴资本市场的政策制定者提出了制定投资者保护的制度，根据模型（2）可知，只是强调制度的制定有失偏颇，我们认为，新兴资本市场的政策制定者不仅仅需要政策的制定，更需要把制定的政策推进和落实，我国最高法院颁布的《关于审理证券市场因虚假陈述引发的民事赔偿案件的若干规定》就是最好的反例。伍利娜等（2010）也认为，2003 年1月9日，最高法院颁布的《关于审理证券市场因虚假陈述引发的民事赔偿案件的若干规定》，提高了审计师的法律风险。Chen et al.（2010）和伍利娜等（2010）的问题在于：第一，把单一法规的出台等同于整个制度环境的改变。第二，他们混淆了制度的预期与制度的现实，他们的研究发现是市场对于低制度风险的渴望，但是制度的现实却相反。第三，从最高法院颁布的《关于审理证券市场因虚假陈述引发的民事赔偿案件的若干规定》的出台至今已经 8 年之久，但是没有一例由于触犯该法律而受到应有的惩罚，这并不能说明我国制度一夜之间就完美了。第四，2005 年在中国开始实行的股权分置改革是一个最好的事件研究，申慧慧等（2009）通过考察股权分置改革对上市公司盈余质量的影响，研究发现，非国有控股上市公司向上盈余管理的程度显著提高；伍利娜、朱春艳（2010）研究也发现，股改后审计师一定程度上配合上市公司实现了向上的盈余管理及审计意见购买；晏艳阳、赵大玮（2006）研究发现，我国股权分置改革中存在较为严重的内幕交易行为。这些表明，制度环境没有发生大的改变，制度风险依然不高，否则的话，盈余管理的程度至少不应该提高。第五，根据模型（2）可知，在新兴资本市场国家，特别是在司法制度较不成熟的国家，制度的执行力才真正决定了政策的经济后果，不能仅仅把政策的制定视为制度的执行力。

总之，现有的文献主要是从公司的经济特征导致内部控制的质量问题及其经济后果，考察其对审计风险和（或）审计师风险的影响，而鲜有文献考察构建内部控制的技术架构所导致的内部控制缺陷，即现有的文献只是把内部控制的技术架构视为外生变量，而在近年来 IT 及其相关技术越来越成为公司内部控制的基础技术，一旦 IT 及其相关技术出现问题，整个公司的运营几乎都要受到影响，特别是我国于 2010 年 10 月 18 日，发布了可扩展商业报告语言（XBRL）系列国家标准和企业会计准则通用分类标准，要求自 2011 年 1 月 1 日起在美国纽约证券交易所上市的我国部分公司、部分证券期货资格会计师事务所施行，鼓励其他上市公司和非上市大中型企业执行。XBRL 国标的采用意味着 IT 技术更深地嵌入到了企业内部控制之中。本文正是基于这个前提，结合我国的制度背景，把内部控制的 IT 技术及其相关技术架构视为内生变量，考察这种技术架构自身的缺陷——安全漏洞对于内部控制的影响，进而影响企业的固有风险、控制风险和（或）信息风险以及审计师的检查风险，最终考察这些风险对于审计风险和审计师风险的影响。根据考察的我国资本市场审计风险情况，考察处于信息化生态环境下的企业内部控制，是否应该引入防范软件中内控机制漏洞风险的架构（陈志斌，2007），根据考察的我国资本市场审计风险和审计师风险情况，考察《企业内部控制应用指引》的实施是否有利于促进我国资本市场的健康发展？同时本文也试图考察 Hogan 和 Wilkins（2008）提出的可能的两种结论解释，进行进一步的澄清和检验。

三、研究假设与设计

（一）研究假设

Arbaugh et al.（2000）和 Jumratjaroenvanit 与 Teng-amnuay（2008）认为，安全漏洞和其他产品一样也具有生命周期的特征，每个安全漏洞都要经历产生、发现、公告、修复和消亡等五个阶段。安全漏洞在不同的生命周期阶段，其危害程度也不一样。Microsoft 公司主要根据安全漏洞对于系统的危害程度划分为四个等级，分别是：危急型的安全漏洞，即无需用户激活的网络蠕虫传播的安全漏洞；高危型的安全漏洞，即该安全漏洞被利用后，会导致用户数据的机密性、完整性和有效性遭到破坏；中危型的安全漏洞，即该安全漏洞被利用比较困难，受到配置、验证等诸多因素的限制，该安全漏洞对系统的影响较小；低危型的安全漏洞，即此安全漏洞被利用非常困难，该安全漏洞对系统的影响非常小。

根据 Microsoft 公司对安全漏洞的划分，我们可知，由于危急型和高危型的安全漏洞破坏力强、危害程度大，各大软件厂商或硬件厂商会通过各种渠道公告其危害性以减少用户不必要的损失，并鼓励用户下载安全补丁及时进行漏洞的修复，同时各种媒体也争相报道，提醒用户这类漏洞对于计算机及其相关系统的危害程度和可能造成的损失，因此，通过诸如网络、电视、报纸等多种渠道，危急型和高危型的安全漏洞受到的关注较多，公众对于其危害程度有足够的认识和防范，从而防止恶意用户利用该安全漏洞进行攻击，而对于企业用户来说，危急型和高危型的安全漏洞对于其内部控制的危害程度更大，因此企业用户更会及时关注危急型与高危型的安全漏洞的防护措施和及时下载补丁修复程序进行修补以保持内部控制的技术基础架构的稳定性、完整性、安全性和有效性，但是，危急型和高危型的安全漏洞的发现并公告以后，企业的反应不可能非常及时，同时，厂商的补丁程序的开发和测试需要时间，在这段空白区的时间内，企业内部控制的缺陷被暴露的概率陡然增加且其缺陷的严重程度也陡增，并且当厂商针对这些漏洞的补丁程序发布后，这些补丁程序也可能导致新的安全漏洞隐患。

因此，我们认为危急型和高危型的安全漏洞的发现，意味着内部控制的缺陷被暴露的概率陡增且其严重程度加剧，也就极大地增加了企业的控制风险、固有风险和（或者）信息风险。根据审计风险模型，当企业的控制风险和固有风险增大时，审计师为控制整体的审计风险，必然会主动去降低检查风险，也即审计师会更加努力以控制审计风险。同样，根据审计师风险模型可知，由于危急型或高危型的安全漏洞的出现导致了内部控制缺陷的危害程度加剧，如果审计师再不努力，那么，审计风险就极其高，这样也就加剧了审计师的个人风险，因此，作为理性经济人的审计师在法律的威慑下必然也会努力，降低审计风险，但是在我国，会计职业界实际所承受的法律风险仍然较低（刘峰、许菲，2002），再者，我国审计市场总体上并不需要，甚至排斥高质量的审计（Wang et al.，2008），造成我国审计市场的审计质量并不太高（杨德明等，2009）。也就是说，在我国，审计师没有太大的激励去付出更多的努力。可是，他们的不够努力可能会受到来自其他非司法方面的处罚，如中注协的处罚，在这种情景下，我国审计师为了避免这些行政类的处罚，需要得到一定程度的风险溢价。基于以上分析，我们提出假设 1 和假设 1a 如下：

假设 1：在其他条件相同的情况下，危机型安全漏洞或者高危型安全漏洞发生的频度与审计风险呈显著正相关。

假设1a：在其他条件相同的情况下，危机型安全漏洞或者高危型安全漏洞发生的频度与审计风险溢价呈显著正相关。

由于中危型和低危型的安全漏洞破坏力较小，产生的负面影响也小，大众媒体就没有激励去报道这些安全漏洞，这些安全漏洞也只是偶尔在一些专业媒体上会提及，造成这些漏洞反而容易被忽视，即使补丁程序或者是更新程序已经出现，许多用户会因为各种原因未及时修补这些看似不起眼的安全漏洞。有些是因为内部控制系统的补丁程序或是更新程序具有一定的副作用，导致内部控制系统的正常运行受到一定程度的影响，而这些中危型和低危型的安全漏洞的危害并没有产生实质性的影响，因此没有得到及时的修补；有些是因为某些中危型和低危型的安全漏洞破坏力较小，不需要安装补丁程序；否则安装了不需要安装的补丁程序，不但浪费系统资源，还有可能导致系统崩溃，影响内部控制的正常运转。

因此，我们认为鉴于中危型和低危型的安全漏洞的危害程度较低，它们的发现，意味着内部控制的缺陷被暴露的概率不大且暴露的内部控制缺陷的严重程度偏小，这些不严重的内部控制缺陷只会稍微增加企业的控制风险、固有风险和（或者）信息风险。根据审计风险模型，当企业的内部控制的缺陷严重性较小时，控制风险和固有风险增加的幅度也较小。审计师如果不减少检查风险，根据审计师风险模型，其个人的审计师风险增幅也不大，这样，由于在我国，公司的内部控制信息自愿性披露激励不足，内部控制自我评价以及审计师的核实评价缺乏统一的标准（杨有红和汪薇，2008），同时在我国对于高质量的审计需要不足（Wang et al.，2008），我国审计市场不成熟（杨德明等，2009），客户压力大（辛清泉和黄琨，2009），我国特有的ST制度以及我国法律执行不力（陈正林，2006）等，都导致了审计师在面对客户的控制风险和固有风险增幅不大时，降低检查风险的激励不大，因此，仍然维持在以前的努力水平上。由于我国经济仍处于转型时期，政府在经济发展中依然起着主要的作用；我国上市公司大部分是国有企业且国有股所占比例较高；我国会计师事务所大部分是经改制而来的且改制前大多为国有的；改制后，会计师事务所与政府部门和国有企业之间仍保持着密切的联系（吴联生、刘慧龙，2008）。

根据审计师风险模型可知，尽管伍利娜等（2010）认为，2003年1月9日，最高法院颁布的《关于审理证券市场因虚假陈述引发的民事赔偿案件的若干规定》提高了审计师的法律风险，但是由于伍利娜等（2010）采用的样本期为2002年1月—2003年1月，为该法律刚刚出台还无法考察该法规的执行效率，只是表明市场的预期以及我国审计市场的问题非常严重，且该文采用的样本期过短，存在一定的噪声，到目前为止，该法律的颁布实施到现在已经有近8年之久，目前还没有看到我国的审计师事务所因为触犯该法律而受到惩罚。陈正林（2006）研究也发现，由于在我国实行“谁主张、谁举证”的制度，中小投资者因诉讼周期长、举证难和预期收益低等问题以及现有的惩罚制度威慑力不够导致监督失效，并且行政处罚的震慑作用也并不明显。因此，在我国，审计市场的制度风险总体水平较低，法律风险近乎于零（刘峰、许菲，2002）。审计师依然我行我素，中国的审计市场依然没有大的改观。

总之，在面对固有风险和控制风险增幅较小和我国特有的制度背景下，审计师没有激励去控制检查风险。由于中危型的安全漏洞和低危型的安全漏洞几乎很难被利用，因此，对于这种安全漏洞的危害程度不需要收取风险溢价。基于此，提出假设2、假设2a和假设2b如下：

假设2：在其他条件相同的情况下，中危型安全漏洞或低危型安全漏洞发生的频度与审计风险呈显著负相关。

假设2a：在其他条件相同的情况下，中危型安全漏洞或低危型安全漏洞发生的频度与审计溢价呈显著负相关。

（二）研究设计

本文采用审计意见作为衡量审计风险的代理变量。本文参照Chen et al.（2010）的做法，对不同的审计意见类型进行不同的编码赋值，即当审计意见为标准无保留意见，设为4，当审计意见为无保留意见加事项段时，设为3；当审计意见为保留意见时，设为2；当审计意见为保留意见加事项段时，设为1；当审计意见为无法发表意见时，设为0。同时本文借鉴伍利娜（2003），Lennox（2005）以及刘继红（2010）的做法，设定模型（3）如下：

$$\begin{aligned}AuditType_{it} = {} & \alpha+\beta_1 Vul_t+\beta_2 Vul_t\times Big4_{ijt}+\beta_3 Big4_{ijt}+\beta_4 State_{it}+\beta_5 Loss_{it} \\ & +\beta_6 Cash_{it}+\beta_7 ROA_{it}+\beta_8 Leverage_{it}+\beta_9 lnSize_{it}+\beta_{10} Growth_{it} \\ & +\beta_{11} Right_{it}+\beta_{12} List_{it}+\sum year+\sum industry+\varepsilon_{it} \qquad (3)\end{aligned}$$

模型（3）中的变量的定义见表1。其中，Vul_t为第t年的安全漏洞情况，包括危急型安全漏洞的发现频率、高危型安全漏洞的发现频率、中危型安全漏洞的发现频率和低危型安全漏洞的发现频率。

为了测度审计师面对不同的审计风险时的行为，我们参照Hogan和Wilkins（2008）的做法，采用审计收费作为度量审计师面对风险的风险溢价或者付出努力的代理变量。同时，参考王守海、杨亚军（2009）和伍利娜（2003）对国内审计收费研究的做法，采用审计收费的自然对数作为因变量。设定审计收费模型（4）如下：

$$\begin{aligned}LnAuditFee_{ijt} = {} & \alpha+\beta_1 Vul_t+\beta_2 Vul_t\times Top5_{ijt}+\beta_8 State_{ijt}+\beta_9 LnAsset_{ijt} \\ & +\beta_{10} Top5_{ijt}+\beta_{11} Loss_{ijt}+\beta_{12} Opinion_{ijt}+\beta_{13} Right_{ijt}+\beta_{14} List_{ijt} \\ & +\beta_{15} Risk_{ijt}+\beta_{16} Leverage_{ijt}+\beta_{17} ROE_{ijt}+\sum year+\sum industry+\varepsilon_{ijt} \qquad (4)\end{aligned}$$

模型（4）中的变量的定义见表2。其中，Vul_t为自变量，其定义见表1。

表1　**模型（3）中的变量定义表**

变量名	变量说明
因变量	
$AuditType_{it}$	审计意见类型，用0~4分别表示
自变量	
$perdanger_t$	危急型安全漏洞的发生频率，危急型安全漏洞占总安全漏洞之比
$perHharm_t$	高危型安全漏洞的发生频率，高危型安全漏洞占总安全漏洞之比
$perMharm_t$	中危型安全漏洞的发生频率，中危型安全漏洞占总安全漏洞之比
$perLharm_t$	低危型安全漏洞的发生频率，低危型安全漏洞占总安全漏洞之比
控制变量	
$Big4_{ijt}$	审计事务所是否为“四大”事务所，是为1，否为0
$State_{ijt}$	上市公司是否为国有控股公司，是为1，否为0
ROA_{ijt}	资产回报率，净利润与总资产之比
$Cash_{ijt}$	现金的期末余额，经总资产标准化
$Loss_{ijt}$	是否亏损，如果前一年度公司亏损，则等于1，否则等于0
$lnSize_{ijt}$	上市公司的规模，等于总资产的自然对数
$Right_{ijt}$	配股达线区间，本年度6%<ROE≤7%，则为1，否则为0
$Listed_{ijt}$	保资格区间，本年度0<ROE≤2%，则为1，否则为0
$Growth_{ijt}$	上市公司的成长性，营业总收入的增长率
$Leverage_{ijt}$	财务杠杆，等于总负债与年初总资产之比
year	年度控制变量
industry	行业控制变量

表2　**模型（4）中的变量定义表**

变量名	变量说明
因变量	
$LnAuditFee_{ijt}$	审计收费的自然对数
控制变量	
$State_{ijt}$	上市公司是否为国有控股公司，是为1，否为0
$LnAsset_{ijt}$	总资产，当年总资产的自然对数
$Top5_{ijt}$	排名前5大的事务所，排名前5大的为1，否则为0
$Loss_{ijt-1}$	是否亏损，如果前一年度公司亏损，则等于1，否则等于0
$Opinion_{ijt}$	审计收费，公司当年被出具非标准审计收费为1，否则为0
$Right_{ijt}$	配股达线区间，本年度6%<ROE≤7%则为1，否则为0
$Listed_{ijt}$	保资格区间，本年度0<ROE≤2%则为1，否则为0
$Risk_{ijt}$	公司风险，等于当年的应收账款与存货之和与当年总资产之比
$Leverage_{ijt}$	财务杠杆，等于总负债与期末总资产之比
ROE_{ijt}	净资产收益率，等于本期净利润与本期期初所有者权益合计之比

四、样本选择与描述统计

（一）审计风险

本文的上市公司的所属的行业、财务数据和安全漏洞数据分别来源于2005—2009年Sinofin数据库，CSMAR财务数据库和中国国家安全漏洞库。剔除金融企业的数据和有缺失值的样本公司，同时，为了避免极端值的影响，我们对控制变量中的连续变量按照1%进行Winsorize处理，最后得到7 131个有效样本。样本的描述统计见表3：

表3 **审计风险样本的描述统计表**

变量	均值	中位数	标准差	最大值	最小值
newaudittype	3.842	4	0.608	4	0
perdanger	6.439	6.729	0.995	7.408	4.727
perHharm	6.640	8.031	4.645	11.367	0.325
perMharm	80.750	79.544	3.656	86.091	77.330
perLharm	6.171	5.118	1.932	9.307	4.534
state	0.637	1	0.481	1	0
top4	0.066	0	0.248	1	0
lose	0.144	0	0.351	1	0
cash	0.054	0.052	0.084	0.297	−0.216
ROA	0.036	0.032	0.092	0.376	−0.329
lev	0.572	0.553	0.290	2.077	0.078
lnsize	21.422	21.337	1.178	24.943	18.601
growth	1.238	1.108	0.912	7.837	0.087
right	0.045	0	0.206	1	0
listed	0.115	0	0.319	1	0

从表3可知，根据中国国家安全漏洞库的危害等级，分为危急型、高危型、中危型和低危型四类。危急型安全漏洞的发生频度（perdanger）的均值为6.439，中位数为6.729，中位数和均值较接近，最大值为7.408，最小值为4.727，这也表明危急型的安全漏洞在2005—2009年年度内，发生比较频繁，并且在年度之间发生的差异较大；高危型安全漏洞占总安全漏洞之比（perHharm）的均值为6.640，中位数为8.031，最大值为11.367，最小值为0.325，这表明高危型的安全漏洞在年度之间差异很大；中危型安全漏洞占总安全漏洞之比（perMharm）的均值为80.750，中位数为79.544，中位数和均值较接近，最大值为86.091，最小值为77.330，这表明中危型的安全漏洞在年度之间分布比较均匀；低危型安全漏洞占总安全漏洞之比（perLharm）的均值为6.171，中位数为5.118，中位数和均值较接近，最大值为9.307，最小值为4.534，这表明低危型的安全漏洞在年度之间分布比较均匀。

表4描述的是审计风险各变量之间的Pearson/Spearman的相关系数矩阵（为了节省篇幅，只列出主要部分），表的左下角为Pearson的相关系数，右上角为Spearman的相关系数。从表3可知，审计风险（audittype）与危急型安全漏洞发生频度（perdanger），高危型安全漏洞频度（perHharm），呈显著负相关；与中危型安全漏洞频度（perMharm），低危型的安全漏洞频度（perLharm），呈显著正相关。

表4　　**审计风险的相关系数表**

	newaudittype	perdanger	perHharm	perMharm	perLharm
audittype	1	0.053 ***	0.067 ***	−0.058 ***	−0.066 ***
perdanger	0.067 ***	1	0.569	−0.889	−0.808 ***
perHharm	0.082 ***	0.833 ***	1	−0.794	−0.875 ***
perMharm	−0.077 ***	−0.905 ***	−0.981 ***	1	0.919 ***
perLharm	−0.086 ***	−0.804 ***	−0.977 ***	0.932 ***	1

注：*** 、** 、* 分别表示检验在1%、5%、10%水平上显著，下同。

（二）审计收费

上市公司所属的行业、财务数据和安全漏洞数据分别来源于2005—2009年Sinofin数据库，CSMAR财务数据库，中国国家安全漏洞库和中国注册会计师协会发布的年度会计师事务所综合评价前百家信息。剔除金融企业的数据，有缺失值的样本公司以及双重审计的样本公司，同时，为了避免极端值的影响，我们对控制变量中的连续变量按照1%进行Winsorize处理，最后得到5 277个有效样本。样本的描述统计见表5。

表5　　**审计收费的样本描述统计表**

变量	均值	中位数	标准差	最大值	最小值
lnfee	13.090	13.017	0.537	14.907	11.918
perdanger	6.450	6.729	0.978	7.408	4.727
perHharm	6.761	8.031	4.678	11.367	0.325
perMharm	80.646	79.544	3.657	86.091	77.330
perLharm	6.143	5.118	1.944	9.307	4.534
state	0.626	1	0.484	1	0
ROE	0.061	0.069	0.266	1.067	−1.358
risk	0.277	0.253	0.177	0.783	0.003
lev	0.572	0.548	0.333	2.575	0.049
loss	0.142	0.000	0.349	1.000	0.000
lnasset	21.351	21.298	1.116	24.407	18.367
opinion	0.082	0	0.275	1	0
top5	0.095	0	0.293	1	0
right	0.047	0	0.213	1	0
listed	0.105	0	0.307	1	0

从表5中，我们可以得到与表3一致的描述统计结果。

表6描述的是审计收费与各变量之间的Pearson/Spearman的相关系数矩阵（为了节省篇幅，只列出主要部分），表的左下角为Pearson的相关系数，右上角为Spearman的相关系数。从表3可知，审计费用（lnauditfee）与危急型安全漏洞发生频度（perdanger），高危型安全漏洞频度（perHharm），呈显著正相关；与中危型安全漏洞频度（perMharm），低危型的安全漏洞频度（perLharm），呈显著负相关。

表6 **审计收费的相关系数表**

	lnauditfee	perdanger	perHharm	perMharm	perLharm
lnauditfee	1	0.112 ***	0.167 ***	-0.140 ***	-0.154 ***
perdanger	0.125 ***	1	0.550 ***	-0.890 ***	-0.813 ***
perHharm	0.169 ***	0.830 ***	1	-0.776 ***	-0.853 ***
perMharm	-0.161 ***	-0.903 ***	-0.981 ***	1	0.923 ***
perLharm	-0.167 ***	-0.802 ***	-0.978 ***	0.934 ***	1

五、检验结果

(一) 样本回归结果

根据相关系数的分析以及研究设计，分别将各类安全漏洞的发生频度逐个放入回归方程进行检验。表7报告了模型（3）的logistic回归结果，表8报告了模型（4）的OLS回归结果。

表7的模型1报告的是危急型的安全漏洞发生频度（perdanger）与审计风险之间的回归结果，模型3报告的是高危型的安全漏洞发生频度（perHharm）与审计风险之间的回归结果。表7的模型1和模型3的自变量的系数都显著为正，这表明危急型的安全漏洞发生频度或者高危型的安全漏洞发生频度越高，审计风险（audittype）越大。

表8的模型1报告的是危急型的信息安全漏洞发生频度（perdanger）与审计收费之间的回归结果，模型3报告的是高危型的信息安全漏洞发生频度（perHharm）与审计收费之间的回归结果。表8的模型1和模型3的自变量的系数都显著为正，这表明危急型的安全漏洞发生频度或者高危型的安全漏洞发生频度越高，审计收费（lnauditfee）越高，即高危害型安全漏洞越多，审计收费越高。假设1得到了验证。

综合表7的模型1和模型3以及表8的模型1和模型3，我们可知，由于危急型的安全漏洞发生频度或者高危型的安全漏洞发生频度越高，内部控制缺陷被暴露得越明显，其危害程度也陡增，即加剧了企业的控制风险，固有风险和信息风险，审计师面临的制度风险也陡增，审计师为了控制其个人的风险，必然对这种风险进行溢价，即增加审计收费，以平衡审计风险。假设1a得到了验证。

表7的模型2报告的是危急型的安全漏洞发生频度与“四大”的交乘项（big4*perdanger）与审计风险之间的回归结果，模型4报告的是高危型的安全漏洞发生频度与“四大”的交乘项（big4*perHharm）与审计风险之间的回归结果。表7的模型2和模型4的自变量的系数都为负，但不显著，这表明“四大”在面对危急型的安全漏洞或者高危型的安全漏洞发生频度越高时，审计

风险没有发生显著变化，表明“四大”具有很好地应对安全漏洞发生频率所导致的审计风险的提升的能力，能够一直控制住审计风险。

表8的模型2报告的是危急型的安全漏洞发生频度与“四大”的交乘项（big5*perdanger）与审计收费之间的回归结果，模型4报告的是高危型的安全漏洞发生频度与“四大”的交乘项（big5*perHharm）与审计收费之间的回归结果。表8的模型2和模型4的自变量的系数都为负，但不显著，这表明“五大”在面对危急型的安全漏洞或者高危型的安全漏洞发生频度越高时，审计收费没有发生显著变化；也就是说危急型的安全漏洞发生频度或者高危型的安全漏洞发生频度越高，“五大”的审计收费没有发生显著变化。

综合表7的模型2和模型4以及表8的模型2和模型4，我们可知，对于非“四大”的事务所，当面对危急型的安全漏洞或者高危型的安全漏洞发生频度提高时，其审计风险越高，为了对这种风险进行定价，非“五大”的审计费用显著提高，这表明，非“五大”的审计师当面对危急型的安全漏洞或者高危型的安全漏洞发生频度提高时，并没有付出额外的努力，而审计费用的提高，是对这种提高的风险的溢价。

表7的模型5报告的是中危型的安全漏洞发生频度（perMharm）与审计风险的回归结果，模型7报告的是低危型的安全漏洞发生频度（perLharm）与审计风险的回归结果。表7的模型5和模型7的自变量的系数都显著为负，这表明中危型的安全漏洞或者低危型的安全漏洞发生频度越高，审计风险（Audittype）越小；也就是说中危型的安全漏洞发生频度或者低危型的安全漏洞发生频度于审计风险呈显著负相关。假设2得到了验证。

表8的模型5报告的是中危型的安全漏洞发生频度（perMharm）与审计收费的回归结果，模型7报告的是低危型的安全漏洞发生频度（perLharm）与审计收费的回归结果。表8的模型5和表9的模型7的自变量的系数都显著为负，这表明中危型的安全漏洞或者低危型的安全漏洞发生频度越高，审计收费越低；也就是说中危型的安全漏洞发生频度或者低危型的安全漏洞发生频度在所有的安全漏洞里的占比越高，其审计收费越低。假设2a得到了验证。

综合表7的模型5和模型7以及表8的模型5和模型7，我们可知，由于中危型的安全漏洞发生频度或者低危型的安全漏洞发生频度越高，内部控制缺陷被暴露的概率不高且其严重性也不高，在我国特有的制度背景下，审计师不减少检查风险，其审计风险增幅也不大，由于制度风险偏低（刘峰、许菲，2002），因此，整体上审计师风险增幅更低。因此，审计师没有激励对低危害型安全漏洞导致的内部控制缺陷进行控制，也就是审计风险和审计收费都显著降低。

表7的模型6报告的是中危型的安全漏洞发生频度与“四大”的交乘项（big4*perMharm）与审计风险之间的回归结果，模型8报告的是低危型的安全全漏洞发生频度与“四大”的交乘项（big4*perLharm）与审计风险之间的回

归结果。表7的模型6和模型8的自变量的系数都为正，但不显著，这表明“四大”在面对中危型的安全漏洞或者低危型的安全漏洞发生频度越高时，审计风险没有发生显著变化，表明“四大”具有很好地应对安全漏洞发生频率所导致的审计风险的提升的能力，能够一直控制住审计风险。

表8的模型6报告的是中危型的安全漏洞发生频度与“五大”的交乘项（big5*perMharm）与审计收费之间的回归结果，模型8报告的是低危型的安全漏洞发生频度与“五大”的交乘项（big5*perLharm）与审计收费之间的回归结果。表8的模型6和模型8的自变量的系数都为正，但不显著，这表明“四大”在面对中危型的安全漏洞或者低危型的安全漏洞发生频度越高时，审计收费没有发生显著变化。

综合表7的模型6和模型8以及表8的模型6和模型8，我们可知，对于非“五大”的事务所，当面对中危型的安全漏洞或者低危型的安全漏洞发生频度提高时，其审计风险越低，为了对这种风险进行定价，非“五大”的审计费用显著下降。

表7和表8的回归结果，在一定程度上检验了《企业内部控制应用指引》第18号——信息系统中的第三章第十三条中规定：“企业应当综合利用防火墙、路由器等网络设备，漏洞扫描、入侵检测等软件技术以及远程访问安全策略等手段，加强网络安全，防范来自网络的攻击和非法侵入。”

表7的模型2、4、6、8与表8的模型2、4、6、8的回归结果表明，对安全漏洞的足够重视，有助于减少企业的内部控制缺陷，为陈志斌（2007）提出的“应该引入防范嵌入在软件中的漏洞风险的内部控制架构”提供了一个实证证据。

以上研究在一定程度上为Hogan和Wilkins（2008）的研究，识别出了审计收费的提高究竟是由于审计师付出了更多的努力还是审计师没有付出更多的努力而是对内部控制缺陷造成的风险的一种溢价。本文研究发现，在中国市场上，对于非“五大”而言，在面对内部控制缺陷时，提高了审计收费，这种收费是对内部控制缺陷造成的风险的一种溢价。

以上研究表明，为了我国资本市场的健康发展，需要提高内部控制的质量。而对于处在信息生态环境中的企业，在实施内部控制，评价内部控制时，需要如《企业内部控制基本规范》第7条规定那样加强信息技术的使用：“企业应当运用信息技术加强内部控制，建立与经营管理相适应的信息系统，促进内部控制流程与信息系统的有机结合，实现对业务和事项的自动控制，减少或消除人为操纵因素。”同时，我们不可忽视信息技术对于内部控制的负面效应，应该加强企业内部控制中的信息技术的管控和相关专业人员素质的提高。以上研究结果也表明，在我国，审计风险模型和审计师风险模型具有较好的解释力，为了培养良好的审计市场，我们需要加强政策的制度，特别是政策的执行力度。

表 7　　审计风险的回归结果

自变量	模型 1		模型 2		模型 3		模型 4		模型 5		模型 6		模型 7		模型 8	
	系数	Wald	系数	Wald	系数	Wald	系数	Wald	系数	Wald	系数	Wald	系数	Wald	系数	Wald
danger	0. 184	16. 037 ***	0. 193	16. 488 ***												
big4 * danger			-0. 134	0. 506												
perHharm					0. 050	25. 47 ***	0. 052	26. 22 ***								
big4 * hharm							-0. 038	0. 896								
perMharm									-0. 063	25. 35 ***	-0. 066	25. 89 ***				
big4 * Mharm											0. 043	0. 73				
perLharm													-0. 108	21. 75 ***	-0. 114	22. 77 ***
big4 * Lharm															0. 098	1. 05
state	0. 392	15. 915 ***	0. 390	15. 75 ***	0. 413	17. 62 ***	0. 410	17. 31 ***	0. 409	17. 27 ***	0. 406	17. 01 ***	0. 410	17. 4 ***	0. 406	17. 03 ***
top4	0. 197	1. 06	1. 042	0. 75	0. 184	0. 93	0. 416	1. 77	0. 188	0. 97	-3. 305	0. 65	0. 185	0. 93	-0. 438	0. 48
loss	-2. 350	534. 99 ***	-2. 349	534. 49 ***	-2. 341	529. 9 ***	-2. 340	529. 33 ***	-2. 350	534. 2 ***	-2. 349	533. 8 ***	-2. 330	524. 4 ***	-2. 329	523. 6 ***
cash	0. 080	6. 019 **	0. 080	5. 99 **	0. 079	5. 89 **	0. 079	5. 86 **	0. 079	5. 85 ***	0. 079	5. 8 **	0. 080	5. 98 **	0. 080	5. 96 **
ROA	0. 028	4. 913 **	0. 028	4. 91 **	0. 030	5. 55 **	0. 030	5. 61 **	0. 029	5. 48 **	0. 030	5. 5 **	0. 029	5. 32 **	0. 029	5. 38 **
leverage	-0. 058	5. 721 **	-0. 058	5. 74 **	-0. 062	6. 34 **	-0. 062	6. 42 **	-0. 061	6. 27 **	-0. 061	6. 3 **	-0. 060	6. 13 **	-0. 061	6. 2 **
lnsize	0. 660	205. 98 ***	0. 660	205. 96 ***	0. 659	204. 48 ***	0. 659	204. 4 ***	0. 659	204. 3 ***	0. 659	204. 2 ***	0. 660	205. 5 ***	0. 660	205. 5 ***
growth	0. 016	0. 924	0. 016	0. 898	0. 017	1. 067	0. 017	1. 02	0. 017	1. 06	0. 017	1. 02	0. 017	0. 99	0. 016	0. 95
right	0. 124	0. 153	0. 124	0. 152	0. 130	0. 19	0. 127	0. 16	0. 131	0. 17	0. 129	0. 17	0. 127	0. 16	0. 122	0. 15
listed	-0. 255	2. 398	-0. 254	2. 37	-0. 246	2. 23	-0. 246	2. 23	-0. 250	2. 3	-0. 249	2. 29	-0. 243	2. 18	-0. 243	2. 17
year	control		control		control		control		control		control		control		control	
industry	control		control		control		control		control		control		control		control	
LRChiSq	1 255. 828 ***		1 256. 344 ***		1 265. 247 ***		1 266. 134 ***		1 265. 107 ***		1 265. 835 ***		1 261. 315 ***		1 262. 35 ***	
R-Square	0. 1615		0. 1615		0. 1626		0. 1627		0. 1626		0. 1626		0. 1621		0. 1622	
N	7 131		7 131		7 131		7 131		7 131		7 131		7 131		7 131	

表8 审计收费的回归结果

自变量	模型1		模型2		模型3		模型4		模型5		模型6		模型7		模型8	
	系数	T value	系数	T value	系数	T value	系数	T value	系数	T value	系数	T value	系数	T value	系数	T value
Intercept	5.956	47.90***	5.965	47.50***	6.149	51.34***	6.142	51.12***	7.133	39.10***	7.159	38.60***	6.356	51.72***	6.355	51.71***
danger	0.033	5.54***	0.032	5.15***												
big5*danger			0.010	0.5												
Hharm					0.010	7.83***	0.010	7.70***								
big5*Hharm							-0.003	-0.78								
Mharm									-0.011	-7.26***	-0.012	-7.16***				
big5*Mharm											0.004	0.78				
Lharm													-0.024	-8.00***	-0.024	-7.67***
big5*Lharm															0.002	0.16
state	-0.127	-10.34***	-0.127	-10.35***	-0.122	-9.91***	-0.121	-9.87***	-0.123	-10.01***	-0.122	-9.97***	-0.121	-9.91***	-0.121	-9.89***
ROE	0.005	0.18	0.005	0.18	0.002	0.07	0.001	0.06	0.003	0.12	0.003	0.11	0.000	0.01	0.000	0.01
lnasset	-0.027	-0.82	-0.027	-0.82	-0.014	-0.44	-0.014	-0.44	-0.018	-0.54	-0.018	-0.54	-0.013	-0.39	-0.013	-0.39
risk	0.064	3.29***	0.063	3.28***	0.060	3.11***	0.060	3.13***	0.062	3.20***	0.062	3.22***	0.059	3.03***	0.059	3.03***
lev	0.030	1.56	0.030	1.53	0.031	1.57	0.031	1.6	0.029	1.5	0.030	1.53	0.033	1.70*	0.033	1.71*
loss	0.325	56.95***	0.325	56.88***	0.323	56.52***	0.323	56.49***	0.323	56.58***	0.323	56.55***	0.323	56.63***	0.323	56.56***
opinion	0.138	5.45***	0.138	5.45***	0.142	5.64***	0.142	5.64***	0.141	5.59***	0.141	5.58***	0.143	5.66***	0.143	5.66***
big5	0.305	15.50***	0.237	1.73*	0.306	15.57***	0.329	9.22***	0.305	15.54***	-0.031	-0.07	0.307	15.61***	0.297	4.69***
right	0.0003	0.01	0.001	0.02	0.003	0.13	0.003	0.12	0.002	0.09	0.002	0.09	0.004	0.14	0.004	0.14
listed	-0.035	-1.83*	-0.035	-1.83*	-0.033	-1.76**	-0.033	-1.75*	-0.034	-1.80*	-0.034	-1.80*	-0.032	-1.68*	-0.032	-1.68*
F值	413.53***		379.03***		418.85***		383.97***		417.35***		382.59***		419.32***		384.30***	
Adj R-Sq	0.4782		0.4781		0.4814		0.4814		0.4805		0.4805		0.4817		0.4816	
N	4 952		4 952		4 952		4 952		4 952		4 952		4 952		4952	

（二）稳健性分析

以上的研究结论是以安全漏洞的各个类别的占比对于审计风险和信息风险的影响，考察的是一种相对指标的影响。那么，安全漏洞的各个类别的数量对于审计质量的影响又是怎么样的呢？上面的研究结论能否得到有效的支持呢？基于此，进行如下稳健性测试：

不对样本进行 winsorize 处理，再进行回归，结果的研究结论得到了一致的支持。

采用安全漏洞的各个类别的数量分别进行回归，结果的研究结论得到了一致的支持。

对危急性的安全漏洞和高危型的安全漏洞，中危型的安全漏洞和低危型的安全漏洞进行归类，分别进行回归，结果的研究结论得到了一致的支持。

对模型（3）不控制年度和行业，进行回归，结果与上面的一致。

从以上稳健性检验可知，研究结论具有较好的稳健性。

六、研究结论与不足

在日益发展的互联网以及移动互联网的今天，信息安全对于一个国家的重要性毋庸置疑，本文通过考察威胁信息安全的首要因素的安全漏洞，结合审计风险模型和制度经济学的原理构建的审计师风险模型，研究分析了安全漏洞对于我国审计市场的影响。通过采用中国信息安全测评中心借鉴 Microsoft 公司的做法，对安全漏洞的影响范围、利用方式、攻击后果等情况，将安全漏洞分为危急型、高危型、中危型和低危型四个类别。考察了这些不同类别的安全漏洞对于我国上市公司内部控制的技术架构的影响，进而考察对于审计风险和信息风险的影响，研究发现：在其他条件相同的情况下，危机型安全漏洞或者高危型安全漏洞发生的频度与审计风险呈显著正相关；而中危型安全漏洞或低危型安全漏洞发生的频度与审计风险呈显著负相关。在其他条件相同的情况下，对于非“五大”而言，危机型安全漏洞或者高危型安全漏洞发生的频度与审计风险溢价呈显著正相关；对于非“五大”而言，中危型安全漏洞或低危型安全漏洞发生的频度与审计溢价呈显著负相关。

本文的研究为处于信息化生态环境下的企业内部控制，应该引入防范嵌入在企业管理控制软件中的漏洞风险的内部控制架构（陈志斌，2007）提供了一个实证检验，本文的研究也为《企业内部控制应用指引》的实施提供了一个实证证据。Hogan 和 Wilkins（2008）研究发现，内部控制缺陷越严重，审计收费越高，作者认为造成审计收费的提高，有两种可能：一是审计师付出了更多的努力；二是审计师并没有付出更多的努力而是对内部控制缺陷造成的风险的一种溢价。而本文通过考察 IT 技术对于内部控制的影响，研究发现，在中国市场上，由于制度风险偏低，审计师只会在内部控制缺陷非常大的情况下，才会去控制审计风险，同时对于信息风险视而不见，这表明，审计师只是“头痛医头，脚痛医脚”，并没有实质付出更多努力，只是为了避免自己过于成为“出头鸟”的明哲保身的处世策略。Hogan 和 Wilkins（2008）发现的由于内部控制缺陷导致的审计费用（为审计师努力程度的代理变量）的提高，在中国这种新兴资本市场里，并不是对由于审计师努力的报酬，而是对风险的溢价，也即是对自己可能成为“出头鸟”的风险的溢价。

本文的研究也为促进我国资本市场的健康发展，应该加强对于已制定的政策，法律法规的执行力度提供了一个实证证据。而不是像 Chen et al.（2010）的研究那样，过于强调政策的制定。因为在我国特有的制度背景下，仅仅依赖政府的监管，不足以培育出具有真正审计独立性的资本市场（Defond et al.，2000）。而应该加强政策的推行和强有力的实施。

本文的一个不足在于没有考察每个公司实际受到的安全漏洞的威胁，可能存在一定程度的偏颇。另一个不足在于本文只是采用发现的安全漏洞，并没有考察这些发现的安全漏洞修复情况对于审计风险和信息风险的影响。作者的后续研究将围绕这两方面进行展开以及采用最新的数据进一步实证考察 Hogan 和 Wilkins（2008）和 Chen et al.（2010）的研究结论。

主要参考文献

[1] 财政部驻河北省财政监察专员办事处课题组:《会计师事务所审计收费监管制度分析及政策建议》,载《会计研究》,2005(3),11~15 页。

[2] 陈正林:《审计风险、审计师风险及制度风险》,载《审计研究》,2006(3),88~92 页。

[3] 陈志斌:《信息化生态环境下企业内部控制框架研究》,载《会计研究》,2007(1),30~37页。

[4] 方红星、孙翯、金韵韵:《公司特征、外部审计与内部控制信息的自愿披露——基于沪市上市公司 2003—2005 年年报的经验研究》,载《会计研究》,2009(10),44~52 页。

[5] 李享:《美国内部控制实证研究:回顾与启示》,载《会计研究》,2009(1),87~95 页。

[6] 李艳姣:《内部控制质量与审计定价的相关性研究》,暨南大学硕士论文,2009。

[7] 刘峰、许菲:《风险导向型审计·法律风险·审计质量——兼论“五大”在我国审计市场的行为》,载《会计研究》,2002(2),21~27 页。

[8] 刘峰、周福源:《国际四大意味着高审计质量吗?》,载《会计研究》,2007(3),79~87 页。

[9] 刘继红:《高管会计事务所关联、审计任期与审计质量》,北京大学光华管理学院工作论文,2010。

[10] 刘启亮、何威风、罗乐:《IFRS 的强制采用、新法律实施与应计及真实盈余管理》,武汉大学工作论文,2010。

[11] 申慧慧、黄张凯、吴联生:《权分置改革的盈余质量效应》,载《会计研究》,2009(8),40~48 页。

[12] 夏立军:《盈余管理计量模型在中国股票市场的应用研究》,载《中国会计与财务研究》,2003(2),94~154 页。

[13] 辛清泉、黄琨:《监管政策、审计意见和审计师谨慎性》,载《中国会计与财务研究》,2009(1),90~121 页。

[14] 杨德明、胡婷:《内部控制、盈余管理与审计意见》,载《审计研究》,2010(5),90~97 页。

[15] 杨德明、林斌、王彦超:《内部控制、审计质量与大股东资金占用》,载《审计研究》,2009(5),74~81 页。

[16] 杨有红、汪薇:《2006 年沪市公司内部控制信息披露研究》,载《会计研究》,2008(3),35~43 页。

[17] 王守海、杨亚军:《内部审计质量与审计收费研究——基于中国上市公司的证据》,载《审计研究》,2009(5),63~73 页。

[18] 伍利娜:《审计定价影响因素研究——来自中国上市公司首次审计收费披露的证据》,载《中国会计评论》,2003(1),113~128 页。

[19] 伍利娜、郑晓博、岳衡:《审计赔偿责任与投资者利益保护——审计保险假说在新兴资本市场上的检验》,载《管理世界》,2010(3),32~43 页。

[20] 伍利娜、朱春艳:《股权分置改革的审计治理效应》,载《审计研究》,2010(5),73~81 页。

[21] 吴联生、刘慧龙:《中国审计实证研究:1999—2007》,载《审计研究》,2008(2),36~46 页。

[22] 吴炎太、林斌、孙烨:《基于生命周期的信息系统内部控制风险管理研究》,载《审计研究》,2008(6),87~92 页。

[23] 晏艳阳、赵大玮:《我国股权分置改革中内幕交易的实证研究》,载《金融研究》,2006(4),101~108 页。

[24] 中国国家安全漏洞库,2010-07-22,http://www.cnnvd.org.cn/2010/0722/191.html。

[25] 杨谷:《信息安全国家漏洞库建成》,载《光明日报》,2009-10-25,http://www.gmw.cn/content/2009-10/25/content_998321.htm。

[26] 张涛、吴冲:《信息系统安全漏洞研究》,载《哈尔滨工业大学学报(社会科学版)》,2008(4),71~76 页。

[27] 中国信息安全测评中心漏洞通报,2010-06-08,http://www.itsec.gov.cn/aqld/ldtb/index.htm。

[28] Allen, F., J. Qian. M. J. Qian, Law, Finance, and Economic Growth in China, Journal of Financial Economics, 77, 2005, pp. 57-116.

[29] American Institute of Certified Public Accountants (AICPA), Statement on Auditing Standards No. 47, Audit Risk and Materiality in Conducting An Audit, New York, AICPA., 1983.

[30] Andrew J. Leone, Factors Related to Internal Control Disclosure: A Discussion of Ashbaugh, Collins and Kinney (2007) and Doyle, Ge, and McVay (2007), Journal of Accounting and Economics, Sep, 2007, pp. 224-237.

[31] Arbaugh W. A., Fithen L. W. Mehugh J., Windows of Vulnerability: A Case Study Analysis, IEEE Computer, 33(12), 2000, pp. 52-59.

[32] Ashbaugh-Skaife, H., Collins, D., Kinney, W., The Discovery and Reporting of Internal Control Deficiencies Prior to SOX-mandated Audits, Journal of Accounting and Economics, 44, 2007, pp. 166-192.

[33] Barth, M., W. Landsman, and M. Lang, International Accounting Standards and Accounting Quality, Journal of Accounting Research, 46: 2008, pp. 467-498.

[34] Bedard, J., Sarbanes Oxley Internal Control Requirements and Earnings Quality, Working Paper, Laval University, 2006.

[35] Berenson, A., The Number: How the Drive for Quarterly Earnings Corrupted Wall Street, New York, NY: Random House, 2003, p. 225.

[36] C., Lennox, Audit Quality and Executive Officers' Affiliations with CPA Firms, Journal of Accounting and Economics, 39, 2005, 201-231.

[37] Chan K. C., Barbara R. Farrell and Picheng Lee, Earnings Management and Return-Earnings Association of Firms Reporting Material Internal Control Weaknesses Under Section 404 of the Sarbanes-Oxley Act, Working Paper Series. http://papers. ssrn. com, 2005.

[38] D. A. Cohen, A. Dey and T. Z. Lys, Real and Accrual-Based Earnings Management in the Pre-and Post-Sarbanes-Oxley Periods. The Accounting Review, 83, 2008, pp. 757-787.

[39] DeAngelo, L., Auditor Size and Audit Quality, Journal of Accounting and Economics, 3, 1981 pp. 183-199.

[40] Dechow, P. M., R. G. Sloan, and A. P. Sweeney, Detecting Earnings Management, The Accounting Review, 70 (2), 1995, pp. 193-225.

[41] Doyle, J., Ge, W., McVay, S., Determinants of Weaknesses in Internal Control over Financial Reporting, Journal of Accounting and Economics, 44, 2007a., pp. 193-223.

[42] Douglas F. Prawitt. Jason L. Smith. David A. Wood, Internal Audit Quality and Earnings Management, Working Paper, Marriott School of Management, Brigham Young University, 2008.

[43] Francis, J., R. LaFond, P. Olsson, and K. Schipper, The Market Pricing of Accruals Quality, Journal of Accounting and Economics 39 (2), 2005, pp. 295-327.

[44] Ge, W., and S. McVay, The Disclosure of Material Weaknesses in Internal Control after the Sarbanes-Oxley Act, Accounting Horizons 19 (3), 2005, pp. 137-58.

[45] Jeffrey T Doyle, Weili Ge, Sarah McVay, Accruals Quality and Internal Control over Financial Reporting, The Accounting Review, 82(5), 2007b, pp. 1141-1170.

[46] Jennifer Altamuro, Anne Beatty, How does Internal Control Regulation Affect Financial Reporting? Journal of Accounting and Economics, 49, 2010, pp. 58-74.

[47] Jumratjaroenvanit A., Teng-amnuay Y., Probability of Attack Based on System Vulnerability Lifecycle, International Journal of Intelligent Information Technology Application, 2008, pp. 24-29.

[48] LaPorta, Rafael, Florencio Lopez-de-Silanes, Andrei Shleifer, and Robert Vi shny, Legal Determinants of External Finance, Journal of Finance, 52, 1997, pp. 1131-1150.

[49] LaPorta, Rafael, Florencio Lopez-de-Silanes, Andrei Shleifer, Corporate Ownershi p around the World, Journal of Finance, 54, 1999, pp. 471-517.

[50] LaPorta, Rafael, Florencio Lopez-de-Silanes, Andrei Shleifer, Robert Vishny, Investor Protection and Corporate Governance, Journal of Financial Economics, 58, 2000, pp. 3-28.

[51] Li, C. , Three Essays on the Effect of the Sarbanes-Oxley Act of 2002 on the Audit Environment, Doctoral Dissertation, University of Kansas, 2007.

[52] Mark L. DeFond, T. J. Wong and Shuhua Li, The Impact of Improved Auditor Independence on Audit Market Concentration in China, Journal of Accounting and Economics, 28, 2000, pp. 269-305.

[53] Mei Feng, Chan Li, Sarah McVay, Internal Control and Management Guidance, Journal of Accounting and Economics, 48, 2009, pp. 190-209.

[54] Hollis Ashbaugh-Skaife, Daniel W Collins, William R Kinney Jr. , Ryan LaFond, The Effect of SOX Internal Control Deficiencies and Their Remediation on Accrual Quality, The Accounting Review, 83(1), 2008, pp. 217-250.

[55] Healy, P. M. , and J . M. Wahlen, A Review of the Earnings Management Literature and its Implications for Standards Setting, Accounting Horizons, 13 (4), 1999, pp. 365-383.

[56] Hogan, C. , Wilkins, M. , Evidence on the Audit Risk Model: Do Auditors Increase Audit Fees in the Presence of Internal Control Deficiencies? Contemporary Accounting Research 25, 2008, pp. 219-242.

[57] Jones, J. , Earnings Management during Import Relief Investigations, Journal of Accounting Research. 29 (2), 1991, pp. 193-228.

[58] Krishnan, J. , Audit Committee Quality and Internal Control: An Empirical Analysis, The Accounting Review, 80, 2005. pp. 649-675.

[59] Krsul I. , Software Vulnerability Analysis, West Lafayette: Department of Computer Science, Purdue University, 1998.

[60] Leuz, C. , D. Nanda, and P. D. Wys ocki, Earnings Management and Investor Protection: An International Comparison on, Journal of Financial Economics, 69 (3), 2003, pp. 505-527.

[61] Mitehell F. , Sarbanes Oxley Section 404: Can Material Weakness be Predicted and Modeled? An Examination of the Variables of the ZETA Model in Prediction of Material Weakness, Doctoral dissertation, Walden University, 2005.

[62] Raghunandan K. and Rama D. V. , SOX Section 404 Material Weakness Disclosures and Audit Fees, Auditing, A Journal Practice & Theory, 25(1), 2006, pp. 99-114.

[63] Shimin Chen, Sunny Y. J. Sun, Donghui Wu, Client Importance, Institutional Improvements, and Audit Quality in China: An Office and Individual Auditor Level Analysis, The Accounting Review, 1, 2010, pp. 127-158.

[64] Tang, A. , Xu, L. , Institutional Ownership, Internal Control Material Weakness and Firm Performance, Working Paper, Morgan State University, 2007.

[65] Yan Y. C. , Associations between SOX 404 Opinions and Auditors, audit committees, and executives, Florida International University, 2007.

[66] Wang, Q. , T. J. Wong, and L. Xia State ownership, the Institutional Environment, and Auditor Choice: Evidence from China, Journal of Accounting and Economic, 46, 2008, pp. 112-134.

[67] Wilson, J. Q. , and G. L. Kelling, Broken Windows: The Police and Neighborhood Safety, Atlantic Monthly 249 (3), 1982, pp. 29-38.

深圳市交通运输委员会内部控制体系建设的探索与实践

孙远忱[1]　马妍[2]

（1. 深圳市交通运输委员会财务审计处　广东深圳　518040；
2. 中国内部控制研究中心　辽宁大连　116025）

摘　要　近年来我国政府部门风险频发，凸显出政府部门内部控制之薄弱。如何构建我国政府部门内部控制体系已经成为一个社会关注的重要课题。相对于企业内部控制，政府部门由于业务活动的特殊性与复杂性，其内部控制建设的研究更需要引起重视和投入力量。此次，深圳市交通运输委员会作为先行者，对政府部门内部控制体系建设进行了积极探索和有益实践，希望为我国行政事业单位内部控制规范和相关指引的制定提供参考，并为行政事业单位推行内部控制体系建设工作提供借鉴和经验。

关键词　政府部门　内部控制　预算管理　资金管控

一、深圳市交通运输委员会建设内部控制体系的动因

2009年8月，深圳市政府实行大部制改革，组建了深圳市交通运输委员会（以下简称“深交委”），率先在全国实现了真正意义上的“一城一交”的综合交通运输体系。随着大交通体系的全面建立，深交委的外部环境和自身职能正经历着一些深刻的变化。这些变化为深交委的深化改革提供了难得的机遇，同时也对内部管理工作提出了更高的要求。

（一）建立内部控制体系是全面提升政府部门内部管理工作的有效途径

大部制改革的核心是转变政府职能。随着职能的调整，深交委成为一个“大职能、宽领域”的综合管理组织体制，拥有规划、建设、管养、行政审批、行政执法等多项职能。由此，深交委所面临的情形是：管理的业务广，涉及海、陆、空等整个立体式的交通运输管理，审批事项急剧增多；资金规模大，2010年仅部门预算就达到16亿元；涉及的职能部门多，业务流程繁冗复杂。但是，目前深交委的内部管理工作不但难以适应这一变化，一些政府部门固有的管理体制问题反而更加突显出来，具体表现在：

1. 内部管理基础工作薄弱。各部门整合后，原交通局的制度已不再适用，

加之很多新情况、新问题的出现，致使深交委在很多制度和程序上出现“真空”，职责划分不够清晰、业务流程不够规范、相关标准不够明确、制度执行不够严格等问题迅速突显出来，造成大量的审批依赖人为经验进行判断。这些问题的出现不但会耗费管理者的精力，严重阻碍相关工作的顺利进展，更为重要的是，由于无法实现以制度为依据科学决策、按章办事，会带来较大的行政风险。

2. 预算执行缺乏过程控制。首先，资源分配缺乏合理性与有效性。在财政资金的实际流转过程中，预算单位通常需要通过内部批复进行细化的工作安排，来合理体现财政资金的最终用途①，但是，目前的内部预算批复较多地停留在单纯的细化分类阶段，缺乏一个科学机制按照事情的明确程度进行合理、有效的资源分配，虽然预算指标最终也分解到了各二级处室，但却存在以下问题：一是资源分配没有落实到具体任务的责任部门、直接责任人。职责不明确导致出现问题后互相推诿，财务部门干着急，不但直接影响“问责制”发挥作用，也反映了“全员控制”的失效。二是财权与事权的匹配缺少科学的标准判断，严重依赖财务管理者个人的经验和判断。一项具体任务的执行究竟需要多少资金进行匹配才算合理、“三公”费用如何配置才不会出现浪费等成为关系到财政资金使用效率的重要问题。其次，经费支出管控缺乏有效手段。财务部门虽然最终通过严格的会计核算对资金支出过程进行了记录和反馈，但是这种事后监督手段并不能有效管控到其中经济行为的发生是否合规，尤其对于那些金额没有超出预算金额的经济行为，财务部门仅凭审核单据很难有效判断其在预算执行过程中是否改变资金用途、经济行为是否合法、合规，甚至还会出现一个指标什么费用都往里装、行政费用挤占业务费用等现象，最终造成了“吃饭的钱多、干事的钱少”，严重影响了财政资金的信息真实性和政府部门形象。

3. 管理手段与大交通体系工作形成矛盾。深交委本身具有“体大、量多、事杂”的特点，而以手工记账为主的管理手段已远远满足不了大交通体系的管理要求。领导要取得一个重要的决策数据，通常要由工作人员忙碌很长时间才能得到，会计信息的传递严重滞后，而且数据的准确性还很低，严重影响了决策质量。

深化政府部门内部管理工作绝不是简单地等同于制度堆砌和汇编，而是在于建立健全有效的内部控制体系，确保经济行为的合规性和真实性，以及实现资源配置的合理性与有效性。一方面，按照内控原则、要求和方法全面梳理、整合经济行为领域的各项管理制度，建立和完善各项标准，优化业务流程等，

---

① 政府部门通常在财政年度初或上年末提交财政预算编制，由于这一编制属于事前计划，因此不论其内容细化到什么程度，通常都需要财务部门通过内部预算批复将财政预算批复的结果进一步落实。

才能做到以制度为依据科学决策、按章办事；另一方面，通过内控机制的建立，由事后处理转变为事前防范、事中控制、事后监督，才有可能确保对资金支出实施有效管控。同时，配合信息化系统进行程序化管理，从而真正实现政府部门从“人治”向“法治”的转变。

（二）建立内部控制体系是政府部门防范风险的重要举措

审批事项多、资金盘子大、风险点增多的内部环境变化不但造成深交委内部管理难度与强度剧增，也为其廉政建设工作带来了更大挑战。深交委所处的交通运输业本身就是一个特殊的行业，具有资金链长、涉及范围广、业务难度大和未知因素多等诸多特点。而大部制改革后，深交委仅2010年大、小建设项目合计就达400多项，需政府采购的事项高达486个。从全国交通部门出现的腐败案件来看，尤其是在工程项目采购、招投标及建设环节出现腐败问题的案例不胜枚举，此前铁道部部长在高铁建设项目中的腐败落马再次印证了交通部门是高风险领域。

健全有效的内部控制体系，被实践证明不仅是企业防范风险的“防火墙”，而且是政府部门提高拒腐防变和抵御风险能力的重要举措。正如胡锦涛总书记“在庆祝中国共产党成立90周年大会上的讲话”中所指出：“必须始终把制度建设贯穿党的思想建设、组织建设、作风建设和反腐倡廉建设之中，构建内容协调、程序严密、配套完备、有效管用的制度体系。”通过开展深交委内部控制体系建设，规范相关业务流程与审批权限，有效弥补制度缺陷和管理上的薄弱环节，形成一套事前、事中、事后相结合的控制体系，既是打造“制度化、责任化、高效率”阳光政府工作部门的需要，也是形成一个有效的“免疫系统”，保护干部队伍的重要举措。

（三）建立内部控制体系是政府部门适应外部环境发展变化的必然选择

与此同时，外部环境也对政府部门的财政资金管理提出了更高要求。近年来，公民的“知情权”越来越被认为是一种神圣的权利，“阳光财政”、“透明政府”等一系列新的理念逐渐为民众所认同。媒体的监督力量被网络空前地释放出来，对政府部门如何保障纳税人权益越来越关注，人大、政协对于监督“三公”费用的积极参政议政也得到民众支持。在这一趋势下，国家对包括财政预算、专项资金等政府信息的公开提出了更高的要求。“十二五纲要”明确指出：“要完善预算编制和执行管理制度，强化预算支出约束和预算执行监督，健全预算公开机制，增强预算透明度。”而中央政府推出从中央到地方“三公”经费全公开的时间表，也是顺应民意的举措。将政府信息置于公开、透明的阳光下，是通过满足公众的知情权进而实现社会的监督权，最大限度地将经费支出压缩在合理范围内，防止暗箱操作以及资金浪费，从而保证纳税人的合法权益。

但是，据有关报道，目前包括“三公费用”在内的政府信息公开现状并不能令公众满意，模棱两可的“其他支出”占了相当大比例，对资金的安排使用缺乏具体的分析与解释。有媒体甚至直接指出，倘若信息公开只是‘笼统公开’、‘模糊公开’乃至‘虚假公开’，与不公开其实相差不远，更遑论有效监督。要做到政府信息公开的细化与真实，根本的一条还是依靠内部控制体系的建立。只有严格自律的方法才能使政府部门“内强素质、外塑形象”。完善的预算管理制度能够对财政资金在科学化的基础上实行精细化管理，为保证预算的详细和规范奠定基础，从而使公众清楚政府用多少钱，办哪些事，怎样用钱；同时，内部控制原理的应用能够提供经费支出约束和预算执行监督机制，从源头上控制和降低行政成本，并防止一些不合理的支出隐身于“其他支出”，从而推动各项财政资金落到实处，真正做到“取之于民，用之于民”。

二、深交委内部控制体系建设的初步实践

深交委对于内部控制体系建设的探索始于2010年7月。当时，前国家财政部会计司刘玉廷司长受邀，为深交委作了题为《非营利组织内部控制建设》的报告。报告所阐述的重要意义为深交委的内部管理工作带来了观念上的革新，更坚定了委领导建设内部控制体系的决心。由此，深交委主要领导以“我要内控”的决心，主动提出借助专家力量，开展深交委内部控制体系建设项目，打造“制度化、责任化、高效率”的阳光政府。2011年3月，由中国内部控制研究中心总负责，北京天健融智管理咨询公司和北京艾图科技开发有限公司为主要成员的“深交委内部控制体系建设项目组”正式组建，探索与实践随即全面展开。通过历时4个月的努力，形成了《深圳市交通运输委员会内部控制手册》、《深圳市交通运输委员会预算管理工作手册》和《深圳市交通运输委会计核算手册》以及全面预算管理信息系统，初步建立了一套具有深交委特色的内部控制体系。下面将对其中主要实践及其初步成效进行介绍。

（一）建立健全重点领域的内部控制规范体系

在深入了解深交委内部管理现实需求的基础上，项目组首先立足于近10年的政府部门实务经验，形成了“以预算管理为主线，以资金管控为核心”的深交委内部控制体系建设的基本框架（如图1所示），并以此指导和推进内部控制规范体系的建设。

按照相关要求，预算必须覆盖至政府部门所有的经济行为，所有经济行为也必须以预算作为支撑，并且为保证政府履行行政管理职能，年度收支预算还有着严格、明确的法定程序。因此，在这一框架中，预算管理作为主线，贯穿于政府部门各个环节的经济活动，一方面衔接了外部法定工作规程，如事前的

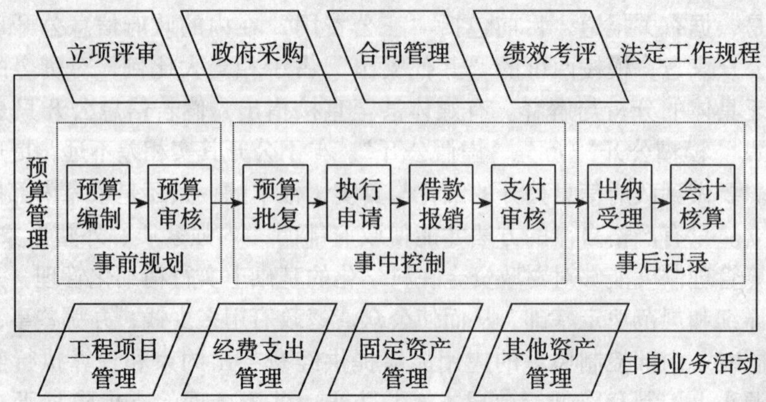

图1　深交委内部控制体系建设框架

立项评审、事中的政府采购和合同管理、事后的绩效考评等。通过内部控制规范体系建设能够确保经济行为符合外部法定的管理要求，并以此为依据合理衔接、细化、完善本单位的内部管理规范，使法律、法规得到贯彻和实施。另一方面衔接了贯穿于预算管理过程中的单位内部自身业务活动，如经费支出、资产管理、工程项目管理、其他资金管理等。对于这些业务活动的内部控制建设核心在于资金管控，因为这些业务活动具有一个共性，即都与资金的取得、使用、管理和分配密切相关，抓住了资金管控这一核心，在一定程度上也抓住了政府部门内部控制的重心和主体，并通过事前规划、事中控制、事后记录三部分，最终形成各环节相互衔接、相互稽核的闭环流程。

围绕这一框架，项目组立足于深交委实际业务情况，针对预算管理、经费支出管理、资产管理、工程项目管理、政府采购管理、专项资金管理、产业财政资助资金管理七大与资金管控密切相关的业务，为深交委进行了内部控制规范建设。

首先，项目组针对七大业务，对以下三个方面内容进行了详细的风险评估：一是制度设计是否合理：重点评估各项制度是否职责明确，是否存在缺失、空白或模糊的领域；二是制度与实际业务流程是否符合：重点评估各项制度是否存在流程断点、是否形成管理闭环；三是各项内部控制制度执行是否有效。通过风险评估，项目组发现，尽管不论是外部监管部门还是深交委自身都颁布和制定了诸多法律法规和内部管理制度。但是，实际上这一制度建设却存在三大问题：制度建设存在缺失和模糊领域、已有的法规和制度执行不到位以及制度之间的衔接出现缺失。针对这三大问题，项目组在方案设计阶段结合深交委自身行业特点，以风险评估为导向，以防范风险、规范管理为目标，明确了业务的主要风险与关键控制点，综合运用各种控制手段，着力规范了业务流程与职责分工，强化制约与监督，并最终形成《深圳市交通运输委员会内部控制手册》，完成了七项业务和四十四个子流程的内部控制规范体系（如图2所示）。

图2　深交委内部控制规范体系图

这一规范体系作为深交委内部控制体系运行的重要规范性文件，有效解决了原先深交委管理制度和标准缺失、弱化、模糊等问题，进一步明确了各部门的职责权限和按流程办事的原则，为职能调整后的大交通体系业务运行提供了系统、翔实又具操作性的制度规范保障。同时，强化了风险防范意识。通过梳理上述七项与资金管控密切相关的重点领域的岗位职责和关键控制点，着力规范了业务流程与职责分工，及时识别、确认了重点领域业务中可能发生的风险，进一步强化了制衡与监督机制，并将控制措施配置于各个业务流程之中，紧紧把控风险关口。这一机制下，各个岗按照规定的程序复核、审验相关业务的合规性、真实性，使相关业务处理实现了依法、规范、高效、透明运转，最终达到管控与高效的双重目的，这对于资金盘子大、风险点增多的大交通体系意义重大。

（二）完成经费支出全过程管控

如前所述，深交委在预算管理中存在缺乏过程控制的问题。为此，项目组为深交委设计了一套经费支出管理模式，以达到对深交委经费支出进行全过程管控的目的。

通常来说，经过同级人大批准后的财政部门年度财政预算批复形成各单位的“财政预算批复结构”。行政事业单位进而负责将财政资金落实到具体经济行为，并通过会计核算工作对经费支出结果进行记录，形成“会计科目结构”。而从财政批复结果到形成会计核算这一过程中，在单位内部要经历确立事由、获取资金、发生经济行为和形成发票等环节。这一过程中经常会发生“预算编制和执行的真实性不符，审核执行不严”等问题①。项目组认为，对

① 刘英来等：《政府内部控制失效溯源》，载《财经》，2007（3），14页。

于这些环节进行过程管控，需要通过内部控制对履行具体职能所需资源的有效性与合理性，以及以此为目的而发生的经济行为的合规性与真实性进行相关的制度设计。

1. 完善内部预算批复，实现财权与事权有效匹配

财政批复口径是按照单位整体职能进行设计的，并按照事项逐一列示例举，但由于预算编制时间较早，所以这一口径并不能做到十分详细。因此，在财政资金的实际流转与运作过程中，预算单位需要进一步进行细化的工作安排，来合理体现财政资金最终的具体用途。但是，目前这种行为尚缺乏科学的机制进行规范。如果没有科学的分类，而只是一味地细化，那么每一个分解后的细项成为一个个独立的事项，对这些事项的一事一议又将高度依赖管理者的经验和判断，而无法进行科学合理的管控。那么，如何设计科学的资源分配机制，就成为现实工作面临的一个重要问题。为解决这一问题，项目组在原有的两大结构中增设了“内部预算批复结构”，在合理衔接法定功能科目的基础上，进一步将预算管理目标和责任按照科学化和精细化的标准层层分解和落实。这一分解和落实标准就是：每一个事项都有其属性，而每类属性都有其相对应的合理管控方式。因此，先按事务的属性先进行科学分类，再进行合理细化，就是一个相对合理的资源分配机制。由此，项目组按照深交委预算执行过程中的事项性质（金额是否可预计与支出方向是否明确），将经济行为预先分为四大类，并根据每类事项的特点制定了相应的管控措施。经过分类管控后，除极小一部分属于需要领导临时评判，其他均有明确的控制手段。即使那些需要临时评判的事情，由于范围已经被界定，评判难度也相应降低。同时，为形成有效的责任传递机制，项目组将内部预算批复的设计一直延伸到责任部门、具体项目、具体责任人的落实，责任到人，责任到岗，形成了协调配合、相互制衡的工作机制。

通过“内部预算批复结构”的设计，可以实现内、外资源的对接与层层细化，并形成有效的责任机制，达到财权与事权的精确匹配，从而在充分保障各单位事业发展目标的基础上，节约和压缩不必的经费支出，实现资源的有效配置。对领导而言，职责更加清晰，管理重点更加明确；对财务管理者而言，资源分配与任务责任人更加明晰；对执行层管理者而言，能够及时明确年度任务分配，便于各处室及早安排相关工作，有效保障年度目标的实现。

2. 设计经费支出管控规则，实现执行与审批有效分离

在细化的预算范围之下，并不一定能保证其中经济行为的发生一定合规。例如，在日常借款报销和财务审核过程中，经常面临问题就是某个发票并没有超出所属的职能范围，金额也没有超出预算，但是这一经济行为并不一定得到了有效控制。因此，为将管控措施进一步延续到经济行为，项目组在内部批复结构的基础上增设了“经费支出结构”。经费支出结构是在对政府部门经费活动进行分类与分析的基础上，对履行其职能的经济活动的总结和描述。设计经

费支出结构，是为了在具体任务一旦明确时，继续细化任务执行的具体方式，通过审批流程、职责、权限以及对支出要素和单据提出要求，对经济行为进行规范。结合深交委自身业务特点和管理方式，项目组初步界定了统筹经费、人员经费、日常运行经费、业务经费、信息化项目经费五类经费支出。在此基础之上，明确各类经费支出的范围、内容、标准、经费支出的归口管理职责、经费支出的审批权限与流程、事前审批程序、事后报销程序及相应的单据规范要求等。

通过“经费支出结构”设计，对履行职能的经济行为进行了更加清晰的界定，明确了经济行为发生的范围、标准、内容以及方式，并与预算管理制度、细则相互配合，达到规范业务行为的目的；同时，通过该结构将业务行为量化为财务数据，为审核和审批提供明确依据，从而规范业务行为，实现财务与业务“一体化”。

“内部预算批复结构”、“经费支出结构”与“财政预算批复结构”、“会计科目结构”相衔接，形成管理循环（如图3所示）。四大结构正向循环反映出预算执行程序，即从财政预算批复结构开始，通过内部预算批复将单位职能细化落实到具体任务和责任人上，再通过经费支出结构对经济行为进行管控，实现财务对业务的支撑和管理的双重作用，并形成会计核算结果；反向循环亦符合预算工作的原理，体现了每一个单位的预算都应该来源于对实际经济行为进行合理计划而形成的内部工作计划，进而形成预算申请的内容。

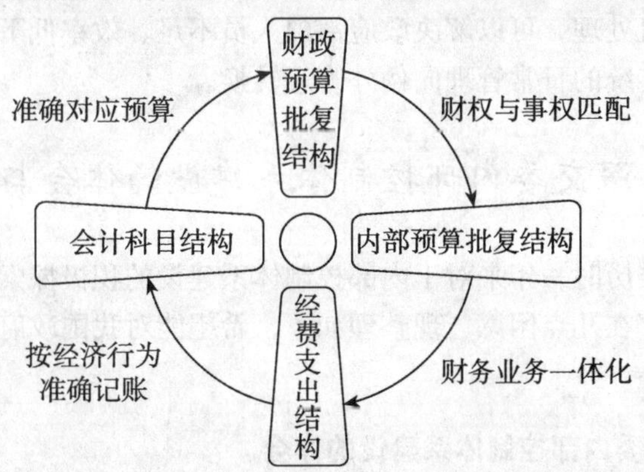

图3　四大结构的有机统一

“四大结构”有机协调，一定程度上克服了目前政府部门在预算管理和支出管控方面“分类不清晰、反映不明细、不能管控经济行为”等现象，清楚地说明政府资金的来源，安排了哪些具体任务，最终通过何种方式用到了何处，将政府部门的内部控制一直延伸到对具体经济行为的管控。“四大结构”与相关制度细则相配合，在深交委内部建立起一个分工合理、互相协调、运转顺畅的预算管理运行机制，进一步提高了财政资金的使用效率，充分体现了市场经济条件下建立健全我国公共财政体系的总体要求和完善支出预算管理体制的新理念。

（三）通过信息化落地，实现内部控制体系程序化与常态化

有效执行是内部控制体系建设的关键，特别是在政府行业推行新举措或对原有制度进行强化，都涉及政府组织行为的变革，实施难度较高。项目组经过多次论证和测试，决定在方案落实阶段主要采取信息化落地的方法，建立“全面预算管理信息系统”，对于稳定的、有规律的控制措施通过信息系统进行程序化和固化，从而切实落实各项管理制度。

通过构建深交委全面预算管理信息系统，初步实现了内部控制体系建设和信息系统建设的有机结合。一方面，借助信息化系统设计，将内部控制管理规定中的部门职责、标准流程、政策法规、权限金额等内容全部“固化”在系统程序中，达到内部控制标准对各项经济业务约束的“自动”实现，任何违背内部控制管理规定的行为都能够得到制止，从而有效推动相关工作的程序化和常态化。另一方面，通过信息的自动生成，能够形成满足日常管理需要的相关信息。各级管理者可以在其相应权限范围内的可视化界面上观察到有关预算执行的各类指标。通过指标的跟踪反馈，各级管理者可以动态掌握管理范围内的预算安排、可用财力、指标执行等方面的信息，为相关资金支出审核提供决策依据，同时，及时、准确获得各责任部门预算具体执行等信息，也可以为各业务部门合理安排工作提供有力的支撑。另外，借助信息化系统，大量的事务性工作由计算机处理，可以解决政府部门人员不足、效率低下等问题，使领导的管理方式由传统的日常管理向例外管理转换。

三、深交委内部控制体系建设的体会与困惑

通过深交委历时一年来对于内部控制体系建设的积极探索与实践，形成了一些体会，也存在几点困惑，现整理如下，希望能对我国政府部门内部控制建设有所裨益。

（一）深交委内部控制体系建设的体会

1. 政府部门内部控制体系建设是“一把手”工程

内部控制运行于控制环境之中，控制环境可以看做影响内部控制质量的内部“气候”，影响着其他控制要素发挥作用。在控制环境中，领导的重视是最重要的因素之一。处于人力资源金字塔尖的领导层的意识和行为将向下级逐级渗透，从而影响单位整体的行为模式。同时，领导的廉正和道德观，也在确定组织道德的高层基调方面扮演了十分关键角色（王光远，2006），尤其是在政府部门，由于现阶段没有强制要求，其内部控制建设更是要完全依靠领导者的自觉意识。因此，从本质上来说，政府部门内部控制建设就是“一把手”工

程，领导的重视程度直接影响到内部控制实施推行的成败，没有领导支持的内部控制建设往往会流于形式。

本次深交委对内部控制建设的探索，正是植根于深交委领导层的责任感和使命感，从而完成了从"要我内控"到"我要内控"的理念转变。在整个项目实施过程中，以党组书记、主任为首的深交委领导对内部控制建设表示了高度重视，并给予了大力支持。为加强相关工作的组织与领导，深交委领导特成立深交委内部控制体系建设工作领导小组与工作小组，明确了各小组成员及工作职责，并强调深交委机关各处室、所属单位负责人一定要高度重视此项工作，并指定专人配合项目组工作，确保相关工作顺利进行。领导的重视与支持，对营造和维持一种良好的控制环境起到了非常重要的作用，也为内部控制体系的全面推行打下了良好的基础。

2. 政府部门内部控制体系建设应当借助外力

在内部控制建设的探索中，还有一项工作至关重要，那就是政府部门内部控制建设应当借助外力。一方面，与企业通过企业内部控制体系提高经济效益不同，由于缺少利润这一驱动力，政府部门内控建设完全依靠的是领导层的自觉意识，加之长期形成的"惯性"，导致政府部门内部控制意识淡薄。如果仅仅依靠政府部门对自身进行内部控制体系建设，相当于既是"运动员"又是"裁判员"，不但难以客观地找到自身问题所在，更很难对自身长期形成的问题"下手"，即使建设也是流于形式；另一方面，作为职能部门，政府部门也缺乏精力和相关专业知识去完成内部控制项目建设和信息化实施，特别是在政府部门内部控制基本规范和相关指引尚未出台的情况下，政府部门更加需要借助资深权威、经验丰富的内部控制专家和项目团队进行指导和协助。在本次项目中，与深交委共同合作的专家团队为本次内部控制体系的建设和实施提供了良好的条件：一是专家、学者能够从政策与业务指导的角度为完善内部控制度体系提供专业建议和理论支撑；二是咨询团队和信息化团队具有丰富的实务经验，使深交委内部控制体系在理论依据的基础上有利于实践操作，保证项目的顺利实施。

3. 政府部门内部控制体系建设应当突出重点

政府部门所掌握的公共权力不仅包括对公共资源的分配，还包括诸如特许经营权等审批权的控制。如果对审批权控制不加以规范，那么很可能会引发滥用职权的风险等。因此，政府部门内部控制边界究竟限定在涉及资金的所有经济业务之内，还是将其延伸到审批权的控制是建设内部控制体系应当首先考虑的重要问题。此次，项目组立足于深交委现实情况的基础上，将内部控制边界确定为"以预算管理为主线，以资金管控为核心"，并不是否定审批权控制的必要性与重要性，而是基于可操作性和阶段性建设的考虑。

首先，政府部门的经济业务具有一个共性，即都与预算的取得、使用、管理和分配密切相关。按照相关要求，政府预算必须覆盖所有的经济业务，所有的经济业务都必须以预算为前提。"预算管理为主线"建立内控体系建设，自然会带动政府采购、工程管理等所有相关经济行为的内部控制的改进与完善。这些经济业务中有的环节与资金直接相关，例如政府采购与工程项目的付款业务、资产购置、修理与报废等；有的业务环节虽然不直接涉及资金，例如工程项目的立项、招标与投标等审批环节，但归根结底要通过资金进行支付，抓住了资金管控这一核心，在一定程度上也抓住了政府部门内部控制的重心和主体。比如，政府采购的资金支付控制必然要求编制和审批需求计划等业务的规范操作，如果这些业务不规范，那么在资金支付环节就要受到限制。因此，"以预算管理为主线，以资金管控为核心"，做到重点突出，才能取得真正突破，并带动其他方面逐步规范起来。

其次，政府部门的内部控制规范建设无现成经验可借鉴，理应循序渐进，先重点后全面。政府部门的业务涉及很多方面，如果面面俱到，往往事倍功半。从已有的案例来看，政府内部控制往往也都是在资金管理环节出现问题，这主要和政府资金运转特点密切相关，规模较大，沉淀时间较长，对资金使用缺乏问责机制，这一问题的解决也直接涉及人民群众切身利益，因此，把住资金管控，就等于把住控制风险的最重要的一道"关口"。现阶段围绕重点建设政府部门内部控制，有利于解决主要矛盾，再以此带动外围业务活动的内部控制建设，从而保证项目的顺利实施和及时应用。

4. 政府部门内部控制体系建设必须通过信息化落地

内部控制体系作为一套人造的免疫系统，标准制定是内部控制的基础，有效实施是内部控制的灵魂（王军，2006）。我国许多政府部门并不是没有制度，但却由于执行不力，造成实施效果不理想。审计署科研所在的《政府部门内部控制研究》报告中指出：尽管政府部门内部控制主体条件比较健全，大多数单位规定了内部控制执行形式，但内部控制信息化程度有待提高，并存在一定的重内部控制制度建设、轻内部控制执行的倾向。对于如何将控制和制约落到实处，深交委充分尊重了项目组专家的意见，认为内部控制制度必须通过信息化才能有效实施，否则就会流于形式。内部控制的科学理念并不是体现在制度的堆砌，而是根植于组织持续运行过程之中，而要做到这一点，就要有严密的系统程序作支撑。项目组为深交委量身定制的信息化系统，为一系列内部控制管理理念提供了载体，并将内部控制规范体系"固化"在系统程序中，达到内部控制标准对各项经济业务约束的"自动"实现，推动制度和流程达到常态化，保证了各项内部控制得到最大限度的执行，真正实现从"人治"管理向"法治"管理的转变。

（二）深交委内部控制体系建设的困惑

深交委在建设内部控制体系的过程中，也产生了几点困惑。

1. 政府部门内部控制体系建设急需参照规范

由于我国政府部门内部控制的基本规范和配套指引仍处于理论研究阶段，

企业内部控制规范又不能适用于政府部门。因此，作为政府部门内部控制体系建设的先行者，深交委在探索与实践过程中，对于实践过程中出现的很多难题和困惑，尚没有规范和指引可以借鉴，只能摸索着前进。因此，呼吁财政部会同有关部门，借鉴企业内部控制规范制定和推广过程中所积累的经验，尽快出台政府部门内部控制的基本规范和配套指引，为我国政府部门内部控制体系建设提供政策支持和理论依据。

2. 政府部门内部控制体系建设缺乏外力推动

由于企业的基本目标在于追求公司价值最大化，健全有效的企业内部控制体系，自然会提高企业形象和经济效益，从而使管理者和员工受益。从这一角度来看，企业有充分的动力去进行自身内部控制建设。政府部门则不同，利润在政府单位没有驱动力，其内控建设的根本目的在于“加强内部管理、提高公共资金使用效益和为人民服务水平”，完全依靠的是领导层责任感和使命感。但是，责任感和使命感是因人而异的，不具备传递性，也不能保证其持久性。长期以来，政府部门发展规模及资金的具体安排等大部分是依靠行政手段管理，承担的责任有限，长期形成的“惯性”导致政府部门缺乏风险管理的认识，内部控制意识淡薄，甚至可能还会有人认为政府部门建设内控实际上是在“自缚手脚”，很难形成建设内部控制体系的“大气候”。因此，要想切实推动政府部门内部控制体系建设，不能完全寄希望于政府部门领导层的自觉意识和自发动力，只有获得国家强制力的支持方能促进政府部门的内部控制建设，不然，即使出台规范也是流于形式。建议我国审计署、纪检监察部等有关部门，借鉴国际经验，建立以国家立法为保障，内部审计机制、信息披露机制和外部审计机制等为辅助的内部控制实施机制，来保证和促进我国政府部门内部控制的实施力度和效果。

历时一年来的内部控制体系建设探索与实践，作为先行者，深交委进行了很多探索与尝试。诚然，任何单位的内部控制体系建设必然是一个循序渐进、逐步完善的过程。深交委内部控制体系建设也将持续改进、不断完善。今后，深交委将继续发扬和落实科学发展观的精神，持续探索，为我国政府部门内部控制体系建设尽绵薄之力。

主要参考文献

[1] [美]爱德华·卡尼等:《联邦政府内部控制》,王光远等译,北京,中国时代经济出版社,2009。

[2] 刘玉廷、王宏:《美国加强政府部门内部控制建设的有关情况及其启示》,载《会计研究》,2008(3),5~10页。

[3] 审计署:《中国审计研究报告2006》,北京,中国时代经济出版社,2007。

[4] 刘英来等:《政府内部控制失效溯源》,载《财经》,2007(3),14页。

［5］王光远:《借鉴国际经验 建立健全政府内部控制机制》,http://www.china.com.cn/zhuanti2005/txt/2006-03/10/content_6150253.htm。

［6］王军:《加快健全我国企业内控标准体系和会计师事务所内部治理机制,在企业内部控制标准委员会、会计师事务所内部治理指导委员会成立大会暨第一次全体会议上的讲话》,2006(7),15页。

盈余质量、财务绩效与内部控制实证研究①

张曾莲　谢佳卫

（北京科技大学经济管理学院　北京　100083）

摘　要　盈余质量、财务绩效与内部控制三者紧密相关，以我国50家上市公司的数据为研究样本，通过建立三者的相应指标，讨论三者的相互关系及作用机理。实证结果表明，上市公司内部控制与其盈余质量显著正相关；若以内部控制作为盈余质量和财务绩效的中介变量，财务绩效也与内部控制正相关。

关键词　盈余质量　内部控制　财务绩效

一、引言

20世纪80年代以来，内部控制相关理论在我国逐渐发展，但和西方内部控制近年来的高速发展相比，我国企业内部控制仍然存在很多的问题，企业内部控制研究还亟待加强。COSO委员会在1992年到1994年的报告中对促进公司内部控制制度的完善和推动内部控制理论的研究发挥了积极的作用。很多跨国公司根据COSO报告要求积极地完善自身的内部控制制度，改善内部管理。其中最为重要的内容便是内部控制的整体框架，该框架指出了内部控制的五个要素：控制环境、风险评估、控制活动、信息和沟通、监督。刘玉廷论述了《企业内部控制的基本规范》的制定背景、总体思路、形成的过程及主要内容，并就内部控制和会计控制的相关关系、会计控制规范和其他相关会计法规的关系、规范的试行等做了有关说明，并强调了《内部会计控制规范》作为《会计法》的配套规章，是解决当前一些单位机关内部管理松弛和控制弱化的重要举措，是从源头上治理腐败的一项制度。1968年Ball和Brown在Journal of Accounting Research中发表了An Empirical of Accounting Income Numbers，这便是对盈余质量最早的研究。Information perspective、contract perspective、valuation perspective则是对盈余质量的三种不同的观点。夏立军和杨海斌（2002）一致认为，盈余质量程度高的公司被出具非标准审计意见的可能性也

① 本文系教育部人文社科青年基金项目（10YZC790367），北京市教育科学课题（CCA10088）研究成果。

就越高，这就意味着审计师能够在一定的程度上揭示出上市公司的盈余管理行为，盈余管理和审计意见之间也存在着一定的相关性。胡艳（2003）指出了内部控制系统局限性的克服不仅只是依靠系统本身的完善，还有赖于公司治理和内部控制两者的无缝对接。公司治理和内部控制都产生于委托—代理关系，但是两者委托—代理的层次却不同。杨德明和胡婷曾指出在我国证券市场成立的初期，审计市场的发展不是市场自身的有效需求，而是管制机构效仿国际惯例的一个附带产物（刘峰，2002）。我国的上市公司并不会努力地去追求高的审计质量，相反地，一些独立性较高的会计师事务所甚至可能会降低自身的审计质量。

本文随机抽选了深圳证券交易所的50家公司进行实证分析，并根据内部控制理论，建立了一个以控制环境、控制活动、风险评估、监督评价、信息与沟通为基础要素的内部控制评价系统。盈余质量程度越高的公司被出具非标准审计意见的概率也就相应越高，这说明审计师能够在一定程度上揭示出上市公司的盈余管理行为，盈余质量和审计质量之间也存在一定的相关性。本文以应计利润的持续性和稳定性来建立有关盈余质量的评价指标体系。在《企业内部控制——整合框架》中曾指出，确定内部控制系统是否有效的依据是评估五个要素是否存在以及是否有效发挥作用，这些要素同时也是有效内部控制的标准。按照这个思路，很多公司都曾经采用的方法是：以内部控制的框架为参照，根据内部控制框架的相关要素是否存在再来评价内部控制的有效性，并研究内部控制运行的合理性，最后通过综合的设计与运行对内部控制的有效性做出总体评价，并评估内部控制实现的风险，确认其是否存在着重大漏洞，最后再来确定内部控制的有效性。这一思路现仍在很多大公司中普遍适用，为很多企业的内部控制和监管提供了方法与便利。综上所述，笔者决定着手对盈余质量、内部控制和财务绩效三者的关系进行分析与研究，希望能为内部控制制度建设提供理论支持；对企业的管理结构具有指导意义；对上市公司盈余质量模型研究具有借鉴意义；对企业建立高效的财务机制具有参考价值；引起管理层对内部控制和财务绩效的重视。

二、研究设计

（一）指标体系的构建

我国企业的内部控制起步于20世纪90年代，经过近20年的发展，特别是随着公司治理结构的逐步完善和发展，企业内部控制制度也相应地由内部牵制过渡到系统的风险管理阶段，在制度建设方面，政府监管层充分地借鉴国际经验并结合我国实际，制订了一系列的内部控制的制度措施，这些制度对于提高我国企业的内部控制水平和风险管理能力，完善公司的治理层结构，降低进入国际资本市场的成本都起到积极的作用。盈余质量和财务绩效是衡量一个公司综合实力的重要标准，盈余其实也就是利润，盈余质量和财务绩效都涉及公司存在和发展的根本——利润。国外很早以前就对财务绩效给予了足够的重视。不断提高财务绩效的质量才能不断地推进公司的管理制度更加合理化。盈余管理直接决定着盈余质量的高低，而公司管理层的效率也决定了财务绩效的好坏。鉴于内部控制在企业中的作用越来越明显，企业也越来越关注内部控制；而盈余质量和财务绩效关系企业的命运，同样也是重中之重，因此笔者尝试探讨三者的关系。

1. 内部控制指标

根据《评估框架》，研究、制定一套具有公认性和完善性，既符合实际又具有可操作性的评价标准体系，应从目标的定位、内容范围以及设置方式等方面来综合进行考虑，既可以从企业管理和控制目标入手，也可以从内部控制的要素入手。其中，要素的评价标准可以分为内部控制的 5 个方面，包括内部控制环境、控制活动、风险评估、检查监督、信息与沟通，建立内部控制评价指标体系也可以从这 5 方面来设计。不同方面笔者将结合所搜集的数据选用合适评价指标来完成研究的需要，这一共涉及 15 个评价指标（见表 1）。

表 1　**内部控制指标**

内部控制环境	公司高管是否持有公司的股份（A1）	若公司高管持有股份取 1，否则取 0
	高级董事成员是否兼任总经理（A2）	若兼任取 1，否则取 0
	公司是否注重内部文化建设（A3）	若注重取 1，否则取 0
企业控制活动	董事会有关内部控制的活动安排（A4）	若年报中说明安排取 1，否则取 0
	企业是否存在绩效评价制度（A5）	若存在取 1，否则取 0
	公司独立董事占董事会的比例（A6）	按实际比率来统计
企业风险评估	公司是否存在关联交易（A7）	若存在取 1，否则取 0
	年报是否有风险提示和对策措施（A8）	若年报有取 1，否则取 0
	借款人的集中度（前五个）（A9）	按实际比率来统计
企业检查监督	公司财务报告的审计类型（A10）	若无保留意见取 1，带强调意见取 0
	公司是否自己出示内部控制报告（A11）	若出示取 1，否则取 0
	内部控制报告是否揭露公司缺陷（A12）	若揭示取 1，否则取 0
企业信息与沟通	公司是否有投资者关系管理制度（A13）	若有取 1，否则取 0
	公司董事会会议的次数（A14）	该年度董事会会议的总次数/100
	公司监事会是否有独立意见（A15）	年报内披露讨论取 1，否则取 0

（1）企业控制环境指标。以《上市公司内部控制指引》为凭据，对公司测评。其主要包括：企业治理层的结构是否完善，股东大会、董事会和监事会

等架构是否合法运作且符合科学的决策；公司管理层是否开展了内部控制培训，让内部风险的防范成为公司高层管理者的共同认识；是否培育了良好且有效的公司精神和内部控制文化，是否创造了工作人员充分了解并忠于职守的环境；企业的高层管理者和采购人员是否签订了诚信的承诺书；是否建立了长期有效的激励约束机制且树立了相关风险防范意识等。根据此次实证研究搜集的数据，结合《评估框架》，笔者采用的三个基本指标是：公司高管是否持有本公司股份，董事长或者副董事长是否兼任总经理，公司是否注重公司内部文化建设。

（2）企业控制活动指标。公司管理层为了保证风险对策的执行和措施程序的落实，采取了批准、授权、验证、复核、定期盘点、记录核对、财产保护和绩效考核等措施。在对公司内部控制活动进行相关测试时，需要审核的要点是组织机构所采取的内部控制活动和内部控制制度方面所采取的控制活动。组织结构方面需要重点审核：岗位、机构及职责权限是否得到最合理的设置与分工，是否成立了相关的法律部门，不相关的职务之间是否得到了相互的分离，对采购和验收等环节是否设置了相互监督制度，并且做到人员分离。在内部控制制度建设方面需要重点审核：公司是否制订了董事会的议事规章、公司总经理的事权规章、子公司的管理制度、采购的相关管理制度、财务的管理制度、合同的管理制度、投资的管理制度、内部控制的检查监督制度等。笔者从董事会内部控制的活动安排、企业是否有绩效评价制度、独立董事占董事会的比例这三方面进行考量。

（3）企业风险评估指标。公司管理层应对影响公司目标实现的各种内、外部风险因素进行分析，充分考虑它的可能性与影响程度，并制定相应的措施。在对公司的风险防范做测评时，需要重点关注公司是否建立了完整有效的风险评估体系，是否建立了审计委员部门和风险管理部门，是否对已经发现的公司各类风险配置了相应的内部控制措施，以及是否对经营风险、市场风险、财务风险、道德风险和政策法规风险等进行持续的监控。同时，需要关注对业务项目和已知风险是否进行了定期的检查、评估、提示与完善，如是否对公司的客户建立了资信档案、是否定期地梳理完善与公司发展战略不相符的业务和项目等。笔者选取了和上市公司内部控制质量审核关系最密切的三个方面进行相关考核：借款人的集中程度、是否存在关联方交易以及年报中是否有风险提示和对策措施。

（4）企业检查与监督指标。在对企业的经营活动进行测试时，应当重点审核的是公司是否制定了内部控制和检查监督相关制度，以及该项工作是否在董事会或监事会的直接领导控制下进行，且有审计部门负责具体的实施，并具有相关的制度。例如，重要领导的离任是否实施了责任审计、基建项目是否具有竣工审计相关制度、担保、重大投资、关联交易、抵押是否建立了相应的审核制度以及是否存在对公司的设备、重要物资和原材料进行定期盘点和不定期的抽查制度，对公司银行账户和现金的抽查制度等。在此，财务报告的审计类型、企业是否自己出示内部控制报告和内部控制评价报告是否揭露缺陷被用来作为指标。

(5) 企业信息与沟通指标。在对公司的信息活动进行相关测试时，应重点审核公司是否已经制定了内外部信息的管理政策，确保董事会、监事会、高级管理人员及审计部门能够及时了解公司及其控股子公司的经营和风险状况，并确保准确无误的传递信息，确保风险隐患和内控缺陷都得到了妥善的处理。根据所选取上市公司的特点，结合我国实际，笔者决定采用企业是否有投资者关系管理制度、董事会会议次数以及监事会是否有独立意见三者来进行研究。

2. 盈余质量指标

Dechow 和 Schrand（2004）认为，公司高的盈余质量应当满足三个条件：反映目前的运营状况；未来运营状况的良好预测指标；真实反映公司的内在价值。美国的通用会计准则（GAAP）与国际会计准则（IFRS）的概念框架中均将相关性及可靠性作为会计信息最基本的质量特征。研究盈余质量需要注重其五个属性：应计利润的质量、持续性、可预测性、价值相关性和平稳性。基于各方面考虑，结合国内实际，笔者仅选取了应计利润的持续性和稳定性进行相关研究（见表2）。

表2　**盈余质量的指标**

应计利润的持续性	若有持续性取1，否则取0
应计利润的稳定性	如有稳定性取1，否则取0

(1) 应计利润的持续性。它是盈余质量很重要的一个属性。应计利润持续性越好，盈余质量越佳，因为持续的利润会再次发生。通常将当期盈余和后期盈余放入回归模型中，当期盈余的斜率作为衡量盈余持续性的标准。斜率越大，说明持续性越好；反之，说明持续性越差。持续性能够较准确地反映财务绩效水平，因为利润是一个公司存在的根本所在，只有持续的利润才能为公司不断地注入新的血液，才能保证公司不断发展。

(2) 应计利润的稳定性。稳定性往往是评价很多指标的重要因素，越稳定预示着越好。波动性越小的盈余越平稳，平稳的收益则被认为是高质量的，因为平稳的盈余能排除很多其他因素而给管理者或经营者提供一个可靠的收益，即平稳性能够降低风险，避免给公司运营造成不必要的麻烦。

3. 财务绩效指标

《中央企业总会计师工作职责管理的暂行办法》指出，财务绩效的评价是指对企业一定期间的盈利能力、资产质量、债务风险和经营增长四个方面进行定量对比分析与评判。财务绩效定量评价标准将根据不同的行业、规模及相关类别，相应地评出优秀、良好和差三个级别。盈利能力是指企业在一定时期内赚取利润的能力，利润率越高，盈利能力就越强；而债务风险是指债权人在法律保护范围内面临的债款损失风险。根据近期相关文献，盈利能力和债务风险能够更好地反映财务绩效的水平，因此笔者选取这两个指标。

(1) 盈利能力。笔者采用公司最近两年平均利润比上相应两年的平均总资产的值来衡量盈利能力，即总资产收益率（ROA）。若公司近两年为亏损，则指标为负。净资产收益率（ROE）是证券会对上市公司发行IPO考核指标，其可靠性不如ROA强，因此笔者选用ROA为评价标准。

(2) 债务风险。笔者采用借款额最大的前五个公司占总借款额的比例来进行分析，若比例值越大，债务风险就越大。之所以选用债务风险，是因为其水平能够很直观地得到较准确的数据。

（二）研究假设

我国企业普遍存在的问题是管理者和控股者拥有绝大多数权利，这很容易给控制者以方便，给其他小股东和投资者造成侵害。学术界普遍认为，企业的盈余质量和财务绩效呈正相关关系，即盈余质量越高，财务绩效越优秀。随着近几年企业财务丑闻的屡屡曝光，政府和企业越来越重视内部控制，内部控制在企业的作用也逐渐被重视。高水平的内部控制能够提高企业应对财务风险和经营风险的能力，高水平的内部控制也是当今每个企业所需要的。财务绩效的优秀程度和盈余质量的高低在一定程度上直接影响着一个企业的利润，当然，任何企业都追求最大限度的利润，因此笔者提出以下假设：

P1：上市公司的盈余质量与内部控制水平正相关。

P2：上市公司的财务绩效与内部控制水平正相关。

根据MacKinnon D P.、Warsi G et al. (1995) 提到的中介变量，即Y通过和L作用到X，则L起到的就是中介变量的作用（见图1）。本文内部控制介于盈余质量和财务绩效之间，因此笔者再做如下假设：

P3：内部控制水平是盈余质量和财务绩效的中介变量，盈余质量和财务绩效也正相关。

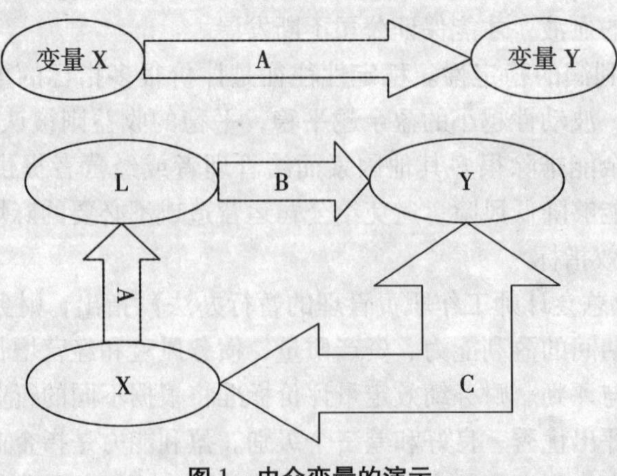

图1 中介变量的演示

（三）建立模型

由于内部控制的公司财务年报的审计类型（A10）指标能反映外部独立事务所对公司内部控制的综合评价，而内部控制的其他 14 个指标都是内部指标，而内部控制是盈余质量和财务绩效的中间变量，因此用 A10 代替内部控制。为了验证本文的三个假设，笔者分别构建以下模型。

（1）模型 1：盈余质量和内部控制水平的关系

$$A10=\alpha+\beta_1 A1+\beta_2 A2+\beta_3 A3+\beta_4 A4+\beta_5 A5+\beta_6 A6+\beta_7 A7+\beta_8 A8+\beta_9 A9+\beta_{11} A11+\beta_{12} A12+\beta_{13} A13+\beta_{14} A14+\beta_{15} A15+\beta_{16} EQ_1+\beta_{17} EQ_2+\varepsilon$$

（2）模型 2：财务绩效和内部控制水平的关系

$$A10=\alpha+\beta_1 A1+\beta_2 A2+\beta_3 A3+\beta_4 A4+\beta_5 A5+\beta_6 A6+\beta_7 A7+\beta_8 A8+\beta_9 A9+\beta_{11} A11+\beta_{12} A12+\beta_{13} A13+\beta_{14} A14+\beta_{15} A15+\beta_{16} FP_1+\beta_{17} FP_2+\varepsilon$$

A10 是因变量也是中介变量。上文已将 A10 给出，无保留的标准意见取 2，有保留意见取 1。其中，EQ 和 FP 分别是盈余质量和财务绩效的相关评价指标，ε 为误差项。EQ_1是盈余质量指标中的盈利能力，即 2010 年的净利润比上总资产的值，公司亏损则值为负数；EQ_2是债务风险指标，取得是上市公司对外借款中借款额最多的前 5 家占总借款额的比例，若比例越大，则容易发生死账或呆账的几率也就越大。在模型 2 中，FP_1 指应计利润的持续性，是结合上市公司前几年的年度报表中的利润对比分析得到的，若大致持续则取 1；FP_2指稳定性，数据来源于最近几年的净利润额，若上下波动不大，则持续性良好。α 是截距，β 是相应变量的系数，若相关性不大，则系数愈发趋向于 0，若显著正相关则趋向 1，若显著负相关则趋向-1。通过线性回归，自动省略掉和因变量没有线性关系的变量，最终得到需要的变量。

（四）数据来源

相关数据取自深圳证券交易所 50 家上市公司，50 家上市公司由笔者在剔除一些不符合研究要求的公司之后随机选取，所有信息都来源于公司 2010 年的财务年报、内部控制评价报告和外部审计报告，所有数据均系笔者查阅相关上市公司的年报手工搜集，具有一定的及时性和准确性。由于数据量较少，可能研究结果不具有代表性和精确性。本文采用 SPSS18.0 对数据进行分析。

三、实证分析

1. 描述性统计与相关性分析

对本文的 19 个指标进行描述性统计。由表 3 可知，所有工具变量的极小值都为 0，极大值都为 1；独立董事占董事会的比例最少为 25%，最高为 57%，均值为 37%，差异很小；借款人的集中度最低为 8%，最高为 100%，均值为55%，差异较大；董事会会议次数最低为3次，最高为19次，均值为8.6次，差异很大；总资产收益率最低为-54%，最高为13.5%，均值为0.8%，差异较大；借款额最大的前5家公司占总借款额的比例最低为8%，最高为700%，差异很大。

表3 **相关指标的描述性统计**

评价指标	观测次数	极小值	极大值	均值	标准差
公司高管是否持有公司股份	50	0	1	0.48	0.505
高级董事成员是否兼任总经理	50	0	1	0.76	0.431
公司是否注重内部文化建设	50	0	1	0.06	0.240
董事会有关内部控制的活动安排	50	0	1	0.26	0.443
企业是否存在绩效评价制度	50	0	1	0.06	0.240
独立董事占董事会的比例	50	0.25	0.5714	0.373	0.0576
公司是否存在关联交易	50	0	1	0.80	0.404
年报是否有风险提示和对策措施	50	0	1	0.04	0.198
借款人的集中度	50	0.0814	1.0000	0.55	0.2548
公司财务报告的审计类型	50	0	1	0.74	0.443
公司是否出示自己内部控制报告	50	0	1	0.76	0.431
内部控制报告是否揭露公司缺陷	50	0	1	0.04	0.198
公司是否有投资者关系管理制度	50	0	0	0.00	0.000
董事会会议次数	50	0.03	0.19	0.086	0.0326
公司监事会是否有独立意见	50	0	1	0.74	0.443
应计利润的持续性	50	0	1	0.56	0.501
应计利润的稳定性	50	0	1	0.42	0.499
总资产收益率	50	-0.5359	0.1349	0.008	0.098
借款额最大的前5家公司占总借款额比例	50	0.0793	6.9985	0.968	1.078

对19个指标进行相关性分析（表格太大没有列示）发现，内部控制单个指标与盈余质量的相关性较高，企业是否存在绩效评价制度、独立董事占董事会的比例、年报中是否有风险提示和对策措施、公司是否有投资者关系管理制度、董事会会议次数、公司监事会是否有独立意见这6个内控指标都与应计利润的稳定性显著正相关；公司是否有投资者关系管理制度和董事会会议次数都与应计利润的持续性显著正相关。内部控制单个指标与财务绩效的相关性并不太大，只有公司是否有投资者关系管理制度与盈利能力显著正相关，是否有投资者关系管理制度与债务风险显著负相关，董事会会议次数与债务风险显著负相关。盈余质量与财务绩效显著相关，其中应计利润的持续性与财务绩效两指

标都正相关，应计利润的稳定性都与财务绩效的两指标负相关。

2. 模型 1 的检验

对模型 1 进行回归分析（见表 4）。EQ_1的系数 β_{16}为正，说明总资产盈利能力和公司内部控制水平正相关。EQ_2的系数 β_{17}为负，说明债务风险水平和公司内部控制水平负相关。高的盈余质量定义为盈利能力强且债务风险低，则盈余质量和内部控制水平正相关，初步证明假设 1 成立。此处，$\beta_{16}=1.482$，$\beta_{17}=-0.144$，说明就盈余质量评价指标而言，盈余能力和内部控制水平的显著性大于债务风险。可见，内部控制对公司的利润有着直接的作用，内部控制对企业非常重要。

表 4　**盈余质量和内部控制的关系**

	系数 β	标准差	t	Sig
α	0. 397	0. 377	1. 051	1. 051
公司高管是否持有公司股份	0. 033	0. 080	0. 418	0. 418
高级董事成员是否兼任总经理	−0. 008	0. 113	−0. 075	−0. 075
公司是否注重内部文化建设	−0. 079	0. 192	−0. 412	−0. 412
董事会有关内部控制的活动安排	0. 227	0. 106	2. 140	2. 140
企业是否存在绩效评价制度	−0. 295	0. 330	−0. 896	−0. 896
独立董事占董事会的比例	0. 675	0. 862	0. 783	0. 783
公司是否存在关联交易	−0. 085	0. 105	−0. 815	−0. 815
借款人集中度	0. 003	0. 167	0. 015	0. 015
公司是否出示自己内部控制报告	0. 471	0. 105	4. 487	4. 487
内部控制报告是否揭露公司缺陷	0. 191	0. 373	0. 512	0. 512
董事会会议次数	0. 002	1. 325	0. 002	0. 002
公司监事会是否有独立意见	−0. 174	0. 098	−1. 771	−1. 771
盈利能力	1. 482	0. 439	3. 378	3. 378
债务风险	−0. 144	0. 041	−3. 550	−3. 550
$R^2=0.75$	$AdR^2=0.65$	标准估计的误差＝0. 262	D−W 值＝2. 4	

3. 模型 2 的检验

对模型 2 进行回归分析（见表 5）。FP1 和 FP2 的系数分别为 $\beta_{16}=0.375$ 和 $\beta_{17}=0.105$，则内部审计水平和应计利润的持续性 FP1 及稳定性 FP2 均呈正相关关系。而应计利润的持续性和稳定性是财务绩效的 5 个指标中相当关键的两个指标，且这两者都正向反映了财务绩效水平，即优秀的财务绩效通常都拥有高的持续性和稳定性，说明财务绩效和内部控制也正相关，初步证明假设 2 成立。

表5 **财务绩效和内部控制的关系**

	系数β	标准差	t	Sig
α	0.225	0.419	0.535	0.596
公司高管是否持有公司股份	0.116	0.089	1.309	0.199
高级董事成员是否兼任总经理	−0.043	0.128	−0.341	0.735
公司是否注重内部文化建设	−0.063	0.216	−0.293	0.771
董事会有关内部控制的活动安排	0.297	0.116	2.572	0.015
企业是否存在绩效评价制度	−0.261	0.361	−0.724	0.474
独立董事占董事会的比例	0.192	0.929	0.207	0.837
公司是否存在关联方交易	−0.109	0.114	−0.958	0.345
借款人集中度	−0.081	0.186	−0.437	0.665
公司是否出示自己内部控制报告	0.459	0.119	3.847	0.000
内部控制报告是否揭露公司缺陷	0.135	0.417	0.325	0.747
董事会会议次数	−0.561	1.460	−0.385	0.703
公司监事会是否有独立意见	−0.088	0.110	−0.803	0.427
应计利润的持续性	0.375	0.125	2.998	0.005
稳定性	0.105	0.120	0.874	0.388
$R^2=0.7$	Ad $R^2=0.58$	标准估计的误差=0.287		D-W 值=2.4

借助盈余质量和财务绩效的研究结论，基本上可以得出两者是呈正相关的。拥有高盈余质量的公司通常具有持续稳健的会计政策，公司的债务水平也是相当的、合理的，且高的盈余质量能够指引管理者和相关工作人员稳定地预测出未来的盈利状况即收益情况，这一点正好和财务绩效的稳定性相对应。根据图1，将Audit作为中介变量，在过程A和过程B相应满足时，关系C也应该成立，且结合实际和相关理论，得到的最终结论是：盈余质量、内部控制和财务绩效三者两两呈正相关关系。换句话说，一个公司如果建立了高水平的内部控制和外部监督，根据公司实际情况不断地完善公司的治理机构和经营策略，那么高的盈余质量是容易得到的，财务绩效也将持续稳定地趋于优秀，最终形成三者良性循环。初步验证假设3成立。

此次所作的回归分析将自动排除不具有相关性的指标，笔者发现：高级董事担任公司高管和关联交易均会给内部控制造成负面影响，即它们是负相关的。当董事长或副董事长同时肩负公司高管时，权利的过于集中也许会造成"一人独大"的情况。很多公司的案例告诉我们，一人集权有可能造成很多弊端，比如通过权利满足私利而侵害其他股东的权利，同时这种权利分布现象也不利于内部审计的发展，甚至会阻碍内部审计的公正执行。关联交易也是同一个情况，关联交易中的关系错综复杂，不是一个外部审计机构或者内部机构短时间能查得清楚彻底的，只有完全按照规章制度完成相关关联交易并做记录，才能真正维护交易双方的利益，但是正是因为其中的复杂性，形成了一些壁垒，有可能阻碍内部审计公正开展，但是，其他被排除的指标并非和内部控制没有关系，而是由此次选取数据样本量小的局限性造成的。

4. 稳健性检验

本文前面是将内部控制作为盈余质量和财务绩效的中间变量，由内部控制分别与盈余质量和财务绩效正相关，推出盈余质量和财务绩效也正相关。实际上，盈余质量和财务绩效两者能直接正相关，盈余质量高的公司通常财务绩效都较好，反之也成立。由前面盈余质量与财务绩效的相关分析也能看出。由两者的曲线图也能看出两者正相关（见图2）。

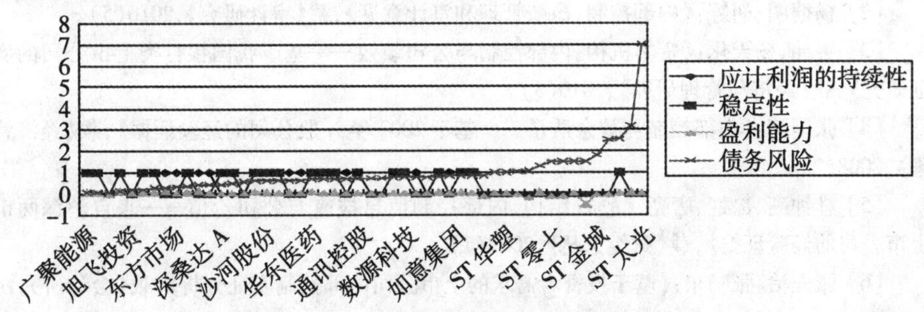

图2　盈余质量与财务绩效的相关分析曲线图

此外，前面只采用内部控制的一个指标（A10）作为因变量，不一定能准确地代表一个企业的内部控制水平，因此，后续研究可以采用因子分析等评价方法对内部控制的15个指标进行综合评价，得出50家公司的内部控制指数，再分别与盈余质量和财务绩效进行回归分析，找出三者的关系。

四、结论

利用我国50家上市公司2010年的相关数据分析发现，在一定程度内，随着内部控制水平的不断提高，公司的盈余质量也将逐渐提高，财务绩效水平也相应地趋向优秀，反之亦然。但是，这只是三者的一个范围趋势，即盈余质量和财务绩效的水平不会随着内部控制水平的提高而无限制的上升，因为三者中任意一个都有很多的评价指标，不受单个因素的绝对影响。通常企业的最终目的在于最大限度地为股东创造最大的利益，即追求利润最大化。资金链是一个公司的生命线，掌握资金链的是公司的财务部门，财务绩效显得颇为重要，持续稳定的收入是一个公司赖以生存和为股东创造利润的根本，只有满足了这个要求，公司才能获得发展。内部控制和财务绩效的正相关性突出了内部控制的重要性，盈余质量的高低能反映出公司的很多问题，特别是财务上的漏洞，也能一定程度地辅助内部控制监督。三者相辅相成，缺一不可。

在激烈的市场竞争中，盈余质量、内部控制和财务绩效三者是一个有机的统一体，只有兼顾三面，面面到位，方能提高公司的竞争力。而内部控制又是三者的重中之重，因此应该加大内部控制的力度，建立完善的内部控制制度和严格有效的监事会规章，有效地降低公司的财务和经营风险。政府和社会都该给予内部控制足够的关注。

主要参考文献

[1] Doyle, J. , Weili Ge, Sarah McVay. Accrual Quality and Internal Control over Financial Reporting. The Accounting Review, 2007, 82(5), pp. 1141-1170.

[2] 杨德明、胡婷:《内部控制、盈余管理和审计意见》,载《审计研究》,2010(5)。

[3] 钟玮、杨天化:《资本机构、内部控制与公司绩效——基于我国银行类上市公司的实证研究》,载《经济与管理研究》,2010(5)。

[4] 张国清:《内部控制与盈余质量——基于2007年A股公司的经验证据》,载《经济管理》,2008(23)。

[5] 林钟高、徐虹、唐亮:《股权结构、内部控制信息披露与公司价值——来自沪深两市上市公司的经验证据》,载《财经论丛》,2009(1)。

[6] 张先治、张晓东:《基于投资者需求的上市公司内部控制实证分析》,载《会计研究》,2004(12)。

[7] 树友林:《上市公司内部控制评价问题研究》,载《商业研究》,2008(11)。

[8] 罗雪琴、李连华:《内部控制信息披露与公司绩效实证研究——基于浙江省2006年上市公司的数据分析》,载《财会通讯》,2009(33)。

[9] 袁晓波:《内部控制与财务风险——来自中国沪市制造业上市公司的经验证据》,载《经济与管理研究》,2010(5)。

[10] 梁松、史本山:《公司控制与公司绩效的相关性实证分析》,载《科技进步与对策》,2010(21)。

中国资本市场对内控评审信息的反应研究
——来自深交所的经验证据

陈淑芳　曹政

（西安财经学院商学院　陕西西安　710100）

摘　要　上市公司管理层与外部投资者之间信息不对称和代理问题，阻碍了资本市场资源的有效配置，而信息披露在缓解这些问题上起到了一个桥梁的作用。通过信息披露，管理层及时向市场传达内部信息，减少了信息不对称和代理成本，从而达到监管要求或者公司管理层自身的目的。本文选取深圳证券交易所A股市场的60家上市公司为研究样本，考察了注册会计师对上市公司与财务报告相关内部控制出具不同审计意见报告时对股价的影响情况。实证研究发现：我国深市对2007—2009年披露的内控评审意见是具有信息含量的，资本市场对CPA出具标准内控评审意见的上市公司股价有显著的正面反应，非标准审计意见则与其相反。之后根据理论和实证研究结果，向相关部门提出一些政策性建议。

关键词　内控评审　市场反应　累计超额收益模型　多元回归分析法

一、引言

新千年以来，世界资本市场风起云涌，昔日无比辉煌的跨国公司折戟沉沙，而一些扣住了知识经济时代脉搏的中小企业一蹴而就，但其经营的可持续性却连遭市场质疑。可以看到，由于经营业务的全球化、复杂化以及竞争的激烈化，企业内部控制的难度不断增加，上市公司的兴衰史与内部控制的有效性产生了非常密切的联系。为解决环球通信、世界通信、施乐、默克制药等国际性大型上市公司出现的财务造假事件而暴露出的内部控制制度徒具形式的问题，经过立法机构和各大利益集团的艰苦博弈，《萨班斯—奥克斯利法案》历经5年终于得到全面执行。然而，次贷危机作用下的雷曼兄弟和贝尔斯登次贷投资巨亏破产、美国AIG保险公司、房利美和房地美的被接管等事件则为法律执行的巨大滞后敲响了警钟。

对于发展内部控制较早的美国如此，更何况我国研究内部控制较晚呢？新加坡的中航油事件，以及与中航油几乎同时发生的伊利股份高管的经济问题，创维数码董事会主席黄宏生被拘，金正数码和深圳石化原董事长被捕等事件，使人们开始意识到内部控制失败给企业和国家带来的双重损失。这些惨痛的教训提醒着我们的证券监管部门立法工作进度必须加快。

被称为“中国萨班斯法案”的《企业内部控制基本规范》由财政部等5部委于2008年6月28日联合发布。其中，要求上市公司对本公司内部控制的有效性进行自我评价，披露年度自我评价报告，并可聘请具有证券、期货业务资格的中介机构对内部控制的有效性进行审计。此外，2008年7月1日发布的《企业内部控制鉴证指引（征求意见稿）》要求从下年7月1日起，所有上市公司在发股、配股时都需出具内部控制专项鉴证报告。据此，我国强制性要求的上市公司内控评审意见产生。

与董事会和公司管理层对内部控制评价相对的是外部审计师内控评审。顾及到审计报告的可靠性，管理当局需发布管理声明书，就提供的会计资料进行真实、可靠性声明。上市公司要保证会计资料真实、可靠的前提条件就是要有一套健全、完善、有效的内部控制体系；而要得知公司的内部控制是否健全、完善、有效的先决条件，就是必须经过对内部控制的评审。内部控制、审计报告与会计资料有着密不可分的关系，投资者进行投资决策的重要依据之一便是包括内部控制信息在内的上市公司披露的年报审计信息。由此可见，投资者对上市公司内控评审的预期将会对股价产生一定的影响。就目前国内外研究进展而言，关于内部控制的研究很多，但是关于内部控制的实证研究涉及很少，本文以一种新的角度探讨内部控制对股价数据变动的影响，使企业在实践中更好地找到其利润产生点，更有效地为企业的生产经营服务。

二、理论分析与研究假设

由于上市公司管理层与外部投资者之间存在信息不对称和代理制度缺点阻碍了资本市场资源的有效配置，信息的有效披露在缓解这些问题方面的作用显得尤为重要。通过信息披露，管理层能够及时向市场传达内部信息，减少信息不对称和代理成本，从而达到监管要求或者公司管理层自身的目的。具体来说，根据审计需求传递理论，信息的发布与信息的质量成本是成反比的，通过定期的公布财务报表和对财务报表进行审计的信息，可以向市场有效传递有关上市公司状态的信息，从而缓解市场中由于信息不对称产生的逆向选择问题。林斌等（2009）认为，高质量公司的高层管理者有动机将上市公司高品质的信号（如较好的业绩、较好的内部控制及完备的风险防范信息）及时、有效地传递给投资者，其内部控制的信息能够显示出该公司具有良好的内部控制系统。在非强制性披露信息的情况之下，如果是一家自愿披露详细内部控制评审信息的上市公司，意味着该上市公司建立了较为完善的内部控制框架并有效负责其执行的效果。Dvald. M. Will（2000）认为，上市公司愿意提供内部控制报告可以堪称良好的公司治理实践。从这一点来看，内部控制报告有利于增加企业价值，良好的内控评审报告与股价有正相关性。方红星等（2009）根据

2003—2005 年年报数据分析发现，自愿性披露内部控制信息与外部审计意见类型显著正相关。因此，内部控制评审信息的披露对投资者来说是一个优质信号，理性的投资者可能会认为该公司的管理处于有序经营执行状态；能够合理有效的规避经营的风险；保障公司经营管理的效率、效果；保证披露的其他信息具有可靠性。因此，上市公司被 CPA 出具标准审计意见的内控评审报告与出具非标准审计意见的上市公司相比，其股价在内控评审信息披露前后会在一定范围内向上波动。据此，本文提出如下统计假设：

H1：被 CPA 出具标准审计意见的内控评审报告将会对股价产生正面影响。

风险转嫁理论被认为是审计需求保险理论的基础，也就是说 CPA 在审计失败时，需要向投资者进行一定的赔偿。在以风险导向为审计的模型下，内部控制的风险是决定上市公司审计风险高低的重要因素之一。依据风险的传导效应，被审计单位的内部控制风险越高，审计的风险也就越高。审计风险决定了诉讼风险，针对各上市公司的诉讼风险，作为理性人的 CPA，基于风险规避的动机，更倾向于出具非标准审计意见。基于风险的传导效应，当上市公司内部控制效率越低，内部控制风险和财务风险也就越高，财务报告出现重大错报的可能性则越大，审计失败的风险也就越高。

内部控制质量的高低直接影响了审计的程序。如果假定对上市公司的审计收费一定或基本无法改变，那么 CPA 可以选择的审计程序也会是比较有限的，在审计程序选择受到限制的条件下，导致审计师面临的诉讼风险则增加。较低的内部控制效率，一方面增加了审计风险；另一方面，审计师还需要扩大控制测试的范围和改变实质性程序的性质、时间和范围，进而增加了审计的成本，其结果是 CPΛ 不愿意看到的。所以 CPΛ 为了避免审计诉讼，倾向于出具非标准审计报告。基于上述分析，可以看出内部控制信息披露程度反映了内部控制的总体水平，它是衡量内部控制效率的重要指标，即内部控制效率越高的上市公司，越倾向于披露详细的内部控制信息，而内部控制效率低的公司不愿意过多地披露内部控制信息。McMullen、Dorothy 和 Ragahunandan（1996）实证研究表明，财务报告有问题的上市公司不大可能会提供内部控制报告。Harnmersley、Myers、Shakespeare（2008）研究发现，在一个较短的事件窗口内，资本市场对内部控制缺陷的披露有所反应，得到负的累积非正常回报率。由于上市公司内部控制效率越低，上市公司越有可能被 CPA 出具非标准的内控评审意见，继而影响投资者投资的热衷程度，导致上市公司股价的下跌。故而本文得出如下的统计假设：

H2：被 CPA 出具非标准审计意见的内控评审报告将会对股价产生负面影响。

财务报告内控评审信息的披露，属于公开信息披露形式，因此根据有效市场理论及我国股票市场的一般特点，本文将我国股市划为所有公开信息都已经反映在当前证券价格中的半强式有效市场，而至于股票能多快调整至可以反映一些特定重大经济事件则可通过股票对新信息的快速价格调整测试得到。

三、研究设计

（一）样本选取

本文样本选自于2007—2009年3年在深圳证券交易所连续上市发行A股的上市公司。本文剔除了如下类型的上市公司：（1）金融保险业上市公司。由于金融保险类上市公司数量较少，而且相关法律法规规定此类上市公司强制披露内部控制信息，所以本文研究中未予以考虑。（2）在各年4月30日之后披露年报的上市公司。（3）有重大违规事件发生的但出具标准意见的上市公司。（4）事件期内公布了季度报告或股利公告的上市公司。（5）在研究范围内连续2天以上（不包括2天）无股票价格信息的上市公司。（6）由于事务所变更引起的审计意见不一致的上市公司。（7）部分数据缺失、数据无法获取的上市公司。

由于上市公司3年非标准的内控评审意见总数量较少，且有股价信息的数据有限，符合本论文筛选条件的一共有30个样本。为了对比两种不同类型审计意见对累计超额收益影响的趋势情况，所以标准意见本文采取等距抽样的统计方法选取。由此，进入本文研究的上市公司样本数量共有60家。

（二）主要变量的定义

1. 解释变量定义

当CPA出具非标准审计意见时赋值为1，标准意见时赋值为0。

2. 被解释变量定义

通过事件研究法确定 CAR_i（t_1，t_2）为股票i在窗口（t_1，t_2）内的累积超额收益，表示股价的变动情况。其步骤如下：

（1）确定事件日期起点（t=0），即内控评审年报披露日期。然后再定义相对于时间起点的时间段。本文事件选取［-5，5］的时间段。用数轴表示如图1所示：

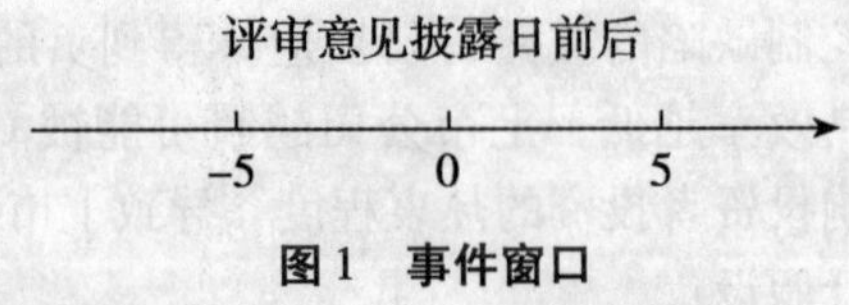

图1 事件窗口

（2）在整个估计期（估计期一般定义为宣布期之前1个月到6个月的时段）。为了研究与事件最接近期间的超额收益情况，所以本文将估计期确定为事件宣布日之前30天，即［-35，-6］。用数轴表示如图2所示：

（3）计算事件时期内股票的期望收益率（ER，expected return），异常收益率（AR，abnormal return），累计异常收益率（CAR，cumulative abnormal

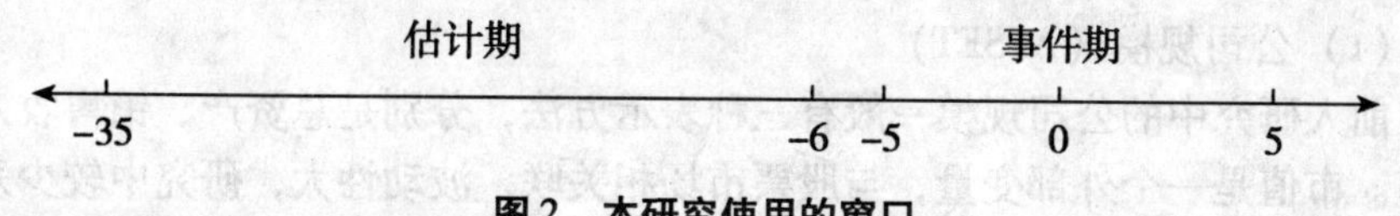

图2　本研究使用的窗口

return）。

本文中正常收益率使用市场模型估计得出：

$$R_{it}=\alpha_i+\beta_i R_{mt}+\varepsilon_{it} \quad (1)$$

式中：$E[\varepsilon_{it}]=0$，$Var[\varepsilon_{it}]=\sigma_2$，$Cov(\varepsilon_{it}, R_{mt})=0$

期望收益率为：

$$E(R_{it})=\alpha_i+\beta_i R_{mt} \quad (2)$$

式中：R_{mt}代表第t日市场证券投资组合（指数）的收益率，本文R_{mt}选取深证综合指数；R_{it}代表第i种股票在t日的收益率；α_i代表第i种股票α的估计值；β_i代表第i种股票β的估计值；ε_{it}是随机误差项。首先取［-35，-6］30个交易日的数据来估计得出α、β值后，再根据α、β值和R_{mt}计算事件窗口［-5，5］共11个交易日的期望收益率$E(R_{it})$。

异常收益估计模型为：

$$AR_{i,t}=R_{i,t}-E(R_{it}) \quad (3)$$

式中：$AR_{i,t}$是指第i家股票在第t天的异常收益。对异常收益进行加总求和，即AAR_t整个样本（各组30个样本数据，即N=30）在t时刻的平均异常收益率；$CAR(t_1, t_2)$是所有样本在(t_1, t_2)期间内的累积异常收益，式中$-5\leqslant t_1\leqslant t_2\leqslant 5$，因此异常收益的时间序列和截面上的加总依次为：

$$AAR_t=1/N\ \sum AR_{i,t} \quad (4)$$

$$CAR(t_1, t_2)=\sum AAR_t \quad (5)$$

（4）判断累计超额收益是否显著超过0。

3. 模型构建

依据前面的理论分析和研究假设，我们建立如下回归方程进行实证检验：

$$CAR_i(t_1, t_2)=a_{0t}+a_{1t}OPINION+a_{2t}ASSET+a_{3t}EPS+a_{4t}H_5+a_{5t}ST+a_{6t}SIZE_{10}+N_{it}$$

如前所述，$CAR_i(t_1, t_2)$为股票i在窗口(t_1, t_2)内的累积超额收益，表示股价的变动情况。OPINION为解释变量。另外式中的控制变量包括5个：（1）公司规模，用总资产（ASSET）替代表示；（2）公司的盈利能力，用每股收益（EPS）替代表示；（3）股权集中度，用前十大股东的持股比例（H_{10}）表示；（4）公司的声誉（ST），当上市公司为ST公司时取0，否则取1；（5）事务所规模（$SIZE_{10}$），当上市公司所聘请的会计师事务所为“前十大”[①]时赋值为1，否则为0。

① 使用中国注册会计师协会（http：//news. esnai. com/33/2008/0519/37773. shtml）公示的2008年会计师事务所百强中剔除“四大”后的前十名的数据资料，分别是中瑞岳华、立信、信永中和、大信、万隆、利安达信、天华、中审、浙江天健、天职国际会计师事务所。

(1) 公司规模(ASSET)

前人研究中的公司规模一般有三种表示方法,分别是总资产、销售收入和市值。市值是一个外部变量,与股票市场相关联,波动性大,研究中较少采用此指标。销售收入在所参阅的内部控制实证研究文献中还未见到,所以本文选择总资产作为控制变量进行进一步的研究。

(2) 企业的盈利能力(EPS)

宋绍清、张侠(2009)验证上市公司盈利能力与内部控制信息披露程度显著正相关,盈利能力较强的上市公司的内部控制信息披露程度较高。故本文采用每股收益控制累计超额收益。

(3) 股权集中度(H_{10})

股东持股数之和占公司股票总数的比例称为股权集中度。股权集中度在一定程度上反映了一个企业对市场信息做出快速反应的能力。

(4) 公司声誉(ST)

声誉机制是现阶段一种成本较低的维持市场交易秩序的机制,是法律机制一定程度的补充。特别有时候法律无能为力时,声誉的存在使其得以解决。张维迎(2002)讲到当人们没有积极性讲声誉的时候,法律就失去了声誉基础。法律制度的运行也离不开执法者的声誉。根据证监会的相关法律规定,上市公司如若财务状况出现异常,上市公司将被特殊处理(ST)。此类上市公司内部控制的有效性与财务状况未出现异常的上市公司相比,应该更弱一点,所以公司声誉对上市公司信息披露是有一定影响的,所以将该变量作为控制变量选入。当该上市公司为ST时赋值为0,否则为1。

(5) 事务所规模($SIZE_{10}$)

"十大"会计师事务所由于其所创立威信的不易,其众多合伙人相互担保,事务所内部大多已成立了具有专业标准控制的部门,而且由于"十大"在2008年综合评价中继续教育培训在97.57% ~100%之间,明显高于其他事务所,审计收入也排在前面。因此在本文的研究中,选取该指标为控制变量,当被聘请的会计师事务所为境内"十大"时赋值为1,否则为0。各变量经济含义、计量方法以及预期符号见表1。

表1 各变量经济含义、计量方法以及预期符号

变量类型		变量名称	变量计量方法
被解释变量	累计超额收益	CAR	衡量股票价格
解释变量	审计意见类型	OPINION	审计意见类型是哑元变量,当CPA出具非标准审计意见为1,标准意见为0
控制变量	公司规模	ASSET	公司总资产的自然对数
	企业的盈利能力	EPS	公司每股收益
	股权集中度	H_{10}	公司前十大股东股数所占总股数的比值
	公司声誉	ST	当该上市公司被特别处理为ST时赋值为0,否则为1
	事务所规模	$SIZE_{10}$	当审计机构为境内"前十大"时赋值为1,否则为0

四、实证结果分析

（一）深市内控评审整体趋势的描述性统计及分析

1. 描述性统计

德勤自2007年连续3年发布的“中国上市公司内部控制现状的调查报告”显示：（1）清楚了解监管机构对内部控制的要求的上市公司从74%上升到79%；（2）现有的内部控制体系不能完全满足监管要求的上市公司从80%下降到21%；（3）在对内控评审的认识水平上，2007年近80%的上市公司不确定是否能够识别内部控制的固有缺陷以及运行缺陷，73%的企业不能确定内部控制的设计和有效性是否可行，76%的公司不了解或不完全了解基于内控之上的财务报告审计可靠性问题的存在，到2008年96%的公司认识到应有统一框架或模型指导内部控制的实施，84%的公司认为主要障碍是缺乏完善的指导性和可操作性强的理论框架或模型，63%的公司认为企业实施内部控制的主要障碍是缺乏硬性的监督检查机制要求，而57%的公司认为实施内部控制的主要障碍是管理层的意识不到位，不能有力支持和倡导内部控制的工作情况，再到2009年我国上市公司在内部控制体系的实施及评价等各方面都有了积极的进展，并取得了一定的成绩。

2. 结果分析

（1）描述性统计的前两点说明，上市公司内控制度的普及和了解程度有了进一步完善，披露内部控制的机制有所加强。

（2）描述性统计的最后一点说明，在内部控制实施方面的主要障碍是各上市公司有不同的意见，产生这种不同意见的原因可能是各上市公司内部控制健全程度不一引起的。

可见，我国内部控制总体趋势有所进步，但是进步缓慢，内部控制整体水平良好的上市公司只占很小的比例，整个市场的内部控制情况有待进一步改善。深市出具内部控制报告的情况较好的主要原因可能是我国将深市现在发展成为一个多层级的资本市场，有利于各类资本的进入和满足中小企业以及创新高科技企业融资的需求。

（二）累计超额收益的变化统计图

60个样本的累计超额收益变化情况如图3所示：

从图3中我们可以很清楚地发现市场对非标准的内控评审意见有很强的反应，而标准意见变化趋势相对弱于非标准意见，在事件期两侧变化比较明显，特别是［-1，1］的窗口有特别明显的变化情况。在事件公布后，累计超额收益发生明显的变化，说明内控评审意见是有信息含量的，而非标准意见的信息

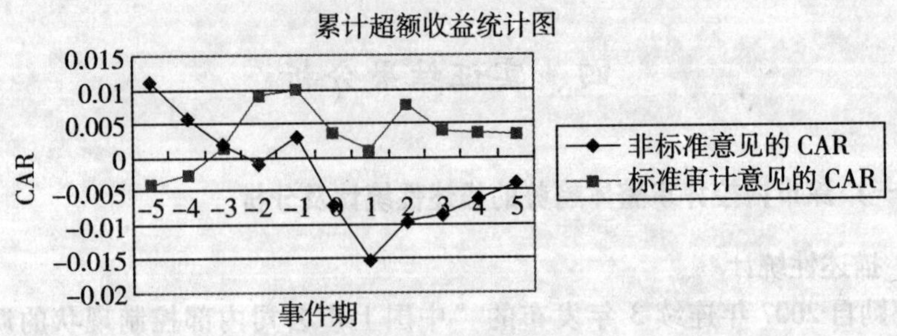

图3 事件期累计超额收益

含量大于标准意见的信息含量。但是，从事件发生的第3天开始，累计超额收益再向0缓慢靠近，但是还是存在异常收益的，因为我国是半强式有效市场，存在异常收益很正常，但不能长期偏离0太远，那么就说明资本市场是弱式有效的，不符合我们前面的本研究基础理论部分假定前提。为了检验CAR与上市公司内控评审意见具体的相关程度，本文做了进一步的相关分析和显著性检验。

（三）皮尔逊相关系数分析

为了对回归模型进行定性的相关性分析，本文对该模型做了双变量的皮尔逊分析（Pearson correlation coefficient），分析结果见表2：

表2 **皮尔逊相关系数表**

		CAR	OPINION	ASSET	EPS	H_{10}	ST	$SIZE_{10}$
CAR	P. C.	1	-0.486**	-0.16	-0.02*	-0.01*	-0.282*	0.184*
OPINION	P. C.		1	0.181	0.373**	-0.14*	0.566**	-0.192*
ASSET	P. C.			1	0.267*	-0.16	0.403**	0.276*
EPS	P. C.				1	-0.074	0.416**	0.021
H10	P. C.					1	-0.282*	-0.264*
ST	P. C.						1	0.082
SIZE10	P. C.							1

注：** 表示检验在1%水平上显著。

* 表示检验在5%水平上显著。

从皮尔逊相关系数表可以看出本文假设初步的验证结果：上市公司内控评审意见与股价有明显的相关关系。由于我们选取的审计意见是一个哑元的0~1变量，所以皮尔逊相关检验的相关度绝对值是一致的，当上市公司被出具标准的内控评审意见时，股价与审计意见是正相关的，相关度是0.486，在$\alpha=0.01$水平下存在显著相关性；当上市公司被出具非标准的内控评审意见时，股价与审计意见是负相关的。本文选取的控制变量中，企业规模，每股收益、股权集中度和上市公司声誉均与CAR呈负相关关系，而事务所规模与CAR正相关。股权集中度、声誉和事务所规模都与本文预期一致，企业规模和每股收益与本文预期不一致。预期不一致原因可能是美国次贷危机影响了我国股市走势，从而影响了企业规模、每股收益与股价的关系。

（四）回归分析

为了更完善地说明本文研究的内容以及所构造模型的合理性，定量分析其结果，本文对累计超额收益模型实行了回归分析，结果见表3：

表3 回归分析表

变量名称 CAR	相关系数 a_{it}	协方差	T检验值	Prob
OPINION	-0.289775	0.010968	-19.35941	0
ASSET	-0.003784	0.004046	-0.93536	0.3538
EPS	-0.169594	0.022508	7.534773	0
H_{10}	-0.121201	0.011407	-10.62549	0
ST	-0.046051	0.021537	-2.138254	0.0371
$SIZE_{10}$	0.055683	0.006036	9.225129	0
R-squared	0.894871	Prob（F-statistic）	0.000000	

从表3可以看出，非标准的内控评审意见与股价是负相关的，标准内控评审意见与股价正相关，并且通过T检验，在1%的水平上相关。而企业规模、每股收益、股权集中度和上市公司声誉均与CAR呈负相关关系，而事务所规模与CAR正相关，并且在1%的水平上相关。股权集中度、声誉和事务所规模都与本文预期一致，企业规模和每股收益与本文预期不一致，并且企业规模这个控制变量未通过检验。至于回归系数没有普通线性回归那样的变化关系，预期不一致的原因可能是美国次贷危机影响了我国股市走势，从而影响企业规模和每股收益。本文所建立模型的拟合优度 $0 \leqslant R2 = 0.894871 \leqslant 1$，表明回归方程拟合程度较高，并通过F检验。

五、研究结论、展望与局限

1. 结论

本文以2007—2009年3年在深圳证券交易所A股上市公司的内控评审信息为研究对象。在初步的描述性分析的基础上，通过采用超额收益法和多元回归分析法考察了我国股票市场对内控评审信息的影响。研究结果发现，我国深市对披露的内控评审意见是具有信息含量的，资本市场对CPA出具标准内控评审意见的上市公司股价有显著的正面反应，非标准审计意见则与其相反。由此可见，我国股票市场对上市公司的内控评审信息有着显著的影响，内控评审信息的获得能够为投资者的决策提供更多的决策相关信息。

笔者认为，我国上市公司的内部控制虽然已渐趋完善，但仍存在着问题。内部控制信息披露格式不规范、评价标准体系不一致、内部监督和外部监督不明显等不足之处。提出以下几条政策性建议：尽快建立统一的上市公司内部控制披露报告格式，特别对内部控制缺陷需要进行更为详尽的体现；加快制定遵循统一的内部控制制度评价标准体系；注重发挥“人”的主观能动性，倡导开展文化教育建设，建立健全反舞弊举报机制，加强审计人员的审计职业道德教育和继续教育培训；更加关注企业的内控评审，提高认识水平；积极构建“四位一体”的新型公司治理结构；研究对内控审计与财务报表审计进行有机结合的可行性。

2. 展望和局限

本文对我国深市的上市公司内控评审信息披露进行的分析是基于深圳证券交易所2006年发布的《深圳证券交易所上市公司内部控制指引》为切入点的，所以样本选择是从2007—2009年3年的数据资料。2007年是深市上市公司执行《上市公司内部控制指引》的第一年，这一指引有力地推动了我国上市公司内部控制制度的建设和建立评价报告制度的进程。同时，由于我国上市公司内部控制基础较为薄弱和准备时间较短等原因，上市公司在执行《上市公司内部控制指引》并出具内部控制报告中出现了不少问题，可能在制度执行方面只是起步阶段。我国2008年6月发布的《企业内部控制基本规范》、《企业内部控制评价指引（征求意见稿）》、《企业内部控制应用指引（征求意见稿）》、《企业内部控制鉴证指引（征求意见稿）》等一系列内部控制法规，在以后成熟阶段可能会更具可比性。可见，上市公司内部控制评审在我国还不是很成熟，有待于我们进一步进行跟踪研究。

由于本文在收集相关数据披露时间和方式以及计算时间方面的制约，在实证分析中，只是选取了深市部分样本进行分析，未收集沪市上市公司2007—2009年3年的内部控制报告评审统计报告情况，没有对沪深两市上市公司的情况进行对比分析，而且我国现阶段的内控趋势分析是间接获得的，存在数据间接获取真实性问题的存在，有待以后进一步的完善。

主要参考文献

[1] 陈丽蓉、牛艺林：《内部控制有效性对审计意见影响的实证研究》，载《会计之友》，2010(25)，66~71页。

[2] 林斌、饶静：《上市公司为什么自愿披露内部控制鉴证报告》，载《会计研究》，2009(2)，45~52页。

[3] Willis. , D. M. , Management Reports on Internal Controls, Journal of Accountancy, 10, 2000, pp. 55 ~ 58.

[4] 方红星、孙翯、金韵韵:《公司特征、外部审计与内部控制信息的自愿披露——基于沪市上市公司2003—2005年年报的经验研究》,载《会计研究》,2009(10),44 ~ 52页。

[5] McMullen, Dorothy, Raghunandan, Internal Control Reports and Financial Reporting Problems, Accounting Horizons, 14, 1996, pp. 67 ~ 75.

[6] Hammersley, J. S. , L. A. Mayers, C. Shakespeare, Market Reactions to the Disclosure of Internal Control Weakness and to the Characteristics of Those Weakness Under Section 302 of the Sarbanes-Oxley Act of, Review of Accounting Studies, 1, 2008, pp. 141 ~ 165.

[7] Fama, E. F. , Efficient Capital Market: A Review of Theory and Empirical Work, Journal of Finance, 2, 1970, pp. 383 ~ 417.

[8] 宋绍清、张侠:《关于上市公司内部控制信息披露影响因素的实证研究》,载《财会月刊》,2009(2),6 ~ 9页。

[9] 张维迎:《法律制度的信誉基础》,载《经济研究》,2002(1),25 ~ 27页。

由“国美控制权之争”引发的思考
——基于公司治理与内部控制的视角

易金翠

（广西财经学院会计系　广西南宁　530003）

摘　要　持续两年多的“国美控制权之争”终于落下帷幕。受控制权争夺战的影响，作为家电零售连锁行业老大的国美电器付出了丧失市场先机、员工士气低落的沉重代价，公司发展缓慢。本文基于公司治理与内部控制的视角对“国美控制权之争”下的国美电器进行分析，认为控制权争夺战源于公司治理中制衡关系的缺失、控制权争夺战直接影响了内部控制目标的实现，公司治理与内部控制在“你中有我，我中有你”的嵌合中主导着内部控制的发展和控制目标的实现，提出建立治理主导型内部控制，积极探索治理主导型内部控制下的董事会制度和监事会主导的监督体系的设计。

关键词　“国美控制权之争”公司治理　内部控制　关系

一、案例回顾①

事件起因：

2008年11月，国美电器创始股东、董事局主席——黄光裕以操纵股价罪被调查，时任国美电器总裁的陈晓主持工作；2009年1月，陈晓正式出任国美电器董事会主席兼总裁。

2009年6月，在大股东违法被捕、金融危机重创公司主营业务和公司极度缺乏资金的困难下，陈晓主导引入美国“贝恩资本”，向其发行18亿港元可转换债券（约占总股份的11%）。国美电器与“贝恩资本”达成融资协议时，双方签订了债权人保护条款，包括“陈晓的董事局主席任期至少三年以上”、“确保贝恩3名董事人选”等，否则，国美电器将构成违约，“贝恩资本”有权要求国美以1.5倍的代价赎回可转换债券。

争议焦点：

1.“贝恩资本”的董事会席位问题：陈晓方面根据融资协议的债权人保护条款，为“确保贝恩3名董事人选”而努力；黄光裕方面认为自己作为拥

① 根据 http：//finance. qq. com/zt2010/gmhgy/资料整理。

有公司1/3以上股权的大股东，自己在董事局中没有代表和话语权，贝恩资本却要占有3名董事，黄光裕担心自己“被不公平地剥夺对公司策略和运营的影响力”。

2. 公司发展战略问题：陈晓认为“中国的零售业最终都要回归到商业的本质上，即以服务制胜”，公司应实施“以提高单店盈利能力”为重点的效率优先策略。黄光裕方面则认为“中国家电零售市场仍处于跑马圈地时代”，公司应以“扩张逻辑”继续推行“狼性发展策略”，先做大再做强。

事件结果：

2010年9月28日晚，由黄光裕提起召开的特别股东大会的投票结果尘埃落定：陈晓提议的三名来自贝恩资本的董事被获准通过，黄光裕的五项提议中的一项提议——“关于撤销董事会拥有的配发及买卖国美股份之一般授权”被获准通过。2011年3月9日，国美召开董事会，陈晓辞去国美董事局主席一职，原大中电器创始人张大中将接替陈晓担任国美电器董事长。持续两年多的“国美控制权之争”终于落下帷幕，投资者以及所有关注者悬着的心终于可以放下。

二、“国美控制权之争”重塑公司治理与内部控制的关系

（一）“国美控制权之争”源于公司治理中制衡关系的缺失

公司治理是随着现代企业制度的产生而产生的。“西方发达的市场经济国家按照资产的组织形式或所有权与经营权是否分离及分离程度来划分企业，把企业分为三种基本形式，即业主制企业、合伙制企业和公司制企业。如果把业主制企业、合伙制企业作为自然企业是古典企业制度的表现形式，则公司制企业中的有限责任公司和股份有限公司作为法人企业是现代企业制度的表现形式”（张银杰，2010）。在所有权与经营权分离的前提下，位于企业外部的所有者与企业内部的经营者就产生了委托—代理关系，所有者通过内部的经营者来控制整个企业。当委托人和代理人利益目标不一致的时候，代理人——企业内部的经营者就会在信息不对称的情况下出现“逆向选择”和“道德风险”，形成“内部人控制”，进而影响所有者的利益，这就需要一种制度安排来合理配置委托人、代理人之间的权力与责任关系，这种制度就是公司治理。从狭义上来理解，公司治理是一种由所有者、董事会、监事会和经理层组成的制衡关系，所有者通过董事会来约束和管理经营者行为，从而尽可能使管理层的目标和所有者的利益相一致；从广义上来理解，公司治理涉及广泛的利益相关者，包括股东、债权人、供应商、雇员、政府和社区等与企业有利害关系的机构、部门及个人。

国美电器是由家族企业发展起来的现代企业。家族企业时期，国美电器是典型的古典企业，所有权与经营权合二为一，所有者的意志决定着企业的发展

方向。现代企业制度下的国美电器产权主体多元化、所有者外在化，为了防止经营者对所有者利益的背离，国美电器建立了股东大会、董事会、监事会及管理者所构成的公司治理结构。但在“国美控制权之争”中，职业经理人陈晓任董事会主席兼总裁，本应由股东会控制的董事会成了管理层操控的工具，监事会淡去了本应有的色彩，“外部人”阵营力量突减，股东会的控制路径变长且控制力度大幅度削弱，余下的只是职业经理人陈晓与大股东黄光裕的争吵，职业经理人置大股东的声音不顾，让人产生国美电器到底姓“陈”还是姓“黄”的疑惑。当公司治理作用的发挥仅维系在职业经理人的职业道德上时，可想而知其治理风险有多大。

“国美控制权之争”中的公司治理变形图如图1所示：

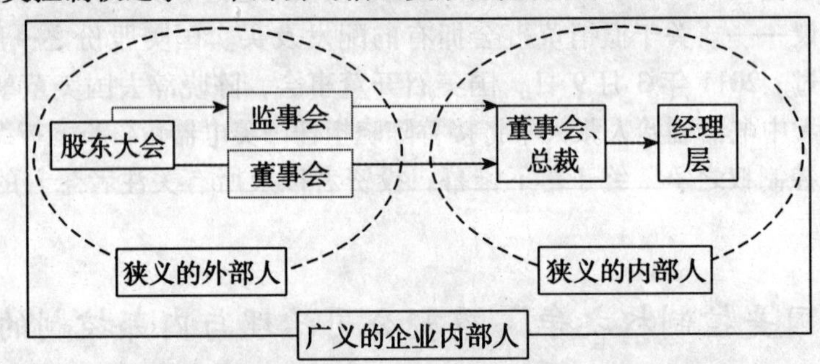

图1 “国美控制权之争”中的公司治理变形图

“国美控制权之争”给公司治理带来了新的思考：

1. 公司治理应该维护谁的利益？一种观点认为公司治理应该维护股东的利益、将所有者的意志贯彻到管理层，即本案例大股东黄光裕的“狼性策略”可以通过董事会直达管理层，使管理层的目标和所有者的利益相一致；另一种观点认为，公司治理不仅仅维护股东的利益，更要维护包括股东、债权人、供应商、雇员等利益相关者的利益，公司发展应注意持续性、稳健性、安全性，本案例中的陈晓就是基于此点引入“贝恩资本”、推行“效率优先策略”，认为这样做都是为了公司除股东以外的更多利益相关者的利益；还有一种观点认为，公司治理维护的利益相关者应该包括政府部门，国美电器是我国家电零售业的老大，陈晓可以为解决公司资金短缺问题想办法，但不一定非得引入“贝恩资本”，甚至让出3个董事席位。

2. 如何分清“内部人”、“外部人”的界限？理论上讲，企业“内部人”与“外部人”阵营界限很容易区分，即所有者与经营者的区分。从公司治理的组成来看，股东会、董事会、监事会应属于企业“外部人”阵营，经理层属于企业“内部人”阵营，公司治理强调“内部人”、“外部人”目标一致，共同实现企业发展战略。本案例中，陈晓一方面是公司的小股东，是“外部人”；另一方面，他作为职业经理人担任公司总裁，又具有“内部人”控制的优势。当陈晓任董事会主席并兼任总裁时，他完全集“内部人”、“外部人”

的权威角色于一身，而这也正违背了公司治理中的制衡初衷。

3. 监事会在公司治理中应该发挥什么作用？在公司治理制度设计中，制衡关系的主要措施是设置了监事会。监事会对股东大会负责，负责监督企业董事、经理及高级管理人员是否依法履行职责，负责调查和审查公司战略、业务活动、财务情况并提出监督意见，将监督情况报告股东大会。本案例中，遗憾的是一直没有监事会的声音，就在黄光裕和陈晓就经营业绩、企业发展策略进行争论的时候，没有人能就双方的数据进行证实，监事会成为一种摆设。

公司治理不仅仅是一种制度安排，更是一种制衡关系，公司治理的重点是突出其制衡作用的发挥。

（二）“国美控制权之争”对内部控制的影响

内部控制 COSO 委员会《内部控制——整体框架》中定义：“内部控制是由企业董事会、经理阶层和其他员工实施的，为营运的效率效果、财务报告的可靠性、相关法令的遵循性等目标的达成而提供合理保证的过程。”企业内部控制涵盖企业经营管理的各个层级、各个方面和各项业务环节。建立有效的内部控制，至少应当考虑以下五个基本要素：内部环境、风险评估、控制活动、信息与沟通、监控。内部环境包括企业发展战略、组织架构、人力资源政策、企业文化等方面内容，企业发展战略决定了企业的发展方向，组织架构包括公司治理和内部机构，人力资源政策让员工在企业中找到目标和自我，企业文化提炼企业的价值取向、影响员工的行为。内部环境是内部控制体系的基础，是内部控制运行的核心，一个良好的内部环境有利于充分调动员工的积极性、促进内部控制目标的实现乃至企业战略目标的实现。

“国美控制权之争”以来，国美电器的企业发展战略由“狼性发展策略”转变为“效率优先策略”，即注重单店盈利能力的提高、对经营不佳的门店予以关闭。在国美采取关店策略的同时，家电连锁零售业老二——“苏宁电器”却借着金融危机商务地产成本低迅速开店。根据两家公司公布的2010年第三季度财务报告，虽然“国美电器”前三季度的营业收入和净利润同期都有较大幅度增长，但与“苏宁电器”相比，其业绩逊色许多，“苏宁电器”正在赶超“国美电器”（见表1）。

表1　**2010年前三季度业绩报告结果对比表**　金额单位：亿元

公司名称	营业收入		净利润		截至9月30日门店数
	金额	同期增长率（%）	金额	同期增长率（%）	
国美电器	372.70	18.6	14.40	49.2	1 255
苏宁电器	543.02	30.61	28.28	43.58	1 235

资料来源：根据“苏宁电器”和“国美电器”公布的2010年第三季度财务报告资料整理。

作为行业老大的“国美电器”受此次控制权争夺战的影响，丧失了市场先机、员工士气低落、部分骨干人员流失，公司发展缓慢。黄光裕曾提出“国美愿景：2015年前成为受尊重的世界家电零售企业第一”，目前的国美急需整合资源，充分发挥公司治理、内部控制的作用，让企业走到正确的轨道上来，让企业的员工一起为企业的战略目标而努力。

（三）公司治理与内部控制关系的重塑

公司治理与内部控制的关系目前仍没有定论。根据相关研究文献分析，目前关于公司治理和内部控制关系的主要观点有“环境论”、“嵌合论”和“互动论”。

“环境论”源自于AICPA的《审计准则第55号：财务报表审计中对内部控制的考虑》和COSO的《内部控制：整体框架》这两个研究报告。这两个文件均把董事会及其对待内部控制的态度认定为内部控制的控制环境。“环境论”认为公司治理与内部控制是环境与主体的关系，实施内部控制制度的同时需要为其营造一个有利的制度环境（阎达五、杨有红，2001）。“环境论”对公司治理和内部控制之间相互关系的描述不准确，降低了公司治理相对于内部控制所具有的重要意义，忽视了内部控制对公司治理具有的反向促进作用（郭永清、夏大慰，2009）。

“嵌合论”认为公司治理结构和内部控制是“你中有我，我中有你”的包含关系（李连华，2005），提出建立公司治理结构和内部控制制度相互关联的共时结构，实现公司治理结构和内部控制的有效对接，实现全空域、分层级控制和全覆盖式连贯一体的监督链，既能提高内部控制效果，又能提高公司治理效率。

“互动论”认为治理结构和内部控制存在着互动关系（程新生，2004）。公司治理机制有效，才能保证不同层次控制目标的一致性，只有从源头实施内部控制，才能维护各利益相关者的权益。有效的内部控制应当能够维护所有利益相关者的合法权益，而不是维护某一类或少数利益相关者的权益。以公司治理为基础的治理型内部控制有助于治理主体与内部控制主体有效沟通，从而为科学决策和效率经营提供保障。

由于公司治理失去了制衡的重心，“国美控制权之争”愈演愈烈，公司的内部控制迷失了目标，导致企业经营和发展受到了重大影响。公司治理不仅仅是内部控制的外化环境，也不仅仅是内部控制发展的基础，而是内部控制的源头，与内部控制在“你中有我，我中有你”的嵌合中主导着内部控制的发展，并且直接决定着内部控制能否有效实现其控制目标。

三、建立治理主导型内部控制的思考

在公司治理中，董事会承载着股东的意志并担负着公司经营决策的重任，对股东大会负责，是公司治理的核心；在内部控制中，董事会负责内部控制的建立健全和有效实施，通过建立一套相互牵制、合理授权的系统来维护企业资产的安全、信息的可靠，以督促经营者合法经营、提高效率，最终实现企业的战略目标，董事会也是内部控制的核心。因此，董事会成为公司治理与内部控制的关键接口。治理主导型内部控制是指公司在建立健全内部控制时应突出公司治理的主导作用，通过董事会这个桥梁，将股东会的意志贯彻到公司的内部控制之中，使整个内部控制系统在董事会的领导下、遵从股东大会的决议，上下步调一致地实现企业目标。治理主导型内部控制如图 2 所示：

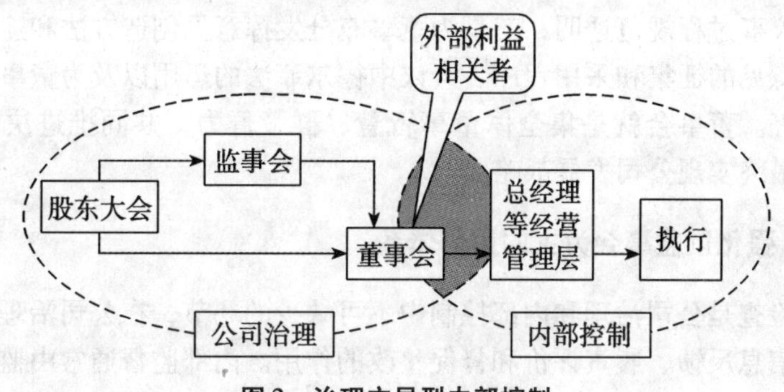

图 2　治理主导型内部控制

（一）完善董事会制度

基于董事会在公司治理与内部控制中的核心地位，“董事会应该代言谁”、“董事会能代言谁”、“董事会是否有能力代言”成为制约董事会发挥核心作用的三个关键因素。“董事会应该代言谁”由公司的性质决定，董事会能“代言谁”由董事会成员的组成决定，“董事会是否有能力代言”由董事会成员的素质决定。在国美电器由家族企业转变为上市的股份有限公司，公司也由黄光裕家族的利益转变为广大投资者、债权人、政府等利益相关者的利益。公司应该以广大利益相关者的利益为出发点来完善董事会制度。

1. 董事会成员的组成要求

打造独立、专业、高效的董事会是取得公司治理效果与实现内部控制目标的有效途径，这对董事会成员的数量、结构和质量都提出了要求。

在董事会成员的结构上，公司董事应该由股东代表、职工代表和外部董事组成，并且规定股东代表、职工代表和外部董事的结构比例。职工代表和外部董事的参与能使董事会兼顾各方的利益，同时对股东代表形成制约、有效防范“一股独大”、损害中小投资者利益的风险。

在董事会成员的素质上，应明确董事会成员任职资格的“硬条件”、建立“公正、公平、公开、透明”的选举程序，确保选拔能力强、水平高、职业道德好的人士成为董事会成员，以引领企业持续、健康、稳定地发展。

2. 建立科学、合理的董事会决策程序

公司董事会职责由公司章程规定，一般包括决定公司经营计划和投资方案、决定公司内部管理机构设置、聘任总经理及财务负责人、负责包括薪酬激励制度在内的多项公司制度的建设、制订预决算方案及利润分配方案等多项职责。董事会会议由董事会主席负责召集和主持，董事会决议的实施情况由董事长组织检查。在董事会决议形成的过程中，为了避免董事会主席工作作风、倾向性意见等不利影响，防范“董事不懂事”的风险，公司需要建立科学、合理的董事会决策程序：一是明确董事会下属各委员会、各董事的职责权限；二是对会议的召开程序、表决方式、提案审议、保密要求和会议记录等做出规定，确保议事过程规范透明；三是为董事充分发挥意见创造方法和途径，如日常管理中意见的征集和采用程序、会议中德尔菲法的运用以及为董事形成提案提供支持等。董事会就是集全体董事智慧、群策群力，共同推进决策的合理性，从而最终实现公司发展战略。

（二）强化以监事会为主的监督体系

监督检查是公司治理和内部控制中不可缺少的环节，在公司治理和内部控制中起到信息反馈、履责评价和督促整改的作用。内部监督通常由监事会、董事会下设的审计委员会及内部审计组成，监事会和审计委员会同属于公司治理范畴，内部审计属于内部控制范畴。治理主导型内部控制的监督体系应考虑监事会和审计委员会在监督体系中的主导作用，而由于审计委员会又隶属董事会，因此，治理主导型内部控制的监督体系应重点突出监事会在监督体系中的主导作用。

实现监事会主导的监督体系的有效路径如下：

一是将审计委员会及内部审计纳入到监事会的监督路线上来，形成三者从上至下的分层监督体系：监事会是公司最高层次的监督机构，审计委员会是公司第二个层次的监督，内部审计是公司最低层次的监督。分层监督体系确定了各层次监督的重点和报告路线：内部审计主要负责企业经营活动、财务管理、资金使用等具体业务的监督，内部审计的信息同时反馈给经理层及审计委员会；审计委员会负责经理层的监督，监督信息同时反馈给董事会和监事会；监事会重点监督董事会是否尽职尽责，并负责指导审计委员会和内部审计的工作。监事会、审计委员会可以把审计监督工作委托给内部审计，也可以外包给外部审计机构。治理主导型内部控制的监督体系如图3所示：

二是多方面强化监事会的职能。一直以来，监事会在公司治理中处于边缘化状态，监事会可有可无、形同虚设。监事会职能的发挥取决于公司治理的监

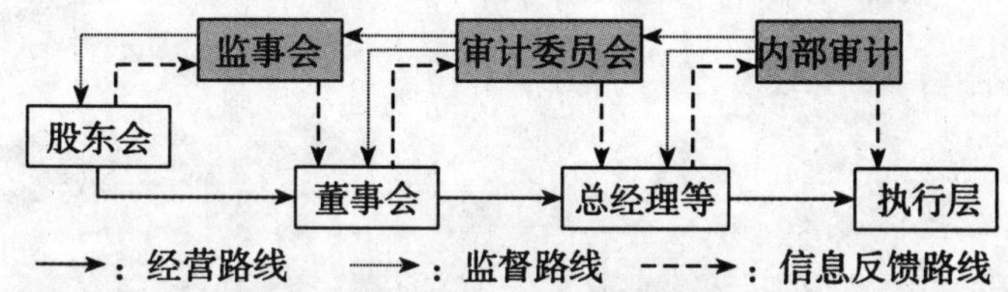

图3 治理主导型内部控制的监督体系

督意识、监事的独立性、监事队伍力量的强弱以及监督水平的高低等因素。强化监事会职能首先，要解决的是增强公司治理中的监督意识，实质就是强化公司治理中的制衡关系；其次，监事的组成要考虑监事的人数、监事的来源、监事的素质水平和能力、监事队伍的结构等方面，监事的来源影响监事的独立性，监事所具备的专业知识以及监事队伍的力量直接影响监督效果；再次，监督水平的高低有赖于先进的审计监督技术，随着企业信息化建设的普及，信息传递和信息储存实现电子化，非现场审计技术在审计监督中发挥了重大作用，监事会应积极探索先进的审计监督技术，不断提高监督水平；最后，监事会应从事后监督为主转变为事中监督、事前监督为主，将问题消灭在萌芽阶段，充分体现监事会在企业发展中的保驾护航作用。

主要参考文献

[1] 郭永清、夏大慰:《基于公司治理的内部控制整合研究》,载《商业经济与管理》,2009(7)。

[2] 杜瑞军:《基于公司治理层面的内部控制研究》,载《财会通讯(综合版)》,2009(3)。

[3] 杨姗姗:《公司治理、内部控制与公司价值的关系研究述评》,载《河南商业高等专科学校学报》,2008(6)。

[4] 李连华:《公司治理结构与内部控制的链接与互动》,载《会计研究》,2005(2)。

[5] 程新生:《公司治理、内部控制、组织结构互动关系研究》,载《会计研究》,2004(4)。

[6] 杨有红、胡燕:《试论公司治理与内部控制的对接》,载《会计研究》,2004(4)。

[7] 阎达五、杨有红:《内部控制框架的构建》,载《会计研究》,2001(2)。

[8] 张银杰:《公司治理——现代企业制度新论》,上海,上海财经大学出版社,2010。

[9] http://finance. qq. com/zt2010/gmhgy.

[10] AICPA, Auditing Standards Board of AICPA: Statement on Auditing Standards (SAS), No. 55: Consideration of Internal Control in a Financial Statement Audit, New York: AICPA, 1988.

[11] COSO, Internal Control-Integrated Framework, COSO, July 1994 Edition.

主要参考文献